Fires Across the Water

Fires Across the Water

Transnational Problems in Asia

Edited by James Shinn

A COUNCIL ON FOREIGN RELATIONS BOOK

The Council on Foreign Relations, Inc., a nonprofit, nonpartisan national membership organization founded in 1921, is dedicated to promoting understanding of international affairs through the free and civil exchange of ideas. The Council's members are dedicated to the belief that America's peace and prosperity are firmly linked to that of the world. From this flows the mission of the Council: to foster America's understanding of its fellow members of the international community, near and far, their peoples, cultures, histories, hopes, quarrels and ambitions; and thus to serve, protect, and advance America's own global interests through study and debate, private and public.

THE COUNCIL TAKES NO INSTITUTIONAL POSITION ON POLICY ISSUES AND HAS NO AFFILIATION WITH THE U.S. GOVERNMENT. ALL STATEMENTS OF FACT AND EXPRESSIONS OF OPINION CONTAINED IN ALL ITS PUBLICATIONS ARE THE SOLE RESPONSIBILITY OF THE AUTHOR OR AUTHORS.

Council on Foreign Relations Books are distributed by Brookings Institution Press (1-800-275-1447). For further information on Council publications, please write the Council on Foreign Relations, 58 East 68th Street, New York, NY 10021, or call the Director of Communications at (212) 434-9400. Visit our web site at: www.foreignrelations.org.

Library of Congress Cataloging-in-Publication Data
Fires across the water : transnational problems in Asia / edited by
    James Shinn.
        p. 000 cm.
    "A Council on Foreign Relations book."
    Includes index.
    ISBN 0-87609-205-9
    1. Asia—Economic conditions—1945– 2. Asia—Social conditions.   3. Asia—Foreign relations.   I. Shinn, James.
    HC412.F477 1998
    330.95—dc21   97-53276
                                                                              CIP

Contents

Foreword

Asia's role in American security and prosperity has evolved over the last century. In the late nineteenth century the United States confronted the European colonial powers to assure free and equal access to Asian markets. Throughout much of the twentieth century, Asia was a geopolitical chessboard on which the United States sought to check first Japanese imperialism and then advancing communism. With Asia now dedicated to market economics and firmly ensconced in the international trade and finance system, a third wave of U.S.-Asian issues has emerged

Transnational issues—such as the environment, international crime, and human rights—will be a major factor in transpacific relations in the 21st century. These issues will be important regardless of economic booms and busts. Increasing prosperity will alleviate the pressures of poverty and migration, but it may catalyze Asian demand for drugs and stress on the environment. Conversely, slower economic growth will heighten the problems of poverty and migration.

Over the course of 1995 and 1996, the Council on Foreign Relations undertook the Asia Project, which included a study group directed by James Shinn and chaired by Robert Oxnam and Robert Scalapino, to explore the salience of Asian transnational issues for the United States. This volume is the result. It introduces interested readers to the broad range of transnational issues that affect both Asians and Americans. Some of the authors offer prescriptive advice, as well as diagnoses, for the new issues they cover.

Gary C. Hufbauer
Director of Studies
Council on Foreign Relations

Prefatory Note

Forty years ago, when the Cold War was in its infancy, international-al relations were tidily focused on arms and diplomacy. In the era of the Korean and Vietnam wars, those brutal military conflicts overshadowed such issues as human rights and population control. Twenty years ago, as Asia's economic takeoff was ushering in a new era in trade disputes with Japan and other Pacific countries, economic issues overshadowed questions of environmental degradation and drug smuggling.

In those days, policymakers focused on guns-and-butter questions and categorized all other issues as "soft issues." Nevertheless, some remarkable pioneers emerged as early advocates of these questions—Eleanor Roosevelt on human rights; John D. Rockefeller III, J. R. D. Tata, and Marshall Green on population; Rachel Carlson on the environment; and Tommy Koh on the law of the sea. Over the past twenty years press coverage of the human cost engendered by these problems has grown—refugees from Afghanistan and Indochina, nuclear disasters in the United States and former Soviet Union, illegal migration from Asia into the United States, repression in the streets of Rangoon and Beijing, and natural disasters afflicting overpopulated areas such as Bangladesh and India.

The United Nations has played a singularly important role in moving these global issues center stage. U.N.-sponsored conferences on human rights, the environment, and population not only created huge fanfare but also produced enduring action plans that are still being implemented. Dr. Sadako Ogata, the U.N. High Commissioner for Refugees—one of the outstanding figures in the U.N. process—has co-authored a chapter in this volume.

As the United Nations has been working at the macrolevel, many other individuals and institutions have been fostering new attention at the regional and local levels. The United States remains the leader in terms of developing issue-oriented constituencies on every one of these problems. With the support of private foundations, new analytical and action institutions emerged around these rising concerns in the 1960s, 1970s, and 1980s. Within many Asian countries, voluntary organizations have sprung up to galvanize public opinion, shape press coverage, and exert public pressure. India, for instance, has spawned important institutions to deal with such issues as balanced economic development, population control, and mass literacy. Even China, where nongovernmental lobbying organizations have little tradition, now has a human rights organization and a strong opposition movement to the building of the Three Gorges Dam on the Yangzi River.

So we approach these global issues at a curious twilight moment in international affairs; they lurk on the visible horizon, occasionally grab our attention, but often remain elusive on political and diplomatic agendas. To be sure, the 1990s have seen some dramatic successes—much better handling of refugee crises in Asia and new government commitments to population policy in several U.N. member nations. A few countries have been successful in addressing critical problems. Japan, for instance, has emerged as an Asian leader in its domestic environmental policies, often prodded by citizen's action groups with roots that go back to the campaign against Minamata disease a quarter century ago.

Despite some notable successes, the cluster of global problems addressed in this book will continue to bedevil Asia and U.S.–Asia relations well into the next century. Indeed, the prognosis is bleak on several fronts, as James Shinn notes in his opening chapter, which skewers the conventional wisdom notion that these problems are being resolved by Asian "business as usual." In a similar tone Stephen Flynn analyzes the mushrooming traffic in drugs and weapons, in which very modern forms of computer-driven communications often assist age-old evils, a traffic in which narcotics and laundered money are just another commodity in Asia's booming international commerce. Elizabeth Economy details the environmental disasters that already are afflicting much of the developing world in Asia, including the one-third of the world's population that lives in China and India. She observes that economic growth extracts a terrible price and that many Asian countries will be paying that price for decades to come. Paul Smith describes the knotty problem of illegal migration in Asia, another boom business, prompted by both "push" and "pull" factors. Illegal migration has grown by tenfold in a decade, making inter-Asian relations more fractious and leading to a huge increase in illegal Asian migration into the United States.

In their chapter Sadako Ogata and Johan Cels are guardedly optimistic about the decline in refugees under the care of the United Nations in Asia but call attention to the high numbers of internally displaced refugees in Asia, cut adrift by civil wars or ethnic conflicts, and the challenge of a new diplomatic paradigm to deal systematically with the refugee problem in Asia.

Sidney Jones is less optimistic in her chapter on labor and human rights abuses in Asia. The root causes—stubborn autocratic governments and the Dickensian conditions of laborers in Asia's developing economies—are clear enough. What is lacking is political will for reform, both within the region and in Asia's trading partners. Indeed, political will—or the lack of it—is the centerpiece of James Shinn's concluding chapter of this volume, in which he pulls together the recommendations of all the chapters and submits them to a policy "reality check."

Asia's collision with the transnational problems is bedeviled by a double-edged condition captured in Robert Scalapino's phrase, "dynamic economies and fragile politics." All of these global issues—including pollution, migration, increased crime, and population growth—are by-products of rapid economic growth. These problems form the downside to the remarkable Asian success story of the past few decades; the problems become more acute as more people are swept into Asia's takeoff tornado.

The only short-term antidote to these contentious problems is firm leadership. Yet, ironically, as Asia speeds ahead economically, it is also moving into an era of increased political fragility and weakened institutions of governance. While these political transitions may enhance attention to some human rights issues (particularly political and legal rights), they also make it harder to create and enforce regulation on other questions (environment, population, and crime). And, with rising regional and local political forces, there is a natural temptation to pass the buck to authorities outside central governments.

Thus, in much of Asia, these transnational issues often receive mere lip service. Governments are quick to issue proclamations on drugs and crime or to set up agencies for the environment and population control but very slow to give sustained attention or to allocate the necessary financial support. Flurries of activity occur in the spotlight of international conferences or state visits, but attention quickly reverts to what are seen as higher priority questions.

Few Asian political leaders have taken strong stands or given enduring attention to any of these global issues. No matter how obvious the transnational threats, domestic political and economic realities force attention in other directions. Developers have more political sway than environmental activists do in most of late twentieth-century Asia. Corruption often links political figures to investments that scoff at concerns for pollution, land and forest degradation, water supplies, and labor standards. In some countries, criminal organizations have tacitly acknowledged public standing (including the yakuza in Japan and the triads in China, as discussed by Stephen Flynn in chapter 2). And one has to look far and wide to find true supporters of human rights issues among Asian political elite.

One potentially positive trend is that some Asian regional organizations, particularly the Association of Southeast Asian Nations (ASEAN) and Asia Pacific Economic Cooperation (APEC), have set up subgroups to address many of these questions. Such attention, often emanating from the annual leadership summits, enhances public concern and often outlines important strategies. In many cases, however, the output is long on suggestions and short on actual results. Sometimes these issues also are featured in bilateral discussions, most notably in the U.S.–Japan dialogue that has given special emphasis to Asian environmental questions since President Clinton's meeting with Prime Minister Hosokawa in 1993.

So most of these issues have a tricky nature—they are relatively easy to spot but devilish when it comes to creating real solutions. It is easier, both financially and politically, to postpone implementing remedies. Then, like a long-predicted earthquake, a sudden disaster produces great tragedies, huge headlines, and endless recriminations. Unfortunately, unless a constellation of new leaders emerges with strong commitments to these issues, the seismic cycle is likely to continue in the decade ahead.

These "global issues" have virtually no coherence in terms of U.S. policy, and they vary enormously in terms of political attention. The hottest short-term issues will probably be those of human rights, illegal immigration, drugs, and weapons smuggling. More remote will be such questions as environmental crises in Asia and migration flows among Pacific nations. Lobbying groups, media organizations, and political leaders will be critical to how, when, and whether these issues will be raised.

America's own internal transition—which resonates with Asia's condition of "dynamic economics and fragile politics"—makes these issues both unpredictable and potentially volatile. The question of how to curtail illegal immigration, from both China and Latin America, may well become a serious battleground between a Republican Congress and a Democratic White House. On the other hand, issues that do not directly affect American voters—such as urban air pollution in countries across the Pacific—are less likely to be drawn into the cockpit of domestic politics.

The enormous vacillations in the Clinton administration's human rights policy make the issue a difficult one for the immediate future. Sidney Jones suggests ways of rethinking human rights strategies for Asia, emphasizing the universal nature of our policies (not country-specific formulations) and the changing agenda of human rights (especially labor rights in future years). Contrary to the current wisdom, she expresses doubts about whether rapid economic development sets the context for greater sensitivity to human rights in Asia. The alternate view is that development has tended to precede political pluralization in much of Asia, creating important conditions (such as the rise of a middle class and rapid increases in literacy) for better protection of human rights. This pattern, which some have called an "Asian form of development," in which economic liberalization occurs before political liberalization, can be seen in Korea, Taiwan, and parts of Southeast Asia.

Perhaps the biggest problem for Americans is where human rights fits into overall foreign policy. A recent report by the Council on Foreign Relations Asia Policy Panel gave special attention to human rights, concluding that

> Human rights should have a strong place in American diplomatic relations with Asia, as with other regions. Human rights should be part of a global U.S. strategy, and should explicitly emphasize international values as set forth by the Universal Declaration of Human Rights. The United States should consistently express its support of such common values in keeping with American tradition, but it should principally employ persuasion rather than sanctions and pressures and should avoid official hectoring. Wherever possible, the United States should employ multilateral approaches and private negotiations focused on particular cases.
>
> In recent years, some Asian leaders have argued that "Asian values" require different approaches to human rights from those of countries with "Western values." [While acknowledging that] many Asian countries emphasize societal obligations over individual prerogatives, and rightly give much attention to economic well-being in rapidly developing societies . . . we do not accept the view that . . . Asian societies should be exempt from universal standards of human rights. . . . Despite a trend towards political liberalization, [there is no regional consensus that democracy should be the goal for all Asian societies.] The United States should therefore support and encourage any efforts by Asian governments to liberalize their political systems.[1]

But all of these concerns, not just human rights problems, often suffer in terms of U.S. policy because the problems are new, they vary in their volatility, they have amorphous positions in the U.S. bureaucracy, and they lack coherence in lobbying groups. Nevertheless, as James Shinn suggests in his concluding chapter, the transnational problems are not "soft issues." They are serious policy problems, with substantial American interests at stake. These problems can and should influence U.S.–Asia policymaking in the 1990s and beyond.

Despite the pessimistic projections that infuse many of the chapters in this volume, there are reasons for cautious optimism over the longer term. Ultimately, those hopes rest with two forces on both sides of the

Pacific—greater public awareness coupled with more enlightened leadership. These global issues deserve priority attention or they will surely compromise both the economic development and the regional security that shape U.S.–Asia relations at the turn of the century.

Robert B. Oxnam
Co-Chair, Asia Policy Project

---

1. Council on Foreign Relations Asia Policy Panel, *Redressing the Balance: American Engagement with Asia* (New York: Council on Foreign Relations, 1996).

About the Authors

JOHAN CELS is Executive Assistant to Sadako Ogata, the United Nations High Commissioner for Refugees (UNHCR). He has worked for the UNHCR in Hong Kong, Turkey, Iraq, and Bulgaria, and has published several articles on refugee issues. He holds degrees from the Catholic University of Louvain in Belgium, the Johns Hopkins University, and a Ph.D. from the University of Notre Dame.

ELIZABETH ECONOMY is Fellow for China at the Council on Foreign Relations. Dr. Economy has written on both Chinese domestic and foreign policy. Her recent publications include *Managing the Taiwan Conflict: Key Is Better Relations with China*, with Stephen Friedman (Council on Foreign Relations, 1995); a forthcoming report and edited volume with Michel Oksenberg, *Shaping U.S.-China Relations: A Long Term Strategy* (Council on Foreign Relations Press, 1998); a forthcoming book with Miranda Schreuers, *The Internationalization of Environmental Politics* (Cambridge Press, 1998); and an American Academy of Arts and Sciences monograph, *Reforms and Resources: the Implications for State Capacity in the People's Republic of China*.

Dr. Economy previously taught Chinese foreign policy and international environmental politics at the University of Washington. She received her B.A. from Swarthmore College, her M.A. in political science from Stanford University, and her Ph.D. in that same subject from the University of Michigan.

STEPHEN E. FLYNN is Assistant Professor of International Relations and member of the permanent commissioned teaching staff at the U.S. Coast Guard Academy. Upon graduation and commissioning from the Coast Guard Academy in 1982, he began his professional career as a sailor, assigned first as Operations Officer of one Coast Guard cutter and then Commanding Officer of two others. He received the M.A.L.D. and Ph.D. in international politics from the Fletcher School of Law and Diplomacy, Tufts University. In 1991, he was selected as the Coast Guard's first Council on Foreign Relations' International Affairs Fellow and since that time has been engaged in policy-oriented research on the illicit drug trade and international organized crime.

SIDNEY JONES has been Executive Director of Human Rights Watch/Asia for eight years. A specialist on Indonesia, she previously worked for four years as the Indonesia/Philippines researcher at Amnesty International in London, and from 1977 to 1988 was a program officer with the Ford Foundation, first in Jakarta, later in New York. She holds degrees in Oriental studies and international relations from the University of Pennsylvania. Ms. Jones has written on human rights in Asia and on the relationship between human rights and economic growth, and is an adjunct professor at Columbia University, where she teaches a course on human rights documentation.

SADAKO OGATA assumed office as the United Nations High Commissioner for Refugees on February 18, 1991 and was re-elected in 1993 for another five-year term, ending in December 1998. Mrs. Ogata has held a variety of public positions: Minister, Envoy Extraordinary and Minister Plenipotentiary at the Permanent Mission of Japan to the U.N. (1976–79); Chairman of the Executive Board of UNICEF (1976–78); Independent Expert of the United Nations Commission on Human Rights on the Human Rights Situation in Myanmar (1990); and Representative of Japan on the United Nations Commission on Human Rights (1982–85). Mrs. Ogata was Associate Professor, diplomatic history and international relations, at the International Christian University in Tokyo from 1974 to 1976 and Dean of the Faculty of Foreign Studies at Sophia University from 1989. Mrs. Ogata has published numerous books and articles on diplomatic history, international relations, and refugee issues. She received a Ph.D. in political science from the University of Cailfornia at Berkeley, and an M.A. in international relations from Georgetown University.

ROBERT B. OXNAM was named President Emeritus of the Asia Society, after a seventeen-year career as the Society's President (1981–92), Vice President and Director of its Washington Center (1979–81), and Director of its China Council (1975–81). He is Senior Adviser to the Bessemer Group. He is also Special Adviser to the Society of International Business Fellows in Atlanta, Georgia. From 1993 to 1996 Dr. Oxnam was Senior Research Fellow at Columbia University. In 1995 he was the Arnold Bernhard Visiting Professor at Williams College. From 1993 to 1994 he was the on-air narrator and author of a nine-part special on China that aired on the NewsHour in late 1993 and early 1994. Dr. Oxnam received his B.A from Williams College (Phi Beta Kappa), and his M.A. and Ph.D. from Yale University. His major publications include *The China Challenge: American Policies in East Asia* (1991); *China Briefing, 1980; China Briefing 1981; Ruling from Horseback* (1975); and *Dragon and Eagle* (1978).

JAMES SHINN served as the C. V. Starr Senior Fellow for Asia from 1994 to 1996 and as Senior Fellow for Commercial Diplomacy from 1996 to 1997. He managed the Council's multiyear Asia Project, whose results were summarized in the Council on Foreign Relations report *Redressing the Balance: American Engagement with Asia*. Another result of the Asia Project was his book *Weaving the Net: Conditional Engagement with China*, published by the Council on Foreign Relations Press in 1996, a critique of the strategy of constructive engagement. Mr. Shinn served in the East Asian Bureau of the State Department in Washington, D.C., working on trade and economic matters. He left government to spend fifteen years in Silicon Valley, beginning with Advanced Micro Devices, a manufacturer of integrated circuits, and then cofounded Dialogic Corporation, a publicly held engineering firm in call processing and Internet telephony technology. Mr. Shinn received a B.A. from Princeton and an M.B.A. from Harvard.

PAUL J. SMITH is an Adjunct Fellow with the Hawaii-based Pacific Forum/CSIS, where he specializes in international migration and Chinese politics. He is editor of *Human Smuggling: Chinese Migrant Trafficking and the Challenge to America's Immigration Tradition* (Center for Strategic and International Studies, forthcoming). His essays and articles on international migration topics have appeared in the *Christian Science Monitor, International Herald Tribune, Japan Times, Korea Times, Survival* (IISS Quarterly), the United Nations *International Migration Bulletin*, and the *Washington Times*.

Mr. Smith received his B.A. in East Asian studies from Washington and Lee University, his M.A. in Far East area studies from the University of London's School of Oriental and African Studies (SOAS), and his J.D. in law from the University of Hawaii.

Chapter 1

Introduction

JAMES SHINN

*Across the water, people are fighting a fire. On this
side, people are watching, emotionless as ice.*[1]

"Transnational problem" is a bland euphemism for the grim mis-
eries of narcotics addiction, crime, illegal migration, disease pandemics, pollution, refugees, labor abuses, and human rights
violations that form the subject of this book. These problems are not "fires
across the water" from the standpoint of the United States. Today the vast
Pacific Ocean is an ineffectual barrier to narcotics, triad criminals, and
deadly viruses—"drugs, thugs, and bugs," as an American diplomat once
described them.

Indeed, activists and pundits now claim that these transnational problems are the prime concern of American foreign policy in Asia, that they
are the "new agenda." Yet world–weary diplomats still dismiss these problems as "soft issues." When government leaders have finished grap-
pling with the serious security and economic agenda at an Asian summit,
a few moments at the end may be devoted to polite rhetoric about the
need for cooperative solutions to the transnational problems—then the
briefcases are snapped shut and the press releases handed out.

But this book makes the strong and unsettling case that the transnational problems are not new, they certainly are not "soft," and they will
shove themselves onto the diplomatic agenda with urgency and very little *politesse*. They will grab headlines, puzzle the politicians, and continue
to befuddle the diplomats, in Asian capitals and in Washington, D.C.

In recent years, transnational issues have made headlines internationally,
including the pandemonium over Hong Kong's deadly "chicken flu" virus
in December 1997; the hanging of migrant Filipino Flor Contemplacion
in Singapore in March 1995; the suffocating smoke from forest fires in Sumatra that blanketed much of Southeast Asia in 1994 and 1997; the furor over

Taiwan's trial balloon to dispose of low-level nuclear waste in North Korea in 1997; the panicked stampede of illegal Chinese immigrants from the grounded vessel *Golden Venture* into the cold surf of Rockaway Beach in New York City in June 1993; and the bitter fight to extradite Thai parliament member Thanong Siriprichaphong to face a charge of drug smuggling in the United States in January 1996. The last two cases make clear that the United States does not have the option of gazing across the Pacific as Asians try to extinguish the smoldering fires of the transnational problems. Both sides have a great deal at stake. Unsolved, Asia's transnational problems will find their way to America's doorstep.

Why is it that Asia's problems become America's problems? What is it that makes these problems "transnational," as opposed to garden-variety social ills? What, if anything, is uniquely "Asian" about them? What are the policy options for solving them, and why is it so hard to craft a multilateral solution to these problems? What is the size and trend of America's stake in these problems, and how do they fit within overall U.S. foreign policy in Asia?

In this chapter I explain why the problems are so intractable by debunking six conventional wisdom notions about how the New Asia easily will brush aside transnational problems, and then I propose a simple typology that ties this bundle of disparate problems into a common analytic framework. In the next five chapters our expert authors delve into the details of the problems, with insight and often with passion, and issue a call for solutions. In the final chapter I pull these problems together again and examine the policy recommendations for solving them, extract a "recipe for success" in overcoming the barriers to a solution, and then place the pursuit of solutions in the broader context of U.S. foreign policy in Asia.

Conventional Wisdom Errors

The transnational problems discomfit politicians and diplomats on both sides of the Pacific because they defy six conventional wisdom notions about the new Asia.

1. Money Will Solve These Problems

On the contrary, rapid economic growth in Asia will make some of these problems worse. It will remedy others only over the long term.

Evidence presented in this volume suggests that higher incomes ameliorate some types of environmental pollution, many infectious disease hazards, and most labor abuses. Yet, perversely, economic growth compounds problems such as greenhouse gas pollution, drug trafficking, and illegal migration.

The globalization of the Asian economy, driven by international trade and highly mobile factors of production—capital, technology, and labor—continues to boost incomes throughout the region. Over the last decade, the average economic growth rate in the region has been 7 percent, and close to 10 percent if Japan is excluded. Trade has doubled its proportion of gross domestic product (GDP) in the region over the same period, from 15 percent to 30 percent in 1995. But globalization also has created a series of widening gaps in the reach of the state, through which illicit commodities are being traded. This witches' brew includes not only narcotics but also illegal migrants, "black" money, dangerous weapons, toxic waste, and even black-market plutonium.

But the thrust of this volume is not antigrowth. Staying poor will not solve any of these problems. Dreadful environmental degradation in Asia occurs in nations on the lower rungs of the income ladder, such as China and Indonesia. Poor Asian states have the highest population growth rates and are wellsprings of illegal migrants and disease. The worst pollution and human rights abuses, the most vicious traffickers and venal officials, flourish on the bottom rung—the "failed states" of Myanmar, Cambodia, and North Korea.

2. *Asian Democracy Will Solve These Problems*

The end of the Cold War, political pluralism, and democratic enlargement in Asia are no "silver bullet" for the transnational problems.

The relaxation of Cold War tensions removed the urgency, and much of the political will, for states in Asia to deal cooperatively with a common external threat to their security. As they turn their gaze inward, many Asian states—especially the newer states, authoritarian states, and those with weak domestic legitimacy—see the transnational problems as internal security threats, to be repressed or stamped out, rather than as opportunities for collaborative solutions. Yet ironically the transition to political pluralism can make it harder to deal with transnational problems such as drugs, illegal migration, and (in the case of China) population control.

All of the authors in this volume agree that political pluralism is a necessary but not sufficient condition for Asian states to solve the transnational problems. Pluralism makes state authorities publicly accountable for crafting solutions for these problems, and it encourages the rule of law that enforces those solutions. But the road to political pluralism in Asia is a rocky one; the path to the rule of law is even rougher and longer.

In the meantime, Indonesia, Malaysia, and the Philippines are still forging national identities after centuries of colonial domination and only a few decades of self-governance and institution-building. They are quick to suppress ethnic or regional minorities that challenge that still shaky national identity, although Malaysia, with the longest tradition of parliamentary democracy and federalism, has demonstrated its ability to deal with ethnic tensions without bloodshed through compromise and bargaining. China and Vietnam are wide open to environmental and labor abuses during their transition to a market economy, due to poor enforcement and corrupt officials. Political pluralism itself is no guarantor of official probity, as evidenced by the scandals of official corruption and political payoffs in Japan, Korea, Taiwan, and Thailand. And organized crime, particularly the smuggling of illegal migrants, flourishes stubbornly throughout Asia, under dictator and democrat alike.

Asia's bumpy transition toward political pluralism has been paralleled by rapid urbanization and the decline of traditional social values. As old structures of village, clan, and religious authority have been undermined, the state has been slow to assert an even-handed secular authority. Asia's booming megacities are fertile ground for drug abuse, crime, the sexual exploitation of illegal migrants, disease pandemics, and Dickensian labor abuses of the worst sort. Law enforcement lags far behind.

Reverting to authoritarian rule, however, will not solve the problem of enforcing laws developed to combat transnational problems—these problems call for good governance, not the iron fist.

3. All Asian Governments Want to Solve These Problems

Not all Asian governments are on the side of the angels in solving Asia's transnational ills. For example, the Philippines depends heavily on remittances from overseas migrants—legal and illegal alike. The ruling State Law and Restoration Council (SLORC) junta in Myanmar has no regard for the Burmese refugees who are huddled in misery along the Thai border, and Hanoi was utterly callous about the fate of its "boat people." Thai politicians and officials have enriched themselves by abetting drug traffickers and snakeheads, or criminal gangs, for years. By the same token, some prominent Japanese politicians and bureaucrats have close ties with criminal yakuza and sokaiya gangs.

Moreover, not all Asian governments believe that the transnational aspect of these problems warrants much of their attention. From the standpoint of Chinese officials, for example, sulfur dioxide emissions from coal-burning power plants are a domestic Chinese problem; they choose more pollution over higher power production costs. Chinese officials dismiss complaints from Seoul or Tokyo that acid rain from these smokestacks is killing their forests, even when the Koreans or Japanese are willing to pay to install stack-scrubbers and other clean technology in Chinese power projects.

In the extreme case, some Asian governments deny that sensitive problems are transnational at all. Indonesia has voiced strong objections to efforts by Western nations to ensure labor standards in Asian manufacturing plants. And Chinese leaders characterize human rights practices as an "internal" issue as a defense against their international critics.

4. "Asian Values" Will Solve These Problems

Proponents of Asian values, including the eloquent spokesmen of the so-called Singapore school,[2] argue that the transnational problems are caused by a moral decay stemming from "Western" social decadence. The best way to resolve the transnational problems is reversion to traditional Asian values of communal responsibility, respect for authority, responsible media, and political consensus.

This line of argument may ring true with regard to narcotics addiction; few would deny that drug abuse is one result of a tattered social fabric. Yet there is no obvious link between Asian values and solutions for crime, pollution, illegal migration, or the other transnational problems.

Proponents of the Asian values also lash out at "sensationalist" media and fractious democratic politics. Yet neither press censorship nor political consensus has been able to stamp out transnational problems. On the contrary, crime, pollution, corruption, and labor abuses flourish in the dark. As for so-called Asian consensus, this is a often convenient justification for the monopoly of power by narrow elites. As the authors in this book ask: Who makes the trade-off between economic growth and transnational problems? Who decides when a transnational problem has become intolerable?

5. NGOs Will Solve These Problems

Not all nongovernmental organizations (NGOs) are positive, not all NGOs agree on the solutions, and NGOs are not equipped to deal with many aspects of the transnational problems.

"NGO" is a slippery term. Not all NGOs are benign. Chinese triads and Japanese yakuza criminal gangs are certainly "nongovernmental organizations," but they are clearly part of the problem, not part of the solution. Some powerful NGOs, such as organized religion and population control charities, hold values that are antithetical to each other. NGOs are better organized to focus on transnational problems such as human rights or the environment than on problems of drug addiction and public health. Some NGOs are locked into antagonistic relations with the very governments in Asia whose policies are needed to solve the transnational problems.

6. *Multilateral Institutions Will Solve These Problems*

Progress so far is sketchy and modest. Two U.N. agencies—the United Nations High Commission on Refugees (UNHCR) and the United Nations Populations Fund (UNFPA)—have tackled refugee and population problems with some success. The multilateral development banks (MDBs) have added some transnational problems to their lending criteria, such as environmental and public health impact, while carefully avoiding more politically controversial problems, such as labor standards or human rights.

But neither the Association of Southeast Asian Nations (ASEAN) nor the Asia-Pacific Economic Conference (APEC), the two regional Asian multilateral fora, have had much success in breaking out of the talk-shop mold in dealing with these problems; they are stuck at the polite rhetoric level. Efforts to craft a multilateral solution have been frustrated by stubborn institutional barriers to solving these problems, including diplomatic distaste and least-common-denominator sluggishness.

What Makes a Problem Transnational?

What elevates a garden-variety social problem to the prominence of a transnational problem in Asia? What do the transnational problems have in common, and how do they contrast with each other?

One way to answer this question is to evaluate each problem in terms of six defining characteristics, which roughly correspond to the six conventional wisdom errors discussed earlier. These six characteristics are the transnational problem's correlation with income growth, its link (if any) to security threats and political pluralism, the nature of the "spillover transaction" by which each problem crosses national borders, the public consensus regarding the severity of the problem, the NGO network associated with each problem, and the set of multilateral treaties that enable governments to work together to solve these problems.

These six characteristics provide a useful typology for thinking about transnational problems in a systematic way; for defining a transnational problem with precision; for predicting whether a transnational problem will get better or worse over time; and for assessing the odds of crafting a solution—a subject that will be addressed in more detail in chapter 7. (Table 7.1 summarizes the details of the following discussion.)

The Paradox of Prosperity

The first defining characteristic in our typology is income growth. How does Asia's rising economic tide affect each transnational problem? More bluntly, why won't money fix these problems?

Money can buy a lot of things in the new Asia, but it can't purchase freedom from illicit drugs or from rising organized crime. On the contrary, higher incomes appear to increase the demand for narcotics by providing more money for consumers to indulge in this (often expensive) form of entertainment. Increased demand for drugs in richer Asian states provides an incentive for poorer states to become drug suppliers. Unfortunately, higher incomes in opium-producing states also have had little or no effect on reducing supply, which is why Stephen Flynn argues in chapter 2 that crop-substitution schemes, of the artichokes-for-poppies variety, are a policy failure.

Money can buy solutions to infectious disease transmission by funding sanitation and public health delivery. Rising national incomes in Asia's poorer countries are rapidly pushing down mortality rates from diseases such as cholera and malaria. At the same time, business travelers, tourists, and long-haul truckers are increasing the speed of infectious disease transmission, from influenza to drug-resistant tuberculosis to human immunodeficiency virus (HIV). So the risk of garden-variety disease in Asia is falling but the risk from exotic viruses and drug-resistant mutations of infectious disease continues to climb.

Money also can buy cleaner air and water—eventually. Elizabeth Economy argues in chapter 3, that there is a U-curve relation between economic growth and pollution.[3] The initial stages of economic growth at low incomes usually causes dreadful pollution, but the curve begins to turn around as incomes rise (around $10,000 GDP per capita) and governments invest in pollution abatement, and better regulation.

The cleanest nations in Asia passed this income level years ago, including Japan and Singapore. Korea, Taiwan, and Malaysia are doing a pollution U-turn now, and Thailand is getting close. (See Table 1.1.) As Economy predicts, environmental concerns have become a contentious vote-getter in local politics, and the authorities in Seoul, Taipei, and Kuala Lumpur are clamping down on the most egregious polluters. Bangkok's choking traffic has brought down prime ministers and even prompted a rare public complaint by King Bhumibol Adulyadej.

Yet the Philippines and Indonesia will not cross the $10,000 per capita U-curve point for at least a decade, while late starters such as China and Vietnam will take even longer. Asia will get a lot dirtier before it gets cleaner.

It is *income differentials* between states more than *absolute income levels* in the source or host states that fuel the flow of illegal migrants. As for refugees, higher incomes in a source state can reverse the flow of refugees after peace has been reestablished. But higher incomes alone can't prevent violence and civil disorder, the root cause of refugee suffering in Asia and Europe alike.

Table 1.1   GDP Per Capita (at purchasing power parity)

	1995	2000
Japan	21,400	24,300
Singapore	22,000	25,400
Taiwan	13,600	16,000
South Korea	13,100	17,100
Malaysia	9,700	12,100
Thailand	7,100	9,300
Indonesia	3,500	4,300
China	2,900	4,200
Philippines	2,500	2,900

Sidney Jones is even less optimistic about solving labor and human rights abuses with economic growth. "There is no correlation between increasing incomes and human rights," she argues in chapter 6. She dismisses the "development first" argument, that an authoritarian government may be more effective in the early stages of economic growth, and casts doubt on the argument that higher income will create a middle class that will then demand labor and human rights. She also argues that economic growth may bring about new sorts of labor abuses, the marginalization of ethnic groups, and the mistreatment of indigenous peoples.

In sum, according to our authors, rising incomes will have a positive effect on public health and the environment over the long run, a marginal impact on human rights and on refugees, and a negative impact on drugs, crime, and illegal migration.

Pluralism and Internal Security

The political context of each transnational problem is the second characteristic in our typology. Do pluralism and the relaxation of Cold War tensions in Asia make it easier to tackle a problem? Which transnational problems are viewed as internal security threats in their own right?

Drug traffickers pose a clear and present danger to several governments in Asia. Stephen Flynn states that narcotics are the sustaining cash flow for guerrilla and terrorist groups in Asia, especially in the notorious Golden Triangle, the intersection of the borders of Burma, Thailand, and Laos. In Myanmar and Cambodia, insurgent forces financed by drug money have challenged the authority of the state with wholesale violence. Portions of Siberian Russia are under the *de facto* control of criminal gangs. In Thailand, Indonesia, the Philippines, China, and even Taiwan, traffickers generally sidestep direct military confrontation with the state, but they have widely corrupted both officialdom and the military. Even in democratic Japan, as Flynn points out, the yakuza have a long and complex relationship with the government, although they prefer intimidation and bribery to outright violence.

Asian nations with large numbers of illegal migrants or refugees fear that these groups may serve as the bridgehead for subversion, espionage, or terrorism. Paul Smith notes in chapter 4 that several Asian states keep resident alien populations under close political scrutiny. Singapore clamps down on any signs of political activity by resident aliens. The Malaysian government is concerned about the one million-plus Indonesians in the Malay Peninsula as well as the tens of thousands of Muslim Filipinos in Sabah, given Malaysia's history of territorial disputes with both "source" nations. The Siberian Russians are terrified of being swamped by Han Chinese emigration across the border.

Authoritarian Asian governments fear that concessions made to labor rights or human rights eventually will erode their monopoly of political power and snowball into popular demand for political rights as well. Sidney Jones argues that the Chinese government fears labor rights as the carrier of "the Polish disease" and is therefore particularly ruthless in suppressing independent labor organizations; the Suharto government in Indonesia is hostile to labor unions and labor organizers for the same reason.[4]

But the end of the Cold War also has made the West less tolerant of abuses by Asian "allies." During the Cold War the United States conveniently ignored decades of political brutality in the People's Republic of China—on a scale that dwarfs the worst abuses in China today—when that nation was a useful ally against the Soviet Union. For the same reason, Washington turned a conveniently blind eye to repression in both South Korea and the Philippines. Sidney Jones suggests that this Cold War expediency is over. Multipolarity in Asia should make the United States less tolerant of abusive regimes in Asia—unless, as Jones warns, growing U.S. commercial interests in Asia edge out U.S. support for human rights in Asia.

Sadako Ogata and Johan Cels point out in chapter 5 that the end of the Cold War may exacerbate the problem of refugees. During the Cold War, refugees from the Communist bloc were considered "asylum seekers" and were welcomed as such, particularly since there were not very many of them. Now that warm welcome has turned chilly. The United States has no ideological reason to welcome Asian refugees with open arms. Nor are the Great Powers inclined to intervene in small regional or civil conflicts, so-called teacup wars, which spawn refugees in increasing numbers. The internal problems of small states are no longer worth the price of intervention to the Great Powers. Yet the end of the Cold War is unlikely to make Tibetans or East Timorese any more enamored of their rulers in faraway Beijing or Jakarta.

In sum, the end of the Cold War has had a mixed effect on transnational problems. It may help bring pressure on crime and on drug traffickers, but it may make things worse for illegal migrants and for refugees. The jury is still out on labor and human rights.

Spillover Scale and Symmetry

The third characteristic in our typology is political will—how seriously are Asian governments motivated to solve the transnational problems? According to our authors, this political will depends on the way that the transnational problems spill over across national boundaries. This includes the physical spillover (how does a problem actually spread from source country A to "host" country B), the scale of spillover (how much the "imported" problem aggravates country B's domestic problem), and the symmetry of spillover (is source country A affected by the problem in the same way as host country B?).

Physical spillover is palpable in the case of drugs, crime, and disease. Drugs, thugs, and bugs clearly cross a border in order to wreak their damage. Less obviously, pollutants still ooze, flow, or waft across borders. Although the damage done to the "commons" such as the Pacific Ocean and the ozone layer of the troposphere is difficult to measure, the spillover from examples such as the Sumatran forest fires and acid rain cases cited by Elizabeth Economy is painfully obvious.

The large-scale population flows that are essential elements of the Asian economic miracle—businessmen, tourists, students, and legal foreign workers—usually mask the spillover of illegal migrants and refugees. The spillover transaction associated with labor standards or human rights abuses is much less obvious. Exports of products made with prison or child labor may be an exception, as this transaction knits both human rights and labor standards into a physical object that is traded across national borders.

The scale of spillover—the relationship between a transnational problem and the underlying social problem in a host nation—varies widely among the problems. Heroin addicts in the West depend on opium smuggled in from South and Southeast Asia. In this sense, Asia looms large in the scale of its contribution to drug addiction problems in the United States and Europe. But Stephen Flynn points out that drug markets are remarkably flexible. If the supply of one drug is restricted, demand quickly can shift to an alternative imported drug, to a synthetic drug, or to domestic production.

In the case of infectious diseases, almost all epidemics begin with small numbers; the initial virus can cross the border in tiny numbers and then balloon into a domestic health crisis. Thailand's HIV pandemic was triggered by "sex tourists" from abroad and then was propagated within the country by indigenous drug abusers and heterosexual transmission.

In contrast, pollution starts and stays mostly at home. As bitterly as the Koreans and Japanese may complain about acid rain from China, the Chinese suffer far more from this pollution than neighboring countries do.

It is axiomatic that the problems of illegal migration and refugees are caused by foreigners, but how seriously the effects are regarded as "problems" by the host country depends on the local economy and on local politics. For example, a host country with high unemployment may point an accusing finger at illegal migrants and expel them, but a host country with low unemployment will turn a blind eye. As for labor and human rights abuses, the scale of spillover is minor; these are largely "home-grown" problems in Asia, although illegal immigrants are often the victims of the cruelest labor abuses—in Asia and the United States.

Symmetry of spillover is unusual for most of the transnational problems, with the exception of drug smuggling and infectious disease transmission. No state gains by "exporting" disease or, in the long run, by exporting drugs. Eventually drug addiction plagues the exporter as much as the importer. Stephen Flynn points out the swelling numbers of drug addicts in Thailand and Myanmar and in the transshipping border provinces of Yunnan and Guangxi in China. By the same token, a minority of drug kingpins and corrupt officials may profit from narcotics exports, but drug smuggling is a deeply corrosive business that leads to corruption, violence, and economic distortions in the supply country.

On the other hand, some Asian source nations clearly do benefit from the outflow of emigrants, legal or otherwise, as a "safety valve" to relieve population pressures and to earn hard cash. Repatriated earnings of foreign workers are a vital source of income to some poorer Asian economies. Vietnam deliberately expelled many *hua qiao* Chinese as a matter of state policy just when Cambodia in turn expelled many ethnic Vietnamese.

In sum, the spillover associated with drugs, illegal migration, and refugees is quite clear. It is less obvious, although still measurable, for health and environmental problems. It is less clear for labor standards and human rights. The only transnational problems in which both source and host countries have a symmetrical stake are drugs and health problems. The scale of the spillover to the underlying domestic problem is small for drugs, health, and the environment, large for migration and refugees, and unclear for labor standards and human rights.

Clashing Values and the Media

The fourth characteristic in our typology—public consensus on the severity of the transnational problem—is molded by the social values that are challenged or embedded in the problem and by the way that the mass media chooses to cover these problems. Some transnational problems are clearly technical, with little or no disagreement about underlying social values. These are sometimes referred to as "value-neutral" problems. Public health and the environment are good examples. No one in Asia or the United States believes that disease or pollution is a good thing, although politicians and officials may disagree on the economic trade-offs.

But migration and illegal drugs are in a gray area. Source states usually deny responsibility for these problems, and in host states there is rarely much social consensus on how to solve these problems. Citizens around the Pacific continue to use narcotic drugs in huge quantities and continue to employ illegal aliens in large numbers, in defiance of law. Some governments, such as those of Singapore and Malaysia, are serious about enforcing drugs laws and are willing to hang smugglers regardless of public ambivalence. China engages in periodic anticrime campaigns and executes smugglers by the score. By contrast, the United States has been engaged in a so-called war on drugs for decades, spending billions of dollars on interdiction, domestic law enforcement, and prisons, but with little progress. The draconian law enforcement necessary to wage an effective war on drugs collides with concepts of civil liberty and, to some degree, civil libertarianism in the West. An effective war on illegal migrants also collides with labor market realities in Asia. Citizens in higher-income states simply will not perform the most menial, dangerous, and dirty jobs filled by illegal migrants.

Television and print media can crystallize public opinion by the way they choose to cover the transnational problems. Drug busts, triad murders, illegal migrant arrests, the pathos of child prostitutes, and oil spills are inherently telegenic. They make excellent video clips and good TV news. As Paul Smith observes regarding media reports on the *Golden Venture* incident, "nobody in Washington paid attention [to illegal Chinese migrants] until one of these ships practically landed in midtown Manhattan." The less telegenic transnational problems—such as slow-moving environmental degradation, the quiet misery of refugee camps, infectious disease pandemics, and labor abuses—are less well publicized. Although advocacy groups and NGOs are becoming more skilled in using press kits and video clips to take their cases to the mass media, television coverage still favors the more lurid problems.

The effect of media coverage cuts both ways. Stephen Flynn complains that the mass media glamorizes the wealth and power of drug traffickers—the "Miami Vice" syndrome. Sadako Ogata and Johan Cels credit mass media reports of the vicious pirate attacks on the Vietnamese boat people with building public consensus in the United States to keep its refugee quotas in place. But they also lament the way that media rumors of U.S. immigrant amnesty or special refugee permits have triggered new waves of refugees who have stretched the resources of the UNHCR to the breaking point.

In sum, there is a broad consensus among Asian elites and the public that they must deal with public health and pollution problems; the disagreement is over the economic trade-offs. There is little consensus on how to resolve the problems of crime, illegal migration, refugees, and drugs, and there is no agreement over labor and human rights. And the media is skilled at fanning the flames of public anxiety with the more lurid aspects of the transnational problems.

Networking NGOs

The fifth characteristic in our typology is the NGO constituency of each transnational problem. Drug abuse and public health problems are largely the preserve of well-established government organizations, as opposed to NGOs, on both sides of the Pacific. Examples of governmental organizations are the U.S. Center for Disease Control (CDC) and agencies such as the Drug Enforcement Administration (DEA). Because of competition from such powerful governmental organizations, NGOs are less well developed and less influential in these two transnational problems.

Almost every state in Asia has an environmental protection agency, but enforcement varies widely, as Elizabeth Economy points out. Environmental NGOs are sprouting like mushrooms all over Asia—even in China—in part because they are perceived as value-neutral and hence politically neutral. Environmental NGOs were active in setting the agenda and negotiating policy planks at the U.N.–sponsored 1992 Rio de Janeiro Conference on the environment, for example.

The NGOs dealing with migration and refugee problems include relief and charitable agencies such as the International Rescue Committee and religious organizations, which work closely with host Asian government and U.N. agencies "on the ground." These NGOs are less visible and less sophisticated in using the mass media to publicize their activities. Yet they have well-developed networks throughout Asia and deep social roots in the West.

Labor unions are NGOs with an interest in migration policy—at least in those countries where labor unions are legal. Unions frequently blame illegal migrants for low-wage competition and unemployment. The same logic makes labor unions strong advocates of imposing strict labor standards on manufacturing exports from Asia.

NGOs pressing for labor or human rights in Asia are denounced as agents of "cultural imperialism" or "foreign subversion" when they take aid from sister NGOs in richer states in Asia or the West. But Sidney Jones argues that, despite official repression, local human rights NGOs have stubbornly taken root in Asia.

In sum, the problems of drugs, health, and illegal migration have relatively weak NGO networks, due in part to existing strong governmental organizations. The rest of the transnational problems have relatively strong NGO networks in Asia, although there is some disagreement among NGOs regarding population control and on labor standards.

The Legal Standing for Multilateral Cooperation

The sixth characteristic is the legal basis for multilateral cooperation between states in taking concerted action.

The United Nations has elaborate legal mechanisms to deal with some problems, such as the institutional World Health Organization (WHO) for infectious diseases, and weaker mechanisms for others, such as the Narcotics Control Group, which has the difficult task of implementing the 1971 Convention on Psychotropic Substances. Some U.N. agreements have more teeth than others. Both the Rio de Janeiro Convention and the Cairo Convention resulted in paper commitments by Asian states. But China was successful in rallying quite a few Asian states around the 1991 Beijing Ministerial Declaration that discounted the environmental responsibility of the developing world, unless the industrial countries are willing to pay for environmental programs. Sadako Ogata and Johan Cels lament the fact that few Asian states have acceded to the United Nations 1951 Refugee Convention or the 1967 Refugee Protocol.

Human and labor rights are debated by the United Nations every year, in the face of much resistance from authoritarian Asian states. Sidney Jones argues that all governments in the region are committed to upholding basic human rights based on the 1948 Universal Declaration of Human Rights, to which every Asian member has acceded, regardless of the annual human rights debate.

Asian regional organizations such as ASEAN and APEC have very little track record in dealing with transnational problems. The ASEAN ministers periodically bemoan the narcotics problem, and convene, from time to time, the ASEAN Ministry on Drugs (ASOD) to do workshops and seminars on narcotics treatment and law enforcement. But funding has been patchy for any serious ASEAN drug program, and the entry of Myanmar (Burma) into ASEAN has slowed ASEAN's consensus-based decision process to a crawl when it comes to cracking down on narcotics smuggling. China and other authoritarian Asian states have similarly resisted attempts to broaden the agenda of APEC to deal with problems beyond economic issues.

In sum, there is a broad set of multilateral agreements or conventions to tackle all of the transnational problems, at least in principle, but migration and drugs have the weakest legal and institutional foundation for multilateral action. There is much disagreement on the standing of agreements on labor and human rights. There has been little progress on any of the transnational problems within Asian regional multilateral organizations.

Before turning to the details of the next six chapters and then to the question of solutions in chapter 7 let us briefly place the Asian transnational problems in perspective—to each other, against Asia's long historical record, and in a global context.

Tangled Causes

The transnational problems appear intractable partly because they are so closely interrelated. In the following chapters, the authors delineate the transnational problems on the basis of their particular research expertise, professional experience, or agency mandate. But the damage inflicted by the transnational problems in Asia is seamless. An unhappy chain of cause and effect connects all of the transnational problems.

For example, slash-and-burn drug cultivation results in deforestation and flooding. Desperate refugees turn to drug cultivation and smuggling out of sheer necessity. Drug users transmit deadly diseases; 75 percent of registered drug addicts in China are HIV carriers. Snakeheads recruit poor peasants and smuggle them throughout the region, force them into the sex trade, and thereby accelerate the spread of HIV and AIDS. Pollution causes higher morbidity and mortality. And so on.

Old Poison in New Bottles

All of the transnational problems have deep historical roots in Asia. There have been four major waves of migration in Asian history, of which the current flow of labor migrants is only the most recent. Asia has also witnessed four major waves of refugees in this century alone. Deforestation and gross ecological destruction, such as abandoned tin mines in peninsular Malaysia, are nothing new to the region. Pandemics have swept through Asia and across the Pacific many times and in many directions. Drugs and organized crime have figured in the landscape of

Asia for centuries, sometimes allied with the state, sometimes against it.

Our authors argue, however, that two things are new about the transnational problems today. The first difference is in their greater scale. For example, the population density of Asia's megacities such as Jakarta or Shanghai, combined with modern air travel, makes Asia (and the United States) exceptionally vulnerable to infectious disease epidemics. The number of illegal migrants in Asia has grown from an estimated 200,000 in 1980 to between two and three million just fifteen years later. The sheer scale of industrial pollution in Asia is exceeding the absorption capacity of the natural environment. Slum-ringed megacities are swelling and arable land is disappearing; both phenomena are irreversible. Elizabeth Economy illustrates this claim with examples of falling water tables, filthy rivers, and heavily polluted air—with their consequential rise in mortality and morbidity rates.

Second, Asian governments are now more accountable to solve these transnational problems. In contrast to the historical record, this *is* new. Historically, imperial or hard authoritarian states have not concerned themselves with such "soft" issues. Government officials in eighteenth- and nineteenth-century Asia—arrogant colonial overlord and indigenous despot alike—blandly ignored the massive human suffering incurred by the transnational problems under their regimes. Today, with the exception of Asia's three failed states—Cambodia, Myanmar, and North Korea—all governments there are more or less accountable to deliver a minimum of good governance. In addition to pressure from the international community, some are accountable by democratic election (such as Korea or Malaysia), some are accountable to a "selectorate" (such as China or Vietnam). None can completely ignore the transnational problems anymore.

Finally, Asia's transnational problems need to be kept in global perspective. It is easy to get carried away with pessimism as our authors catalog the transnational ills and escort the reader through their particular shop of horrors. But there is no reason to believe that Asian governments and publics may not rise to meet these challenges and that the transnational problems—despite their apparent intractability, and despite the institutional barriers to solutions—are not ultimately manageable. Desperate poverty and war are only a memory to most Asians, particularly those who have grown up in the past two decades.

Moreover, Asia's odds of managing these problems are far better than in many areas of Latin America, much of the Middle East, and nearly all of Africa. High economic growth may add its own complications to the transnational problems, but at least it provides Asian governments with the resources to deal with these problems, if they can summon the political will to do so.

Notes

1. In Chinese *ge an guan huo* means "fire across the water," a classical reference to the act of watching a crisis from a distance but remaining detached. This phrase can be traced to a longer poem by Ch'ien Kang, of unclear dynastic origin. The author thanks Marius Jansen for this reference.

2. See Bilahari Kausikan and Kishore Mahbubani.

3. Economy correctly points out that environmental protection and economic growth are not mutually exclusive. Proper accounting for the side-effects and real resource costs of some economic activity can slash the nominal growth rates and per capita incomes of some Asian states by several percentage points.

4. Poland's Solidarity labor union is widely credited with weakening and eventually destroying the communist regime in the 1980s.

Chapter 2

Asian Drugs, Crime, and Control: Rethinking the War

STEPHEN E. FLYNN

On June 26, 1996, the Chinese government summarily executed several hundred drug traffickers to commemorate the U. N.–declared International Day Against Drug Abuse and Illicit Traffic.[1] The challenge of controlling drugs is by no means a new problem for China. Beginning in the early 1700s, the Chinese had a more than two-century love affair with opium thanks to the matchmaking talents of Portuguese, Dutch, British, and American traders. Efforts by the Qing Dynasty to put an end to this national habit during the nineteenth century were resisted by powerful foreign commercial interests backed by the gunboats of the British empire.

It would take the strong-arm tactics of the People's Republic of China to accomplish what the last emperors could not. From 1950 to 1952, the new Communist regime forcibly detoxified twenty million opium addicts and conducted a nationwide eradication campaign against the cultivation of opium poppy. Declaring victory, the antidrug campaign went into mothballs for three decades. But drugs are back now, and, ironically, it is the growing appetite for heroin in the West that has given impetus to its resurrection.

Opium production in Southeast Asia grew by 19 percent in 1995 over production levels the previous year. With an estimated 175,470 hectares of opium poppy under cultivation, the region has the potential to refine and export 213 tons of heroin.[2] Just ten years ago, heroin from the Golden Triangle region of Burma, Thailand, and Laos was a relative novelty in U.S. drug markets, accounting for only 14 percent of the heroin seized by American enforcement authorities; by 1995, its market share stood at nearly 60 percent, with much of this reaching American shores after first transiting through China.[3] With a reputation for high quality and street purity levels averaging 53 percent, this heroin has displaced long-standing market leaders from Mexico and Southwest Asia.

Not only is the heroin better; it is substantially cheaper. The average price paid by American heroin addicts in 1995 was $1,259 per pure gram, down from $3,374 in 1981.[4] In New York and the Mid-Atlantic states, bags of heroin could be had for as little as $5.[5] Yet even at these new, low prices, heroin remains the Cadillac of drugs, earning over thirteen times as much as an equivalent amount of cocaine.[6]

The U.S. government has met this growing flood of high-quality Asian heroin into the country with a surprisingly muted response, particularly in comparison to the cocaine war. Despite substantial data that heroin abuse is on the rise, intelligence and enforcement resources are overwhelmingly committed to combating cocaine.[7] As recently as 1993 there were only four intelligence analysts assigned to the Southeast Asian region—three in Thailand and one in Hong Kong.[8] With their plates already full by their hemispheric exertions,[9] U.S. drug control agents appear to be reluctant to complicate their lives by making a serious attempt to tackle the Asian drug trade. They have good cause to be hesitant.

This chapter maintains that these tepid Asian drug control programs should be abandoned altogether if they are not part of a comprehensive effort to redress rising drug consumption, political corruption, and organized crime. Well-intentioned enforcement attempts which sidestep the vexing context that motivates and facilitates this illicit trade are destined to fail. Further, this failure comes at a significant cost since such efforts can be sustained only by placing other overarching U.S. regional interests at risk.

This pessimistic outlook is based on an assessment of the sweeping social, economic, and political changes under way within the region and their impact on the drug phenomenon and Asian organized crime. These transformational changes are rendering impotent traditional governmental means to police increasingly sophisticated criminals within and across national borders. As a result, current U.S. programs designed to bolster the drug-control capacity of the region's governments will have no measurable effect on stemming Asian production and trafficking. Indeed, the only "success" these programs can achieve is to reinforce and legitimize the authoritarian tendencies of regimes—especially in Burma and China—that are under growing domestic and international pressure to democratize. A Faustian bargain with Beijing or Rangoon might be palatable if it secured Americans some relief from the array of social ills connected with widespread abuse of drugs. Unfortunately, there is little prospect that such an outcome will be achieved. Thus, the bargain is a decidedly bad deal for wider U.S. national interests.

What can be done? An analysis of the factors facilitating drug production within the region, the makeup and workings of the Asian organized criminal networks that traffic in illicit narcotics, and the durability of the markets that generate the demand for these products shows a more complicated policy environment than politicians and bureaucrats generally acknowledge. A critique of our current efforts must begin with an understanding of this untidy backdrop.

Next we should consider a policy prescription that redirects our efforts along two fronts. First, there is a rational alternative to a strategy that makes the control of drugs themselves the overarching objective. Instead of working on a cure for a specific virus, we could choose to investigate ways to strengthen the overall immune system. Such an approach would acknowledge that the burgeoning trade in drugs suggests not so much a sudden universal craving for mind-altering substances as it does the capacity for Asian organized criminal networks to create markets for their wares by exploiting the legitimate global economy with virtual impunity. It is the capacity for this exploitation that should receive our attention, not the growth in the trade of one particularly noxious commodity. What we need rather than an international *drug* strategy is a comprehensive joint public and private sector campaign to enhance *criminal* safeguards.

The second front is one that already receives universal rhetorical acknowledgment by policymakers—and is almost universally ignored in practical terms. The drug market is sustained by a demand for its drugs. Specific drug control energies therefore should focus on reducing the demand for drugs and the conditions that motivate and facilitate their widespread abuse. While this approach will not be inexpensive or provide for immediate victories, the logic behind making demand reduction the end game is straightforward—if there are few customers, there will be few suppliers.

Fields of Dreams

Any evaluation of the efficacy of U.S. drug control policies for Asia must be grounded in an understanding of where these drugs—primarily heroin—come from; how they are produced, transported, and sold; and who are the consumers.

The Golden Triangle—where the borders of Thailand, Burma, and Laos meet—is the source of two-thirds of the estimated 4,086 metric tons of opium produced worldwide in 1995.[10] The region is approximately the size of Nevada, and its weather and mountainous terrain make it ideally suited to grow the opium poppies that are the raw material for heroin. Opium poppies must be planted annually. They grow for four to five months and flower before the opium is harvested. The harvesting process is labor intensive, as opium bulbs must be individually scored (cut) up to six times during harvesting. Normal harvest yields from six to fifteen kilograms of opium per hectare.

Burma cultivates just under 90 percent of the total opium poppy in the region, generating annual revenues for opiate growers of between $257 million and $293 million.[11] Cultivation traditionally has been concentrated in the mountainous regions of the Shan plateau, which extends the length of the Shan State. Since 1989, however, cultivation has spread to the west bank of the Salween River and into the Chin State along Burma's border.[12] While Burma's overwhelming market share will not be threatened by other regional producers any time soon, the cultivation of opium poppy has spilled over into Vietnam, China, and—if recent reports are substantiated—Cambodia as well. In Vietnam, poor ethnic minority groups, predominantly H'mong in the northern mountainous provinces, have plowed under traditional crops for the colorful and much more lucrative poppy plant. According to a 1993 U.N. estimate, Vietnam was capable of producing 27 to 39 tons of raw opium.[13] In China, while there is no publicly available national estimate of total opium production, there are reports of large opium fields in the Chinese provinces of Yunnan, Sichuan, Guizhou, Inner Mongolia, Guangxi, Hunan, and Qinghai.[14] In Cambodia, there have been rumors of opium cultivation and the presence of heroin labs. Finally, press accounts in March 1995 reported that some North Koreans have begun growing opium in the mountain recesses near Hamhung and Chongjin in response to increasingly desperate economic circumstances.[15]

This surge in drug production throughout the region can be attributed, first and foremost, to its profitability relative to the alternatives. A hectare of poppies in Southeast Asia, on average, can produce raw opium valued at between $925 and $1,050 in 1993 prices.[16] With the per-capita income in most rural areas of Southeast Asia and China below $500, the economic appeal of cultivation is self-evident. Poppies also are relatively easy to grow and harvest, and are far less labor intensive than other traditional crops.

This basic economic appeal can be expected to grow with time. This is because the region's economic boom has bypassed many rural backwaters, leaving farmers to their own devices to cope with a general global decline in the prices of many agricultural products, a persistent rise in the cost of fertilizers, the substitution of machines for human labor, and demographic pressures that inevitably lead to a division of land into smaller and less efficient parcels. By and large, limited government revenues in the region are concentrated on providing basic services to urban areas, or financing industrialization programs and infrastructure development. When the rural poor belong to minority ethnic groups—as is the case in Burma, Thailand, Vietnam, and throughout China—appeals for development aid generally go unheeded.

For farmers in North Korea and Vietnam, their situation has been aggravated by the economic disintegration of the former Soviet Union, and the end of foreign aid and subsidies from their former communist sponsors. While Vietnam has moved toward economic liberalization, the transition from the old economic order to the new has been painful. After two decades of civil war, Cambodia's infrastructure is in ruins, and the fledgling democracy is almost completely dependent on external assistance to run its ministries.

Elsewhere in the region, the incentives for engaging in illicit production are fueled by the absence of governmental authority and widespread conflict in areas where drug crops are grown. In areas such as the Shan State in Burma and along the Cambodian-Laotian border, push-and-pull factors draw farmers into production. Political instability displaces farmers from their traditional villages and disrupts their access to downstream markets where they can sell legitimate goods. In addition, insurgents in need of hard currency to finance their struggles and traffickers motivated by basic greed often force farmers to abandon traditional crops in favor of opium poppy or cannabis. The pull factors include offers by traffickers to provide cash advances for drug crops in combination with minimal real risk of enforcement action. Peasants are further emboldened by "success stories" involving family members, neighbors, and friends.

The explosive growth in the regional economy has introduced technology, infrastructure, and investment to the drug trade. Refinement processes that once could be accomplished only in sophisticated laboratories in the developed world now can be completed near the cultivation sites. This also raises profits, for it reduces the logistical and smuggling problems of moving bulky raw materials over long distances. Field laboratories powered by diesel generators now dot the dense jungle regions along Burmese-Thai and Burmese-Chinese borders. In these remote areas, chemists work converting opium gum into morphine base, treating the morphine base with acetic anhydride or acetyl chloride, sodium carbonate, and hydrochloric acid, and mixing it with sodium carbonate and hydrochloric acid to yield the lucrative, easily transported final product of heroin.

More indirectly, the technological revolution has vastly expanded access to the precursor and essential chemicals required to produce drugs. Of the world's $1.2 trillion chemical industry,[17] East Asia—excluding Japan and China—now produces 3.9 percent of the world's industrial chemicals and 4.3 percent of other chemical products.[18] In general, China, the Republic of Korea, Taiwan, and Malaysia are becoming increasingly important players in the global chemical industry.[19] Suppliers in the chemical industry typically are far removed from the industrial applications of their products and therefore have limited capacity to discriminate among their customers.

Asian Thugs and Drugs

That the region has the capacity to produce enough drugs to satisfy the world's current and future appetite for opiates and other narcotics seems clear. Ominously, Asia is also the base for growing organized criminal networks that possess the means to ensure a steady flow of drugs from remote production areas to major markets around the world. Today these criminal enterprises are aggressively exploiting dramatic regional and global changes to advance the trade in drugs.

Global capitalism has not been the only beneficiary of the widely heralded revolution in the transportation, communications, and financial sectors. These changes have been a boon for organized crime as well. Throughout much of Asia, drug traffickers and other criminals can move as freely across national borders as their legal counterparts. The sheer magnitude of international commercial and financial transactions within the region has made it more and more possible for them to blend their activities into the legitimate economy with little risk of detection. Like searching for the proverbial needle in the haystack, enforcement officials face insurmountable odds in their efforts to interdict drugs and other contraband or to root out money laundering. Additionally, in many places, investment and liberalization trends have been accompanied by a huge growth in corruption.

This development has been particularly pronounced in China, where the liberalization regime and resultant prosperity has been concentrated along the coast under the watchful eye of poorly paid government bureaucrats. The boom atmosphere has swept away most ideological and party loyalties, and collusion between local government officials and businessmen to avoid regulations and taxes is widespread. Further, the fact that the new special economic zones coexist with the highly restrictive and stagnant provincial economies in the hinterland has created a fertile environment for domestic smuggling of an array of legitimate exports and imports.[20]

The Asian criminal networks that are prospering under these conditions fall into three major groupings: ethnic Chinese criminal enterprises associated with Chinese triads or gangs, the Japanese yakuza, and Chinese and Vietnamese street gangs. Chinese triads can trace their origins back to secret societies established in China 2,000 years ago, but the four major contemporary groups—the Sun Yee On triad, the 14K groups, the Wo Hop To Triad, and the United Bamboo Gang—have more recent antecedents. These groups are the modern-day descendants of patriotic societies, geographically centered in the coastal provinces of Fujian and Guangdong, which sprang up in the seventeenth century in opposition to the Qing dynasty. Their power grew as that of the Qing emperors declined. Indeed, they contributed to the downfall of the Manchu emperors, by actively and passively assisting Hong Xiuchuan in the Taiping Rebellion and later backing Sun Yat-sen in the successful Republican rebellion of 1911–12. The ports of Canton, Amoy, and Shanghai became triad strongholds, and the triads increasingly relied on criminal enterprises such as the opium trade, gambling, prostitution, and extortion as a sources of income.[21] After the Communist revolution, many triad members fled to Hong Kong, Taiwan, and elsewhere in Southeast Asia.

The global reach of the triads expanded beyond China's borders as immigration from Fukien and Canton increased during the first half of the nineteenth century. In North America, triad lodges sprang up in San Francisco; Laramie and Cheyenne, Wyoming; Kansas City, Missouri; Seattle, Washington; Vancouver, British Columbia; the Klondike, Alaska; and eventually New York and Boston. Today triad members can be found residing among the twenty million ethnic Chinese living around the world.[22]

The relationship between criminal groups associated with triads in these various cities and countries is flexible. Groups tend to work together temporarily to commit a crime, divide the resultant profits based on a prearranged formula, and then disperse. These groups engage in a variety of criminal activities: heroin smuggling, money laundering, share manipulation, alien smuggling, gun-running, counterfeit credit card fraud, cloning of cellular phones, insurance fraud, automobile thefts, home invasions, prostitution, illegal gambling, murder, extortion, and manufacturing counterfeit passports, visas, and other official documents.

Like their Chinese counterparts, the Japanese yakuza have deep historical roots.[23] During the eighteenth century, these groups attracted outcast samurai displaced by the end of Japanese feudalism during the Tokugawa period. Their power grew during the twentieth century, when they aligned themselves with right-wing nationalist politicians and moved into the construction and transportation businesses. The yakuza prospered during the post–World War II occupation by the United States and since then have had widespread influence in both Japanese political and financial circles.[24]

Today the modern Japanese yakuza has an estimated 88,300 members,[25] 15 percent of whom are ethnic Koreans.[26] The Yamaguchi-gumi is the largest group, with 26,000 members and 944 affiliated subgroups. It dominates the industrialized, densely populated region extending from Kyoto through Osaka and Kobe. Based in Tokyo, the Inagawa-kai, the Sumiyoshi-Kai, and Toa Yuai Jigyo Kumiai are the other major yakuza crime groups, with 8,600, 7,000, and 900 members respectively.[27] A 1988 report by the National Police Agency of Japan estimated that the yakuza earned almost $10 billion in annual revenues—one-third of which came from sales of crystal methamphetamine, or "ice."[28]

Although the yakuza do not have the extensive overseas networks of the ethnic Chinese, they are active throughout the Pacific. They have limited ties with the Chinese triads, primarily as a result of relationships forged during World War II when many Hong Kong and other Chinese triads collaborated with their Japanese occupiers. In addition, Japan's forty-year occupation of Korea during the first half of the twentieth century and Japan's large ethnic Korean community provide links to South Korean criminals. Yakuza-financed laboratories in South Korea supply most of the world's market for ice.

Yakuza syndicates also have moved into Taiwan, the Philippines, and Thailand to set up "sex tours" for male Japanese tourists. Desperate for the hard currency generated by tourism, local government officials are often openly supportive of hosting high-grade brothels. These brothels use women from China, Korea, Thailand, and the Philippines who are smuggled out of their native lands and virtually enslaved into prostitution rings. In 1982 Thai police estimated that there were 700,000 prostitutes in the country, or nearly 10 percent of all Thai women between the ages of fifteen and thirty. The number of Filipino prostitutes was estimated at 300,000, and South Korea was home to 200,000 Korean prostitutes.[29]

In the mid-1970s, the yakuza began extending their reach eastward to ethnic Japanese communities in Hawaii and California. Hawaii has become a major money-laundering center for the yakuza, where they wash their assets through real estate investment and the $1 billion spent annually on the islands by one million Japanese tourists. By one report, yakuza money has purchased close to fifty major properties in Hawaii.[30] Los Angeles, home to nearly 250,000 people of Japanese descent, is another more recent base for yakuza money-laundering activities. In addition, yakuza operatives have managed to corner much of the large Japanese tourist industry in California.

While these overseas ventures are by no means insignificant, most yakuza enterprises are still based in Japan. Over the past decade, yakuza organizations have concentrated their energies on profiting from the mainstream economy—especially in securities and real estate—rather than traditional criminal acts.[31] For example, through shell companies set up in the late 1980s, Japan's largest yakuza syndicate managed to become the second-largest shareholder in Kurabo Industries, a major Japanese textile firm. Since 1992 yakuza syndicates have successfully targeted financial corporations and other legitimate companies with blackmail schemes. One Tokyo-based syndicate compiled a massive computer database of corporate and political scandals reported in newspaper accounts over the past forty years. The data is stored on a $10 million minicomputer, cross-referenced by company name, individual name, and type of scandal. The information is then used to generate outright payments from the victims or used as leverage to obtain access to financial institutions in support of yakuza illicit business operations.[32]

Street gangs make up the third and final major grouping of Asian organized crime. These gangs operate in major cities in the United States and Canada in addition to Hong Kong and Taiwan, and are primarily of Chinese and Vietnamese origins. Chinese street gangs tend to be loosely connected to triads within the many Chinatowns throughout North America. They draw many of their recruits from recent immigrants—often illegal—with limited education and vocational skills and poor English-speaking ability. Many Vietnamese gang members came to the United States as unaccompanied minors after years in the crime-ridden refugee camps in Southeast Asia. Vietnamese gangs tend to be highly mobile, often traveling between states and perpetrating a variety of criminal acts before moving on. An extensive network of contacts made while they were refugees assists in their activities.

Most gangs consist of males in their late teens and early twenties. They typically have a three-tier hierarchy of gang leaders, lieutenants, and street soldiers. The leaders have contacts with other organized criminal elements and tend to stay clear of the actual commission of street crimes. Chinese gangs such as the Ghost Shadows and the Flying Dragons engage primarily in extortion from Asian merchants and also serve as enforcers for the triad groups and tongs.[33] Vietnamese gangs such as Born to Kill (BTK) tend to be more versatile and violent than their Chinese counterparts, with criminal activities including extortion, fraud, auto theft, high-technology theft, gambling, prostitution, narcotics, trafficking, and home invasion robberies.[34]

While the distinctive characteristics of triads, yakuza, and gangs suggest caution in generalizing about Asian organized criminal networks, they share three common attributes: a global reach facilitated by legal and illegal migration; a tendency to exploit opportunities in the legitimate commercial sector; and a willingness to engage in strategic alliances to facilitate profitable transactions. All three characteristics rest upon a foundation secured by the ancient Chinese social practice of *guanxi*.

Guanxi is a bond established between two or more persons for the purpose of satisfying anticipated and contingent future needs. When asked, a member of a guanxi network is obligated to provide goods and services to other members of the network. The requester, in turn, is obligated to respond in kind if necessary at some future date. Guanxi bonds tend to be built around kinship ties emanating from one's family and extended family but also include neighbors, classmates, coworkers, people who were born in the same neighborhood or village, and other contacts of social significance.[35] Once established, they are expected to last a lifetime. An inability or unwillingness to perform as expected usually leads to expulsion from the network and general social ostracism.[36] Therefore, preserving these relationships and satisfying the obligations attached to them tends to transcend obligations to abide by formal rules and laws established by governments—particularly non-Chinese governments. Naturally, such a system is extremely advantageous for individuals engaged in criminal activities. As long as they make requests—that while technically illegal appear reasonable to others within the network—they will have an extensive network of potential accomplices.

The benefits of *guanxi* when conducting transnational crimes are twofold. First, *guanxi* debts provide a means to recruit a vast array of potential accomplices into a long chain of contacts. Second, since these debts are strictly personal versus organizational obligations, each contributor need not—and often will not—know all the members of a particular network.[37] Together these two factors create a situation where the membership within these chains can be very fluid, often changing from one criminal episode to the next. Networks are produced that enforcement authorities find virtually impenetrable and immune to disruption if one or two members are apprehended.

This fluid quality combined with global reach makes Asian criminal organizations an ominous force. They operate somewhat like successful corporations; they comprise decentralized networks of entrepreneurs with global reach, as opposed to vertically integrated behemoths such as IBM and General Motors. Like so many profitable, small international firms, Asian criminal networks can be exceptionally nimble in the face of global change. They take full advantage of the information revolution as well as the revolution in the global transportation sector and the globalization of financial markets. Like their corporate counterparts, Asian criminal organizations benefit from the deregulatory trend by governments. As governments court investors by creating open capital markets and by removing customs barriers that might slow trade and raise transportation costs, they create an economic no-man's land where all entrepreneurs, licit and illicit, can prosper.

The East Asian economic boom has produced a smugglers' paradise. New roads, rail lines, port facilities, and airfields dot the region, linking once-remote areas to the global economy and facilitating a flood of goods that render border inspections entirely impractical. For example, every month more than one million maritime containers transit through the port of Hong Kong and 1.1 million move through the port of Singapore. In the United States, it takes on average five customs agents three hours to inspect just one container comprehensively. But in Singapore, the average time between discharge and reloading an entire ship carrying as many as 3,000 containers is just eight hours.[38] China, Hong Kong, and Taiwan are undertaking port development programs to nearly double their annual container capacity from 28 million today to 58 million in 2000.[39] South Korean shipyards are constructing ships capable of carrying upward of 5,000 containers.

The aviation sector is witnessing similar spectacular growth, with the attendant vulnerability to smuggling. Air service in China has been growing over twice as fast as the national economy and more than four times faster than world averages. China's total passenger volume increased by twelve times between 1980 to 1994, to 78 million passengers.[40] Since 1988, ninety new airlines have been added to the Asian market, forty in China alone.[41] By the year 2000, Chinese and other airlines will be taking off and landing in some five hundred new or renovated airports in the People's Republic.[42] In 1995, Hong Kong was host to 21 million air passengers and the air cargo terminal at Chek Lap Kok soon will have the capacity to process 2.4 million tons of air cargo per year. The explosive rise in air express freight—it climbed by 25 percent in 1995—will be supported by a new facility designed to handled 200,000 metric tons annually.[43]

It is not simply the sheer volume of trade that renders traditional customs controls impractical. Governments themselves are less likely even to make the attempt. Hong Kong and Macao are free ports, with no customs tariffs on imports or exports. Indonesia has created a free trade area in Batam Island. Malaysia has set up eight free trade areas in West Malaysia. The Filipino ports of Bataan, Mactan, and Cavite are all free trade areas. Singapore has six free trade zones, including Singapore Changi International Airport. China has eliminated tariffs for a plethora of imports in its special economic zones (SEZs) in Shenzhen, Zhuhai, and Shantou in Guangdong province, and Xiamen in Fujian province. In addition, there are no tariffs on all exports produced by enterprises within these zones. South Korea has set up two free export zones in Masan City and Iri City.[44]

In general, goods within free trade zones are not subject to the usual customs controls. The idea is to provide a "a no-man's customs territory where goods in international trade can be stored or further processed before they finally become imports for a particular country, or are re-export-ed to another country."[45] Goods entering these zones need not be declared, and customs control is reduced to the absolute minimum. Having elim-inated customs duties for most imports and exports, governments have no real incentive to inspect any cargo passing across their borders.[46]

The communications sector has grown alongside the transportation sector, bringing cellular phones, fax machines, and the Internet to urban areas throughout the region. Once the commercial global communications satellite systems now under development become operational, anyone with the resources to purchase airtime will have an immediate and secure connection to the rest of the world, no matter where he is locat-ed in the Far East. All of this, naturally, enhances the capacity to coordinate the movement of chemicals, drugs, and cash that underpin the illicit nar-cotics trade.

A revolution in the financial sector has made it possible to mask the origins of the profits gained by the drug trade. Flows of foreign direct invest-ment (FDI) have increased dramatically over the past decade.[47] A sub-stantial proportion of these flows has been intraregional, originating from Japan, Hong Kong, Taiwan, Singapore, and South Korea.[48] New rules have allowed residents to transfer capital and hold financial assets abroad, while nonresidents have been permitted to borrow money freely in home markets. Additionally, lending and investment transactions in virtually all East Asian countries can be made in foreign currencies.[49]

These changes provide ample opportunity to smuggle money in and out of Asian banking centers. Cash from drug proceeds can be placed into the luggage of Asian couriers or loaded into maritime containers to be shipped to Hong Kong, Taiwan, Singapore, Malaysia, and Thailand, there to be placed into bank accounts. None of these countries has cur-rency controls in place, nor do any require the reporting of large deposits. The cash also can be deposited in a growing number of regional offshore finance centers that guarantee airtight secrecy for the true owner. These include Vanuatu, the Marshall Islands, Cook Islands, Western Samoa, and Nauru.[50]

Once the profits from illicit enterprises have been placed into the international system, obscuring their origin—by "layering" via multiple financial transactions across a variety of regulatory jurisdictions—is rel-atively straightforward. There is no hope of randomly identifying drug money among all the funds moving by wire transfers. The sheer quan-tity of transactions is overwhelming, totaling 8.1 billion electronic trans-fers in 1993.[51] On an average day in 1994, $800 billion moved through the New York–based Clearing House Interbank Payments System (CHIPS), and $1 trillion passed through Fedwire—the primary U.S. domestic wire transfer system.[52] Money launderers know that even if a suspicious transfer is identified, locating its originator is virtually impossible.[53] This is because, outside the United States, electronic transfer signals have just three parts: the address of the preparing bank, the message, and the address of the receiving bank. If the electronic transfer is sent to an intermediary institution, as they often are by launderers, the identity of the originator is dropped and replaced with that of the intermediary who prepares the new message. Even if there is a paper trail to back up these electronic transfers, if the intermediary institution is a foreign bank, investigators trying to gain access to that paper quickly run into the bureaucratic wall of competing national jurisdictions.[54]

In short, the growth of Asian organized crime is directly related to transformations within the regional and global milieu that the organizations seek to exploit. Today the international system is under extraordinary strain as a result of political, economic, and social changes that together are eroding the capacity of states to regulate the flow of goods, services, and peoples within and across their borders. Like a virus that replicates quickly once the immune system is compromised, Asian organized crime is well positioned to prosper as long as there are consumers who demand the products and services these networks provide.

Global High: The Market for Asian Drugs

There appears to be no shortage of consumers for Asian organized crime's most lucrative product—illicit narcotics. In the United States, Southeast Asian heroin accounts for 60 percent of a market[55] that the U.S. government believes to consist of 586,000 drug users who consume heroin at least weekly.[56] Many observers believe that the heroin population could be more than twice that size, pointing to such data as the 169 percent rise in hospital emergency room episodes involving heroin use between 1988 and 1994.[57]

The recent growth in U.S. heroin consumption is attributed, in part, to the way the drug currently is being marketed at the street level. Traditionally, American heroin addicts consumed the drug intravenously, to maximize the drug's effect by placing it directly into the bloodstream. But heroin is now being sold at purity levels that allow equivalent highs to be achieved by inhalation, negating the need for more unattractive needle use and thereby eroding one of the long-standing "access" barriers for heroin use. In addition, as the 2.1 million hard-core cocaine and crack users grow older, they are experiencing the "burnout" common with long-term stimulant use. Heroin, a depressant, offers a drug alternative that can be used either as a substitute or taken immediately following a cocaine or crack binge to diminish the unpleasant aftereffects.[58]

The sizable market for heroin in the United States still accounts for but a small fraction of the heroin produced globally each year. By one 1993 estimate, the 500,000 regular U.S. heroin users consumed eight metric tons of heroin.[59] Even if Americans consumed twice that amount, they would still be demanding fewer than 4 percent of the total potential global heroin production for 1995.[60] Worldwide seizures represent about 6 percent of the total potential production,[61] leaving other markets to account for at least 90 percent of opium and heroin production.

Europe appears to be a more important market for heroin than the United States. The figures for drug-related deaths and seizure data suggest that there is a large and growing population of heroin consumers. For instance, France saw a 24 percent increase in drug-related deaths between 1993 and 1994, mainly from heroin overdoses.[62] Drug-related deaths in Spain more than doubled between 1994 and 1995,[63] and after several years of dramatic rises, drug deaths in Germany finally leveled off in 1995.[64] In 1993 law enforcement authorities in both western and eastern Europe confiscated 8,008 kilograms of heroin[65] as compared to 1,600 kilograms seized by U.S. authorities that year.[66] These European seizures are up from 4,100 kilograms, just five years before.[67] Improved enforcement hardly would seem to explain this rise, particularly in light of the post-Communist disintegration of law enforcement agencies in the East and the creation of a borderless community in the West in 1992

There is strong evidence of a burgeoning market for heroin and opiates in Asia itself. Beginning in the late 1980s, when traffickers began smuggling heroin from the Golden Triangle to Hong Kong via Yunnan to the Guangdong provinces of China, Chinese authorities noted an alarming increase in addiction. The number of addicts reported officially by the Chinese authorities grew more than fivefold from 1990 to 1994, from 70,000 in 1990 to 380,000 in 1994. Ninety percent of the abusers were below thirty years old with the average age twenty-three to twenty-five years, and the majority was poorly educated males.[68] By the end of 1995, 520,000 people in China were registered as drug abusers. The highest incidence rates were reported in Yunnan, Guizhou, Sichuan, Shaanxi, and Gansu provinces. With addiction has come disease. In a test of over one million Chinese in 1990, 890 cases were found to be HIV positive—657 of whom were heroin addicts from Yunnan Province. In Ruili County bordering Burma, 78.4 percent of heroin addicts were HIV positive.[69]

There are an estimated 400,000 drug addicts in Thailand,[70] and addiction rates among some northern highland villages run at 90 percent.[71] In 1993 about 21,000 addicts either applied for treatment or were arrested for consumption or possession of heroin. While this reflects only a tiny percentage of the overall addict population, it is a 22 percent increase from the previous year.[72] Official estimates in Vietnam place the addict population at between 100,000 and 150,000, although sources suggest that there are as many as 90,000 addicts in the northern mountain areas alone.[73] Additionally, there are reports of rising heroin use in Burma, Laos, Cambodia, Malaysia, Singapore, and the Philippines.

There are also signs of drug use, including rising heroin consumption, in Eastern Europe and the republics of the former Soviet Union. Independent experts place the number of addicts at 100,000 in Poland, and casual users are estimated at 200,000.[74] Russian authorities claim that drug use is now increasing by 50 percent each year, reaching two million consumers in 1995.[75] Ukrainian government officials place their addict population at 500,000.[76] The Central Asian republics of Kazakhstan, Kyrgystan, Tajikistan, Turkmenistan, and Uzbekistan all report rising opium consumption.[77]

Finally, the largest market for opiates appears to be concentrated in Southwest and South Asia. Iran is home to an estimated two million addicts.[78] The Indian government conservatively places its addiction levels at 500,000.[79] According to a 1993 U.N. survey, Pakistan is now home to three million drug addicts.[80] In those countries, heroin addiction has risen from tens of thousands in the late 1970s, to 300,000 in late 1980s, to an estimated 1.5 million in 1995.[81]

The rapid growth in heroin consumption in virtually every corner of the globe makes clear that widespread drug use is not just an affliction of wealthy societies. The ingredients for drug abuse are by no means exacting—one must have an awareness of drugs, access to them, and the motivation to use them. Many factors are making these three elements commonplace even in poor and once-remote societies.

The combination of the reach of global communications,[82] the erosion of state information monopolies,[83] and pervasive Western programming have created a media environment where most Asians are exposed to what one communications scholar has called "messages that hurt."[84] Traditional Confucian values are under daily attack by the consumer-oriented thrill-seeking messages in mass entertainment television, movies, and musical recordings. Tobacco, alcohol, and pharmaceutical companies promote their products throughout Asia. Western tobacco companies have been particularly aggressive in advertising in the region, hoping to capture some portion of a market with one-half billion smokers.[85]

Access to drugs also is increasing with the persistent rise in global production and trafficking. In addition, as economic liberalization continues, potential drug consumers have greater personal freedom, mobility, and control over their incomes. In China, where traditional drug use has been heavily concentrated in rural areas, the recent flood of rural migrants into urban areas has made drugs more widely available to burgeoning urban populations. The actual population in Shanghai will climb from

15 million in 1995 to a projected 21.7 million in 2010. And China is but a part of a regional demographic trend where millions of Asians are abandoning the countryside for the supposed better life of the burgeoning megacities. Over the next fifteen years, Jakarta is expected to grow from 11.2 million to 17. 2 million; Manila, from 10.7 million to 16 million; Bangkok, from 8.5 million to 12.7 million; Rangoon, from 3.9 million to 6.3 million; and Ho Chi Minh City, from 3.5 million to 5.3 million.[86]

The urbanization trend is not only enhancing access to illicit drugs but also is fueling many of the conditions that motivate drug use. First, many of these migrants are young men, often under the age of twenty-five—an age group known for risk-taking behavior and the willingness to challenge social conventions. Second, in cities these new migrants are generally separated from their families, often underemployed, and with little opportunity for schooling. Third, cut off from their cultural support system, they are vulnerable to peer pressure and hedonistic mass media messages. The combination of age and alienation creates a far greater pool of young people at higher risk for becoming drug users.

Reconsidering Drug Control

The manifold factors influencing the growth of the Asian drug trade means that traditional supply-side policies are impractical. Simply eliminating drugs at their source and seizing them prior to their arrival in the United States cannot solve the drug problem. Policies enacted with these objectives in mind are fatally flawed for two reasons. First, the emphasis on enforcement makes these policies inherently reactive. Law enforcement by definition cannot be preemptive—rules must be broken before the authority of the state can be brought to bear to impose sanctions. Second, these policies rest on the fallacious notion that drug production and trafficking activities can be readily rooted out from the context in which they exist.

By defining drugs as "bad," drug control policies rest on the presumption that the phenomenon is alien and that "normalcy" can be restored by isolating and exorcising drugs from the body politic. But the drug phenomenon cannot be exorcised precisely because it is deeply entrenched in modern society. Further, as James Shinn points out in the previous chapter, there is little agreement over exactly what constitutes the evil to be eradicated. While there is nearly universal acknowledgment that the abuse of drugs such as heroin is a bad thing, it is difficult to formulate similar tidy judgments about the array of interwoven activities that ultimately supply the addict with his fix. Farmers, chemists, shippers, and bankers who are directly or indirectly involved in the drug trade rarely see themselves as criminals but instead characterize themselves as "good" businessmen. Importers, exporters, tourists, and commercial carriers are acting in concert with the principles of economic liberalization when they strongly oppose the use of intrusive border controls governments traditionally have relied on to detect and stop contraband. Finally, civil libertarians are embracing the core ideals of democratic society when they fight to restrict the intrusiveness of governmental authority into the individual lives of their citizenry.

So where does this leave policymakers committed to stemming the burgeoning Asian drug trade? By outlining the factors that motivate and facilitate drug production, it becomes evident why U.S.- and U.N.-funded crop eradication, crop substitution, and alternative development programs are not working in the region. Such programs are premised on the notion that if existing growers can be either coerced or enticed to end drug cultivation, the void will remain unfilled. But three rudimentary conditions render this approach unworkable: first, the existence of suitable alternative sites for cultivation; second, the greater appeal of profits from drug production vis-à-vis those of the competing agricultural alternatives; and third, the existence of jurisdictions in which the host governments lack either the means or the will to end drug production. The first condition is a function of geography; vast tracts of the Asian countryside are well suited to cultivation. The second is a function of market demand; it shows no signs of diminishing. The third is dependent on political legitimacy and the effectiveness of regulatory and enforcement mechanisms; all of which are under significant strain throughout the region.

Similarly, interdiction efforts within Asia that aim to stem the cross-border flows of processing chemicals, drugs, and drug monies are ineffectual. As long as smugglers can blend within the increasingly unregulated movements of people, goods, and services, these enforcement efforts are condemned to a futile needle-in-the-haystack exercise.

While acknowledging the dim prospects for real achievement, some might argue that supply-side suppression serves an important symbolic role, providing a tangible demonstration of international support for antidrug norms. This rationale is found wanting, however, once the costs of undertaking this essentially normative effort are considered. For example, crop eradication programs typically end up displacing production into more remote areas, which often are environmentally sensitive public lands. Since farmers do not own the land or expect that their activities will go undetected over the long term, they clear it with highly destructive slash-and-burn practices, plant and harvest a crop, and then move on. If these cultivation activities take place on mountainous terrain, as is commonly the case in Southeast Asia, erosion can produce irreversible harm to the surrounding area.[87]

Pursuing interdiction efforts for largely symbolic reasons also can be largely counterproductive. Since criminal organizations are more nimble than enforcement agents, who are constrained by resources and jurisdiction, new enforcement actions often end up generating incentives for traffickers to exploit new societal vulnerabilities as they burrow deeper "underground." Investing in political corruption and immersing trafficking activities within the legitimate global transportation and financial sectors offer the greatest opportunities for avoiding the reach of state authorities. The consequences are sobering. First, the legitimacy of governmental authority is eroded. Second, the credibility of the current global regulatory regimes that govern those sectors is undermined, inviting widespread rule breaking. Third, the means and the incentives for drug-trafficking organizations to diversify into an array of other nefarious criminal activities, such as alien and weapons smuggling, ultimately are enhanced.

Perhaps the greatest cost of pursuing flawed supply-side policies in Asia is that it requires U.S. authorities to enter into an unholy alliance with authoritarian Asian governments. Antiproduction and antitrafficking initiatives mandates collaboration between U.S. officials and the host government. In the case of Burma, for example, this means cooperation with a military junta that seized power after firing on thousands of nonviolent demonstrators in 1988 and that placed Nobel Prize winner Aung San Suu Kyi under house arrest for seven years. While human rights activists have strongly opposed any conciliatory gesture to Burma's State Law and Order Restoration Council (SLORC), the U.S. Drug Enforcement Administration (DEA) has lobbied hard for a relaxed official posture toward the government. The DEA's logic is straightforward: Burma is home to most of the world's opium production. If drug control is a priority, you can't afford to be offended by the domestic policies of your enforcement allies. From a purely realistic perspective, the DEA's position might be compelling if one could be confident that the SLORC leadership could end Burmese drug production with the assistance of the United States. Unfortunately, the evidence is to the contrary.[88]

Policy Recommendations

We need to rethink the drug war in the Far East. An effective policy for combating the Asian drug trade must be built on a foundation that, first, subsumes antiproduction and antitrafficking efforts into an overall strategy to combat organized crime and political corruption and, second, places greater emphasis on demand reduction programs. For such efforts to be effective, they must be multilateral, and enlist the private sectors as partners in propagating the antidrug message. The following are essential components for such an approach:

- We need an integrated perspective on the drug-and-crime problem. Much of the evidence cited in this chapter came from reports authored by disparate government agencies. Yet, to this author's knowledge, there is not a single comprehensive U.S. government assessment of the Asian drug and organized crime issue. There is little bureaucratic incentive and no interagency mechanism to create a composite picture that outlines transnational linkages.

- There must be a sustained effort to advance public awareness of the methods of organized criminal enterprises. Law enforcement agencies instinctively resist educating the public on the details of organized criminal activities. In part, this is due to practical concerns of compromising an ongoing investigation or a prosecutory effort. The pace of operations also leaves little time or resources to commit to the task of education.

- Finally, an Asian Organized Crime (AOC) task force should be established, with membership drawn from the private sector and NGO community along with representatives from the enforcement, intelligence, financial, and judicial ministries of member nations. The AOC task force would focus on identifying, promoting, and implementing private sector initiatives and legislation throughout the region, with an eye toward enhancing the means to regulate domestic and transnational commercial activities that currently are vulnerable to organized crime. Among the initiatives the task force could consider are:

  1. Strengthening the newly adopted APEC investment code. Particular attention should be paid to developing meaningful and binding guidelines for trade and financial record keeping, and these records should be accessible to enforcement authorities involved in investigatory work. Specifically, access to international maritime transportation hubs should be restricted to those shippers who provide detailed manifests electronically to inspectors at transshipment points and the final destination. Additionally, no one should be allowed to make wire transfers through the interbank payment systems unless the originator and beneficiary of the transaction are documented.

  2. Establish guidelines for a common global database on known criminals and their activities. This information should be made widely available to travel agencies and financial institutions, which should be called upon to conduct speedy background checks and to deny convicted criminals access to international travel and

investment opportunities. Additionally, each member state should have a designated Organized Crime Intelligence Unit that is assigned the responsibility for coordinating crime intelligence collection and analysis within its borders and working with intelligence units from other countries. Finally, the AOC task force should regularly publish an "Accessories to Transnational Crime Report" that spotlights governments, business institutions, or individuals that routinely fail to abide by regional and international crime control conventions.

3. Actively advance legal reforms in East Asian countries, including instituting appropriate legal codes for embezzlement, criminal conspiracies (RICO statutes), corruption, money laundering, and fraud. Provide the technical and material support to build law libraries throughout the region and to upgrade training for prosecutory work. Promote the drafting of common rules and provide training for conducting criminal investigative work, including guidelines on using informants, conducting wiretaps, and safeguarding evidence. Aggressively negotiate extradition treaties with all countries in the region and adopt mutually agreeable procedures and a formula for sharing seized criminal assets.

4. Work to improve cultural understanding and linguistic abilities among the member nations by establishing a common fund to train judicial, financial, intelligence, and law enforcement representatives from member nations and to support exchange programs. Federal, state, and local law enforcement agencies in the United States should take the lead by recruiting Asian Americans into law enforcement, aggressively engaging in community outreach programs in ethnic Chinese neighborhoods. The Canadian Royal Canadian Mounted Police and United Kingdom law enforcement officials with Asian crime experience can serve as liaisons with U.S. federal, state, and local police officers.

Accepting the status quo practically ensures that drugs will become more widely available and, concurrently, that the criminal organizations which advance the trade will become increasingly powerful and corrosive. If we are unprepared to accept the proposals just outlined, we should consider dismantling the prohibitionary regime. This is because a failed prohibitionary approach to drug control does more harm than good, for it ends up serving the interests of organized crime to a greater extent than the interests of collective society. If the global community is unprepared to redress the systemic weaknesses that facilitate drug production, trafficking, and consumption, it will have to accept the fact that widespread drug use is an unfortunate fact of life and a by-product of transnational trade.

Conclusion

The persistent growth of the illicit drug trade, despite the long-standing national and international enforcement regimes designed to contain it, offers a compelling case study in the precarious status of national sovereignty. The production of illicit narcotics has gravitated to the weakest Asian states. Asian criminal enterprises have benefited from the same revolution in communications, transportation, trade, and finance that has made it possible for global businesses to ignore the traditional prerogatives of nation-states.

The success of Asian organized crime also reveals the widening holes within the global economy that are facilitating the free trade of an array of nefarious "commodities," including drugs, plutonium, hazardous waste, counterfeit credit cards and documents, pirated copyrighted materials, stolen vehicles, child pornography, aliens, and indentured prostitutes.

The paradox embedded in the predicament of declining sovereignty is that in order to strengthen their role in the international system, states must agree to act less and less like states. That is, they must agree to abide by international conventions that severely limit their capacity to act independently in the pursuit of their own narrowly defined national interests.

The United States must lead in promoting strategies of cooperative engagement that include a broad-based alliance of international, regional, and nongovernmental organizations and the private sector. Crime and drugs consistently rank at the very top of the list of domestic policy challenges that most worry U.S. voters. By outlining the clear linkages between forces acting in Asia and these "domestic" problems, policymakers in Washington can begin to build the necessary political support for sustained engagement to solve these transnational problems.

Notes

1. The International Day Against Drug Abuse and Illicit Trafficking was established by the United Nations General Assembly in resolution 42/112, adopted on December 7, 1987. Death was introduced as a penalty for drug trafficking under amendments to the Criminal Law adopted by the National People's Congress Standing Committee on March 8, 1982, and came into force on April 1, 1982. In December 1990 a revision to the legislation controlling narcotics lowered the minimum criteria for imposing the death penalty and increased the number of drug-related offenses punishable by death. While the official execution figures are regarded as a state secret, Amnesty

International has recorded 64 executions for drug offenses in 1990, 367 confirmed executions in 1991, 73 executions in 1992, 224 in 1993, and 579 in 1994. See "The Death Penalty: No Solution to Illicit Drugs," Amnesty International Report: ACT 51/02/95 (October 1995), reprinted in *Drug Law Report* 3:24 (Nov.-Dec. 1995), pp. 277–78.

2. The 1995 estimated potential production of opium gum produced in Burma, Laos, Thailand, and the Yunnan Province of China is 2,561 metric tons. *International Narcotics Control Strategy Report* (INCSR), March 1996, Department of State Pub. No. 10324 (Washington, DC: U.S. Department of State, 1996), p. 25. The conversion ratio of opium gum to heroin used by the Drug Enforcement Administration is twelve parts to one.

3. *National Drug Control Strategy: 1996*, Pub. No. NCJ160086 (Washington, DC: Office of National Drug Control Strategy, 1996), p. 49.

4. Ibid., p. 93.

5. *Pulse Check: National Trends in Drug Abuse: Winter 1995* (Washington, DC: Office of National Drug Control Strategy, 1996), p. 6.

6. The average price per pure gram of cocaine in 1995 for purchases of 5 ounces or less was $96. See *National Drug Control Strategy: 1996*, p. 93.

7. For fiscal year 1997, the State Department requested $193 million for its international drug control programs—75 percent of this amount is to fund Latin American programs; 3.3 percent for Southeast Asian programs.

8. *Report of Audit: U.S. Efforts to Reduce Heroin Trafficking in Southeast Asia*, Report No. 3-CI-007 (Washington, DC: U.S. Department of State: Office of Inspector General, July 1993), p. 3.

9. Despite the celebrated victories of the deaths and arrests of many Colombian kingpins from the notorious Medellin and Cali cartels, cocaine is more available today, at lower prices and at a high purity, than it was ten years ago.

10. *INCSR 1996*, p. 25.

11. This figure has been computed by using the estimate of total opium cultivation of 2,340 metric tons and multiplying it by an average selling price in the northern Shan State of Burma of $660 to $750 for the raw opium required to produce one kilogram of heroin.

12. *INCSR 1996*, p. 252.

13. "Vietnam," United Nations International Drug Control Programme, Country Program Network (Sep. 7, 1993), p. 1.

14. Dali L. Yang, "Illegal Drugs, Policy Change, and State Power: The Case of Contemporary China," *The Journal of Contemporary China*, No. 4 (Fall 1993), p. 20.

15. "Opium Growing, Sale Said Result of Food Shortage," FBIS-JPRS-TDD-95-011-L (2 May 1995), p. 35. Two arrests by Russian and Chinese authorities

in 1994 appear to support the rumors that North Korea has entered the heroin trade. Russian drug law enforcement officials arrested two North Koreans attempting to sell 8.5 kilograms of heroin—during the negotiations, the two North Koreans said they had an additional 500 kilograms for sale. In January 1994 two North Koreans were arrested by Chinese authorities in Jilin Province with 30 kilograms of heroin. *The NNICC Report 1994: The Supply of Illicit Drugs to the United States,* Pub. No. DEA-95051 (Washington, DC: Drug Enforcement Administration, Aug. 1995), p. 42.

16. The average is a very rough estimate. As with any agricultural product, there can be tremendous variation in actual productivity depending on soil and weather conditions. The average value of a hectare was determined by dividing total potential metric tonnage of raw opium for Southeast Asia by the estimated number of hectares under cultivation and multiplying by the 1993 per-kilogram price in the northern Shan State of Burma.

17. The figure is for 1991. See *Industry and Development: Global Report 1993/94* (Vienna: U.N. Industrial Development Office, 1993), p. 180.

18. Ibid., p. 22.

19. Ibid., p. 180.

20. Raymond Vernon and Louis T. Wells, Jr., *The Economic Environment of International Business* (Englewood Cliffs, NJ: Prentice Hall, 1991), p. 122.

21. Martin Booth, *The Triads* (New York: St. Martin's Press, 1990), pp. 9–16.

22. The U.S. Drug Enforcement Administration has identified 70 triad groups operating in Hong Kong, 18 in Taiwan, 31 in China, 30 in Thailand and Burma, 82 in Malaysia, 133 in Singapore, 7 in Australia, 20 in Europe, 1 in Paraguay, 5 in South Africa, 16 in Canada, and 39 in the United States. See George F. Harkin, "Chinese Triads, Triad Organizations, and Triad Relationships," Paper presented to the 17th Annual International Asian Organized Crime Conference, Boston, MA, (Mar. 8, 1995), pp. 3–4.

23. The Japanese National Police Agency prefers to use the term "Boryokudan," which translates into "the violent ones."

24. For a comprehensive history of the yakuza, see David E. Kaplan and Alec Dubro, *Yakuza: The Explosive Account of Japan's Criminal Underworld* (Reading, MA: Addison-Wesley, 1986).

25. "The New International Criminal and Asian Organized Crime," p. 14. This is nearly twenty times the size of the 1960s membership level of the Italian Mafia (La Cosa Nostra) in the United States. See Sen. Joseph R. Biden, "Opening Statement" before the Joint Hearing on U.S. International Drug Policy—Asian Gangs, Heroin, and the Drug Trade of the Committee on the Judiciary and the Caucus on International Narcotics Control of the U.S. Senate, 101st Congress, 2nd Session, Aug. 21, 1990 (Washington, DC: U.S. Government Printing Office, 1991).

26. "Testimony of James E. Moody, Section Chief, Organized Crime, Federal Bureau of Investigations," before the Hearing on Asian Organized Crime of the Per-

manent Subcommittee on Investigations of the Committee on Governmental Affairs, U.S. Senate, 102nd Congress, 1st Session, Oct. 3, Nov. 5–6, 1991 (Washington, DC: U.S. Government Printing Office, 1992), p. 21.

27. "The New International Criminal and Asian Organized Crime," pp. 19–20.

28. Testimony of William S. Sessions, Director, Federal Bureau of Investigations, before the Hearing on "Asian Organized Crime" before the Permanent Subcommittee on Investigations of the Committee on Governmental Affairs, U.S. Senate, 102nd Congress, 1st Session, Oct. 3, Nov. 5–6, 1991 (Washington, DC: U.S. Government Printing Office, 1992), p. 16.

29. Kaplan and Dubro, *Yakuza, p.* 203.

30. "The New International Criminal and Asian Organized Crime," p. 17.

31. "Japanese Yakuza Expanding," *Corporate Security Digest* (July 15, 1991), pp. 4–5.

32. Sakurada, pp. 46–47.

33. Howard Abadinsky, p. 259.

34. "The New International Criminal and Asian Organized Crime," p. 13

35. William H. Myers III, *Orb Weavers—The Global Webs of Transnational Ethnic Chinese Criminal Groups and Their Structure and Activities*, (Philadelphia: Center for the Study of Asian Organized Crime, 1995), pp. 4–5.

36. M. Cordell Hart, "On the Chinese Practice of 'Guanxi,'" Paper presented to the 23rd Annual Meeting of the International Society for the Comparative Study of Civilizations," Dublin, Ireland (July 9, 1994), pp. 3–4.

37. M. Cordell Hart, "'Guanxi': An Important Concept for the Law Enforcement Officer," Paper presented to the 17th Annual International Asian Organized Crime Conference, Boston, MA (Mar. 8, 1995), p. 6.

38. Tony Carding, "Fastest Routes to Southeast Asia," *Intermodal Shipping* (Feb. 1995), p. 32.

39. Ibid., p. 30.

40. Michael Mecham, "China Seeks Formula for Foreign Funding," *Aviation Week & Science Technology* (June 5, 1995), pp. 40–41.

41. John Naisbitt, *Global Paradox* (New York: William Morrow and Co., 1994), p. 116.

42. Ibid., p. 193.

43. Michael Mecham, "Continued Prosperity Eyed with 'Super' Cargo Terminal," *Aviation Week & Space Technology* (Jan. 15, 1996), pp. 38–39.

44. *Customs Areas of the World*, Statistical Papers Series M, No. 30, Rev. 2 (New York: United Nations, 1989).

45. Ibid., p. 2.

46. *International Narcotics Control Strategy Report, April 1994* (Washington, DC: U.S. Department of State, 1995), p. 481.

47. The figures for foreign direct investment are the totals of foreign direct investment East and Southeast Asian countries, excepting Japan. See Mark Mason, "Foreign Direct Investment in East Asia: Trends and Critical Issues," Council on Foreign Relations Asia Project Working Paper (Nov. 1994), Table 6.

48. Ibid., Table 5.

49. Yilmaz Akyuz, "Financial Openness in Developing Countries," in *International Monetary and Financial Issues for the 1990s*, Vol. 1 (New York: U.N. Publications, 1993), pp. 110–124.

50. Scott B. MacDonald, "Global Underground Financial Economy: Asia-Pacific Money Laundering," *International Currency Review*, 22: pp. 2, 32. The British Dependent Territory of the Cayman Islands is the prototypical tax haven that money launderers find particularly cozy. With its population of 26,000, the Caymans prospers as host to 23,500 shell companies and 548 banks with more than $400 billion in deposits. See *INCSR: 1995*, 481. Efforts to close down this mecca for money launderers has grounded on the shoals of United Kingdom resistance to classifying money laundering for tax purposes as a crime. *INCSR: 1995*, p. 511.

51. *Statistical Abstract of the United States, 114th Ed.* (Washington: U.S. Department of Commerce, Economic and Statistics Administration, Bureau of the Census, Sept. 1994), p. 522.

52. Among the most important wire transfer networks outside the United States is the Society for Worldwide Interbank Financial Telecommunications (SWIFT). Besides banks, SWIFT provides services to securities brokers and dealers, clearing institutions, and recognized securities exchanges. SWIFT is a cooperative society located in Belgium and has more than 2,600 member institutions in 65 countries.

53. The Office of Technology Assessment determined in 1995 that it would be unfeasible to develop a computer model to monitor wire transfers as they take place for money laundering even if Congress changed current legislation to allow greater access to wire transfer records. See "Money Laundering: A Framework for Understanding U.S. Efforts Overseas," U.S. Government Accounting Office Report No. GAO/GGD-96-105 (May 1996), pp. 35–36.

54. Richard Small, "Introduction to the Federal Reserve System and Wire Transfers," Presentation before the 17th Annual International Asian Organized Crime Conference, Boston, MA, March 8, 1995.

55. *National Drug Control Strategy: 1996*, p. 49.

56. Ibid., p. 42.

57. There were 64,000 hospital emergency episodes in 1994, which would amount to 11 percent of the officially estimated population—an improbably high amount.

58. *Pulse Check: National Trends in Drug Abuse: Winter 1995*, p. 5.

59. Mathea Falco, "U.S. Drug Policy: Addicted to Failure," *Foreign Policy* 102 (Spring 1996), p. 127.

60. There is no published estimate for worldwide potential heroin production. Estimates are made for total opium gum in metric tons. The figure for 1995 was 4,086 metric tons. The official DEA conversion ratio for opium gum to heroin is 10:1. Applying this ratio to the 1995 opium gum figure is how the "4 percent of total potential global heroin production" estimate was arrived at.

61. Worldwide seizures amounted to 23.8 metric tons in 1994. *The NNICC Report 1994*, p. 32.

62. *INCSR: 1996*, p. 351.

63. Ibid., p. 395.

64. Ibid., p. 354.

65. "Heroin Traffic Targets Europe: New Corridors to the West—1993," Report by the International Criminal Police Organization (Feb. 1994).

66. *National Drug Control Strategy*, 1996, p. 145.

67. "Heroin Traffic Targets Europe."

68. Cai Zhi-Ji, "An Overview of the Drug Situation and Its Control in China," in *Report of the Asian Multicity Epidemiology Work Group: 1995* (Minden, Pulau Pinang, Malaysia: Centre for Drug Research, International Monograph No. 7, 1996), p. 200.

69. Cai Zhi-Ji, "Situation of Drug Abuse and Its Control in the People's Republic of China," in *Report of the Asian Multicity Epidemiology Work Group: 1995*, p. 68.

70. M. Nishikawa, "Drug Control Policies in Some Parts of Asia," *Bulletin on Narcotics*, 46: 1 (1992), p. 36.

71. Peter Loverde, "Heroin in the Hills: Changing Patterns of Drug Dependency among Thailand's Hill Tribes," in *Epidemiological Trends in Drug Abuse: Proceedings of the Community Epidemiology Work Group—June 1992* (Rockville, MD: Department of Health & Human Services, 1992), p. 467.

72. Panporn Liewtiwong, "Drug Epidemic Situation in Bangkok," in *Report of the Asian Multicity Epidemiology Work Group: 1995*, p. 61.

73. "Vietnam," p. 2.

74. *INCSR: 1996*, p. 380.

75. Ibid., p. 387.

76. Ibid., p. 411.

77. Ibid., pp. 418–32.

78. Ibid., p. 231.

79. Ibid., p. 227

80. Ibid., p. 237.

81. John F. Burns, "Heroin Scourges Million Pakistanis," *New York Times* (Apr. 5, 1995), p. 5.

82. See Naisbitt, *Global Paradox,* p. 186.

83. The Chinese government's recent failed attempt to control the import and use of satellite dishes is a case in point.

84. George Gerbner, "Stories That Hurt: Tobacco, Alcohol, and Other Drugs in the Mass Media," in *Youth and Drugs: Society's Mixed Messages,* ed. Hank Resnik (Rockville, MD: OSAP Prevention Monograph–6, 1990), pp. 53–128.

85. Stan Sesser, "Opium War Redux," *New Yorker* (Sept. 13, 1993), pp. 78–79. As one tobacco industry analyst stated in commenting on the success of American cigarette companies in capturing the Asian market: "As poor countries get richer they smoke more American cigarettes. That doesn't change until they get rich enough to worry about their health." See Nancy Hass and Steven Strasser, "Fighting and Switching," *Newsweek* (Mar 21, 1994), p. 53.

86. *World Urbanization Prospects: The 1992 Revision* (New York: United Nations, 1993), Tables A.11 and A.13.

87. For an overview of the pernicious environmental effects of drug cultivation, see "Illicit Narcotics Cultivation and Processing: The Ignored Environmental Drama.," United Nations Drug Control Programme Report (Vienna: UNDCP, 1992).

88. The Was and Kokang, in the northern Shan state, have signed cease-fire agreements in 1995 with SLORC and, as a result, the military reportedly does not interfere with their economic activity—which is mainly the cultivation, conversion, and sale of opium. See Josef Silverstein, "Change in Burma?" *Current History* (Dec. 1995), pp. 440–43. Burma's most notorious drug lord, Khun Sa, surrendered his Mong Tai Army and his Ho Mong headquarters to the military rulers in early January 1996. He traveled to Rangoon for meetings with the military in January, February, and March and negotiated an agreement that he would face neither a trial in Burma nor extradition to the United States. See "Burma: Opposition Criticizes Government's Release of Khun Sa," in FBIS-TDD-96-017-L (May 30, 1996), pp. 73–74.

Chapter 3

The Environment and Development in the Asia-Pacific Region

Elizabeth Economy

The nations of Asia are internationally acclaimed for their success in fostering rapid and sustained economic growth while maintaining political stability. These factors have significantly improved the standard of living in much of the region during the past two to three decades. Yet the environmental impact of such rapid growth has been largely ignored in this calculus. As a result, the region suffers from a range of development-induced environmental degradation, including dangerous levels of local and regional air pollution, soil erosion and loss of arable land, and the contamination of major waterways used for agriculture, drinking, and aquaculture. The region is also a major contributor to global environmental problems such as climate change, ozone depletion, and the loss of biodiversity.

These polluted conditions have negative ramifications for the health of the region's populace and the prospects for continued economic growth. Moreover, the region's burgeoning population (despite declining birth rates in the majority of East and Southeast Asian countries), rapidly increasing demands on energy resources, and increasingly high-consumption lifestyles pose a substantial challenge not only to the region's environment but also to the environmental health of the United States and the rest of the world as the twenty-first century approaches.

This chapter addresses three issues. How does rapid economic growth in the Asia-Pacific region affect the region's environment? What is the nature of the interplay between economic growth and the social and political context in which economic and environmental policies are made? How do

Asian environmental policies affect U.S. environmental and security interests?

The Impact of Rapid Economic Growth on the Environment

Rapid economic growth and an increasing population have engendered severe environmental degradation in the Asia-Pacific region. As industrialization and urbanization have progressed, new forms of air, water, and soil pollution have emerged at a rate that substantially exceeds the capacity of the Asian states to respond effectively. The Asia-Pacific region encompasses countries at vastly different states of this industrialization and urbanization process. Countries in the earlier stages of development— such as China and Indonesia—face the greatest future threats to their own domestic environments and pose the most significant future challenge to regional and global environmental health. Vietnam, Indonesia, the Philippines, China, and Thailand also face the challenge of environmental degradation from such sources as the spread of migrant agriculturalists into upland areas; land degradation from cattle grazing; deforestation; air pollution from fuel– or coal–burning stoves; and water pollution from agricultural runoff, domestic waste, and extractive (mining and logging) and processing industries. Cities in these countries often suffer from advanced air and water pollution problems.[1]

Among the more developed and wealthier nations, such as Malaysia, Korea, and Taiwan, as well as the coastal areas of the People's Republic of China (and urban centers of the other developing nations), widespread industrialization and urbanization has engendered an additional set of environmental problems. Untreated industrial waste, which contaminates drinking water and fish stock; air pollution and acid rain from power plants and factories that emit sulfur dioxide; and dangerous levels of airborne lead pollution from heavily congested automobile traffic all challenge environmental protection efforts. Infrastructure projects to support continued economic growth, such as ports, roads, and power plants, further burden understaffed and underfunded environmental protection agencies.

In a third phase of development, such as that now experienced by Japan (and perhaps being approached by Taiwan and Korea), the focus is on improving the quality of life through raising environmental standards. Improvements include elevating the use of environmental technologies; promoting an ecological consciousness among the populace to support government clean-up programs; emphasizing "clean industries" and transferring high-polluting industries to other states; and strengthening the legal infrastructure and state capacity for implementing environmental protection efforts.

The Asia-Pacific region as a whole, therefore, is confronting myriad environmental problems; a brief examination of three issues—water pollution and scarcity, declining air quality, and deforestation—illuminates the challenges for Asian policymakers for the next decade and beyond.

Water Pollution and Scarcity

Many countries within the region are already critically concerned about the future availability of water. Rapid economic growth has significantly increased demand for water in the residential, industrial, and agricultural sectors of these countries. In addition, factories dump their untreated waste directly into streams, rivers, and coastal waters. Throughout Southeast Asia, denuded uplands have contributed to devastating cycles of flooding and drought. Agricultural runoff, untreated domestic sewage, and industrial waste also are degrading ground, surface, and coastal waters.[2] Major cities in China, Indonesia, and Thailand all suffer from polluted water supplies, periodic shortages, and potential long-term scarcities. Sewage treatment is nonexistent in most cities in the region, and according to a World Bank report, groundwater is polluted by "cesspools, septic tanks, leaking sewers, and landfill sites."[3] Moreover, water tables in Thailand and China are sinking, and, in Indonesia, Thailand, and Vietnam, "so much water is being sucked up from wells that sea water has entered the aquifers."[4]

In 1990 China was able to provide safe drinking water to only 72 percent of its population; Thailand, to 76 percent; and the Philippines, to 82 percent. Indonesia ranked far behind with a capacity to provide safe drinking water to only 34 percent of its population[5] In each case, urban dwellers fared far better than the rural population.

Poor water quality and water scarcity threaten both the health of the region's populace and its continued economic development. In the Java Sea, increasing levels of waste, including toxic waste from industrial and processing activities, are causing declining fish stocks and increased morbidity among the human population from the spread of infectious diseases. There also have been minor outbreaks of Minamata disease caused by mercury poisoning and pollution resulting from fisherman using the poison in coastal and marine waters to kill schools of fish. In 1994, in Vietnam and Hong Kong, inadequate water treatment facilities were blamed for outbreaks of cholera. Similar failures led to contaminated seafood and two hepatitis outbreaks in Shanghai, which affected hundreds of thousands of people.

The economic costs of water pollution are significant. In Jakarta, the World Bank estimates that an amount "equivalent to 1 percent of the city's GDP (gross domestic product)" is spent each year on boiling water.[6] Environmental officials in China also have confronted numerous instances in which toxic waste from industries near rivers and lakes has polluted the water and led to widespread illnesses, lack of water for irrigation, and the destruction of fishing industries.[7] The economic losses from one of these cases, the release of toxic waste in the Huai River in July 1994, were estimated at U.S. $75 million.[8] Estimates of economic losses in China due to water pollution totaled U.S. $1.7 billion in 1990.[9]

Even in such wealthy nations as Korea and Taiwan, industrialization continues to threaten water quality. In Taiwan, high levels of cadmium and copper are contaminating several major waterways used for drinking, aquaculture, and agriculture.[10] Korea also has been plagued by untreated industrial waste contaminating several of its primary sources of drinking water.[11] While Japan has successfully reduced levels of mercury and arsenic in its coastal waters, the development of coastal resorts and golf courses has devastated fish stocks. Overall, degraded water resources will hamper continued economic growth throughout the region through increased morbidity and mortality rates, increased costs to industry, constrained supplies to agriculture, and decreased value of freshwater and coastal fisheries.

Air Pollution

The most visible sign of environmental pollution in Asia may be the thick haze that settles over many urban areas throughout the region. The levels of air pollution in the region's major cities typically exceed World Health Organization standards for much of the year. Five of the world's seven most polluted cities are located in the developing nations of Asia: Beijing, Calcutta, Jakarta, New Delhi, and Shenyang. Suspended particulate matter and sulfur dioxide (SO_2) are also at particularly hazardous levels in Beijing, Shenyang, Shanghai, and Seoul. Economic growth and rapid industrialization caused a tenfold increase in SO_2 emissions and suspended particulate matter in Thailand between 1975 and 1988. These pollutants also increased eightfold in the Philippines and fivefold in Indonesia.[12]

The pollution generated from automobile use, patterns of energy consumption, and inefficiencies in the supply and distribution of energy have led to significant health and economic ramifications for the region. In China, environmental protection officials estimate that lung cancer among the *nonsmoking* populace in major cities increased 18.5 percent between 1988 and 1993 due to heavy atmospheric pollution.[13] Auto use also has produced dangerously high levels of airborne lead in Bangkok, where health officials have estimated that excessive exposure to lead has caused an average drop of four IQ points among Thai children.

The rampant air pollution stems, in significant measure, from the region's reliance on coal. Approximately half of Asia's energy needs are met by coal,[14] and it is the dominant source of commercial energy in China, North Korea, and Vietnam. The urban population is expected to triple in Asia by the year 2000, and improved living standards and demand for consumer goods will increase energy demands. Already the demand for electricity in China, Taiwan, Malaysia, South Korea, Indonesia, the Philippines, and Thailand is expected to grow by 8 percent between 1996 and 2010. Growing automobile usage also promises to be a substantial contributor to declining air quality. In 1993 nearly one million cars and trucks were sold in Indonesia, Malaysia, the Philippines, Singapore, Brunei, and Thailand. This represents twice the number sold in 1989, and analysts believe that sales will double again by 2000.[15]

Inefficiencies on both the demand and the supply side also contribute to waste in the energy sector. Overall, energy intensity (the amount of energy consumed per unit of gross national product) in the commercial sector has declined steeply over the past two decades throughout the Asia-Pacific region. However, the energy intensities of Korea and Malaysia, for example, are still triple that of Japan[16] (which boasts the lowest level of energy intensity among the advanced industrialized states), and Indonesia's energy intensity is roughly four times that of Japan.

In part, this poor performance stems from energy losses in transmission and distribution due to theft, poorly maintained transmission and distribution systems, and low-quality operating procedures. In general, however, these losses decrease as states develop and improve their power management infrastructure. In 1988 these losses ranged from 6 to 8 percent in Korea, Taiwan, and Thailand, to 12 percent in China, 17 percent in Indonesia, and 22 percent in the Philippines.[17]

These losses have important ramifications for both the environment and overall production levels. At any given time, approximately 21 percent of enterprises in the PRC are unable to operate due to energy shortages. Moreover, 200 million rural residents have no electricity whatsoever. The introduction of energy-efficiency technologies and appropriate pricing for energy are key components to improving performance in the energy sector and improving the state of the environment. However, as is discussed in the next section, the efficacy of these measures often is undermined during the implementation process.

These problems in the structure of energy usage will have negative consequences for the environment in the future. It is expected that at current levels of energy consumption, Asian countries will produce more SO_2 than Europe and the United States combined by 2005.[18] China currently consumes roughly two-thirds of the total amount of coal used in Asia and contributes approximately two-thirds of the region's SO_2 emissions.

Japan is an exception to the bleak picture painted by prospective levels of energy use and air pollution. While a major contributor to greenhouse gas emissions, Japan is the largest importer of natural gas in the world and is the leading producer of nuclear power in the region. Japan made significant strides in air pollution control during the 1960s and 1970s by enacting strict automobile emission standards and pursuing energy efficiency during the 1970s in the wake of the oil crisis.[19] Tokyo and Osaka also boast the two lowest emission levels of SO_2 and standard particulate matter of the major cities in Asia. However, with high levels of automobile use, Japan has not been able to meet its own ambient air quality standards for nitrogen oxide in Tokyo and Osaka.

Air pollution in Asian nations has engendered high economic and health costs not only within the countries of origin but throughout the region. In 1994 and 1997, for instance, forest fires in Indonesia, due to logging, caused serious respiratory illnesses and headaches among the populations of Malaysia and Singapore.[20] In addition, low visibility caused by such fires has forced airports in east Malaysia and Singapore to close for several days at a time, at significant economic cost. Acid rain from SO_2 emissions—which erodes buildings, destroys aquaculture, and damages habitat[21]—also has emerged as an important problem in China, Korea, and Japan. According to one report, half of the rain in Guangdong, China, is acidic. Moreover, China contributes to acid rain in Korea, Japan, and Vietnam. Many Japanese believe that the acid rain in western Japan is due primarily to China's SO_2 emissions. In response to this transboundary pollution, Japan has funded a Sino-Japanese Friendship Environment Protection Center in Beijing. Moreover, Japan has leased two reduced-cost versions of desulfurization plants to the PRC; according to one Japanese official, however, the Chinese refused a third plant because of the lowered efficiency that the desulfurization process produces.[22]

For most policymakers in the West, Asia's current and future contribution to global atmospheric problems merits grave concern. Future regional economic development trends, including growth rates of up to 20 percent in some regions of China, reliance on coal and fossil fuels for energy, and continued deforestation practices will likely increase the percentage of Asia's contribution to global greenhouse gas emissions. South and Southeast Asia currently account for over 40 percent of the global carbon dioxide (CO_2) emissions from deforestation. China and Japan are two of the top five countries of greenhouse gas emissions, and conservative estimates indicate that China will surpass the United States as the chief contributor of CO_2 by the year 2020 (assuming an average growth rate of 5 percent and modest gains in energy efficiency). In addition, Indonesia, Korea, and Thailand rank within the top 25 greenhouse gas emitters.

Japan has formally announced its commitment to become a global leader in environmental affairs and has pledged to lower its CO_2 and methane emissions to 1990 levels by the year 2000. However, government and business leaders have balked at Ministry of Environment proposals for a carbon tax, and many Japanese acknowledge that it will be difficult for them to achieve their targets.

Consumption of ozone-depleting substances in Asia, such as chloroflurocarbons and halons, also will grow for the foreseeable future. Although per-capita use of ozone depleting substances in the PRC is quite low—approximately 0.3 kilograms per capita—usage is likely to grow significantly in the next decade. Already, China's consumption of ozone-depleting substances has soared from 3 percent of the world total in 1986 to 18 percent of the current total global annual emissions.[23] Even with technology transfer, Chinese environmental protection officials have stated that they will be unable to fulfill their pledges to phase out ozone-depleting substances in aerosols by the year 1997 and in the foam industry by the year 2000. There is a substantial shortfall in the funds that PRC officials deem necessary to implement the substitutions and a lack of cooperation from local level officials.

Deforestation

In addition to the problems of water and air quality caused by economic development, many countries in the Asia-Pacific region have derived a significant portion of their wealth from logging industries. The region boasts the highest average annual deforestation rate in the world (1.2 percent). As a whole, between 1980 and 1990 Asia lost approximately 2.2 million hectares of forested land annually. Domestic needs for agricultural land and firewood for fuel are partly responsible for this deforestation. The substantial income derived from wood-related products, however, is the driving force behind much of the region's loss of forest cover.

In 1993 Indonesia, which has the second largest forest area in the world, exported approximately U.S. $7.5 billion worth of wood-related products, accounting for about one-fifth of the country's total exports. Indonesia alone accounts for almost one million hectares of deforested land and almost one quarter of the global rain forest coverage lost annually[24] The World Bank estimates that Indonesia is harvesting "at least 30 percent more wood each year than is considered sustainable."[25]

The loss of forested land in the region has both local and global consequences. Deforestation damages the local ecosystem, adding to biodiversity loss and contributing to soil erosion and loss of soil nutrients. In addition, the loss of rain forest cover throughout Asia contributes to greenhouse gas emissions through the release of carbon dioxide when trees are felled.

While domestic elites typically view the timber industry through the lens of the revenues it brings to the loggers and the state coffers, environmentalists using natural resource accounting arrive at a radically different conclusion concerning the costs and benefits of the timber trade. In the case of Indonesia, for example, an official annual growth rate of 7.1 percent between 1971 and 1984 drops to 4 percent after deducting for the "loss of forests, depletion of oil reserves, and soil erosion."[26]

Collectively, the developing nations of Asia have undergone rapid increases in the rate of deforestation. Malaysia's annual rate of deforestation is currently somewhere between 2.4 and 3.4 percent, due to land development, dam construction, mining, and wide-scale commercial logging. In both Thailand and Vietnam,[27] growing demand for agricultural land, increased timber sales, and investment by Japan has accelerated the rates of deforestation.[28] (Forest coverage in Thailand, for example, decreased from 53 percent to 28 percent between 1961 and 1988).[29] In China, over 16 percent of the land is desert, and some experts estimate the direct economic loss from sandstorms at almost U.S. $800 million annually. Although Chinese officials have undertaken aggressive reforestation efforts, local-level officials who monitor the forests have reported that of the country's 140 forest bureaus, 25 have almost run out of forest reserves and 61 have indicated that trees are being felled at unsustainable rates.[30]

In addition to its large wood exporters, the Asia-Pacific region is home to some of the most significant consumers of timber and wood products. While Japan maintains a 70 percent forest coverage and strictly regulates domestic timber-cutting, it is the largest net importer of hardwood in the world. In addition, Korea and Taiwan are also significant importers; since 1971 South Korea's imports have more than quadrupled while Taiwan now imports over seven times its 1971 levels.[31] China, too, has become a major consumer. Some experts believe that it will become the leading importer of wood in the future.

Degraded forest resources in Asia will constrain continued economic growth in the region through shortages of wood products, fire and flood damage, and associated transport disruption. While international and national level efforts to counter deforestation by curtailing illegal logging and advancing sustainable development policies for forestry management have intensified during the past few years, their success is predicated on the ability of national governments to strike a balance between national control and local-level management authority, something that remains to be proven.

The Interplay of Economic Growth, Politics, and the Environment

As outlined in the last section, economic growth has had a range of negative consequences for the environment in the Asia-Pacific region. However, this growth also has contributed to increases in public spending and improvements in quality of life as measured by gross national product per capita, access to safe drinking water and sanitation services, improved literacy levels, and reduction in the percentage of the population living below the poverty level.

The experience of Western Europe and Japan in the development of their state capacity suggests that as the immediate needs of survival are met, elites and subsequently the general populace begin to regard environmental degradation as an impediment to future growth and improvement in quality of life. This awareness sets in motion the reorientation of state resources and political reform necessary to implement environmental policy effectively and systematically.[32]

It is also plausible, however, that countries such as China may follow the path of Eastern Europe, where environmental issues provide a state-approved outlet for public discontent. In this scenario, environmental degradation and other political considerations will fuel awareness and political activism. For example, nongovernmental environmental organizations may become the lightning rods through which popular social and political discontent is channeled.[33] In Eastern Europe, however, this path did not lead immediately to an improved environmental decision-making context but to the reconfiguration of the entire system of governance and, in some cases, crisis-level social instability, which actually may delay environmental improvements.

Currently, only the most economically advanced states in the region—Japan and Singapore—have established their capacity to implement environmental protection policies successfully on a national scale. Korea and Taiwan appear poised to develop this capacity within the next decade. Given the current levels of economic development and social welfare of most states in the region—Indonesia, China, Thailand, the Philippines, and, to a lesser extent, Malaysia—such capacity will more likely emerge within the next two decades or beyond.

The economic policies that have fueled the rapid economic growth in Asia traditionally have offered little recognition of the environmental, health, and economic costs that this development has engendered. Officials in every state, however, are now making some effort to reconfigure the package of economic incentives and penalties for development to account for some of the costs inherent in this economic growth. These include more accurate pricing policies through the elimination of subsidies in energy and water, adopting energy-efficient technologies, and implementing permit and fee systems for regulating industrial waste and emissions.

At the same time, the relationships that comprise the sociopolitical context in which decisions regarding economic development and environmental protection are made often undermine these policies. These relationships include tightly linked business, political, and enforcement elites (without clearly defined lines of responsibility and power); ineffectual environmental protection agencies; poorly developed legal infrastructures; and weak institutionalization of nongovernmental organizations (NGOs) and an independent media.

The data offered to illuminate the current social and political decision making context are largely anecdotal. When examined in conjunction with the statistics of current and projected environmental degradation, however, they offer a more nuanced picture of the impact of economic growth on the Asia-Pacific region.

Business and Military Connections

To varying degrees, the business communities in Asia are linked through financial, friendship, or familial connections with political elites responsible for environmental protection. The importance of these ties is enhanced by weak legal infrastructures, which are especially prevalent in the economically less advanced Asian states.

In Malaysia, for example, elected leaders traditionally have held the right to allocate logging concessions to their political supporters. These concessions are estimated to be worth hundreds of millions of dollars; in the process, officials often share in these millions.[34] This fact may explain why in the 2,316 cases of illegal logging that have been brought before the Malaysian courts, those who were punished were typically the workers rather than the license holders.[35] In 1994 the government passed a number of new measures to curtail illegal logging. However, Friends of the Earth and Greenpeace International have both stated that corruption will undermine the new laws, arguing, "The political structure is inextricably intertwined with vested interests." Even the Pahang royal family has been accused of illegal logging practices.[36]

In Thailand, well-connected developers who are backed by the military and other high-level politicians have overrun the national parks division. Poachers and developers have plundered national parkland. The forestry officials themselves are demoralized and often supplement their incomes with payoffs from poachers and developers.[37] This same pattern of behavior emerges in Indonesia and the Philippines, where loggers often bribe forest inspectors in order to log the timber illegally. In the Philippines, the illegal timber trade is valued at four times that of the legal trade.

In addition, in China, the Chinese People's Liberation Army has been implicated in protecting poachers and smugglers involved in trade in endangered species.

Engagement of the legitimate private sector in environmental protection efforts is an important component of successful implementation of new technologies and economic mechanisms for environmental protection. Japan has had significant success in integrating national objectives with business interests. Flue gas desulfurization and denitrification and auto exhaust control technologies were developed through cooperation between the Japanese Ministry of International Trade and Industry (MITI) and private enterprise. Even MITI's intervention, however, is not always enough to induce cooperation from business. In 1992 MITI published a series of proposals urging industry to develop voluntary plans to protect the environment; however, industry responded by claiming that MITI was "overly interventionist."[38] In addition, the Keidanren published a set of guidelines for Japanese businesses abroad, urging them to adhere to Japan's environmental standards. However, fewer than half of companies surveyed were even conducting environmental impact assessments in the countries in which they were doing business. Moreover, according to one Japanese official, only those companies that were exposed by the media for their poor environmental behavior abroad actually changed their behavior or closed down.[39]

Environmental Protection Agencies

Weak environmental protection agencies remain a problem for implementing successful environmental policies in virtually every country in the Asia-Pacific region—albeit to different extents. In part, this is because states typically established environmental protection agencies later in the overall development of their bureaucracies, or the agencies evolved from other ministries whose primary commitment was not to environmental protection. Typically they are plagued with low levels of funding, poorly trained staff, inadequate equipment and technology, and mandates that overlap or conflict with other, more powerful, agencies.

Moreover, while environmental protection agencies may have regulatory power, most have no mandate to influence sector-wide development paths that are responsible for environmental degradation, such as energy or transportation. Even in Japan, the Environment Agency is generally considered among the most ineffective of all the government organizations. In 1993, for instance, when that agency attempted to advance a new Environmental Basic Law, the law was substantially diminished in scope by the resistance of various business and government officials. They were concerned that the law would elevate the status of the Environment Agency and that environmental constraints would hinder Japanese economic development.[40] In Korea the Ministry of Environment did not assume control over monitoring tap water quality from the Ministry of Health and Social Affairs and the Construction Ministry until 1994, after the country experienced a high level of contamination at several key sources of drinking water. However, as the ministry has only two or three employees who possess the qualifications to be classified as professional technicians, it plans to turn over much of the management responsibility to the private sector.[41] In Indonesia the Environment Ministry has had to fight with the Ministry of Health for jurisdiction over hazardous wastes and has no authority over the 70 percent of national land controlled by the Ministry of Forestry.

Environmental protection agencies throughout Asia have attempted to transfer policies from the West to strengthen their standing. The "polluter pays principle" is one such economic mechanism to enhance efficient use of resources and environmental protection that has gained currency in the region. Japan, for instance, charges for garbage collection and waste treatment based on how much waste is generated. The Korean Ministry of Environment has inaugurated a similar policy. China imposes fees on enterprises that violate standards on wastewater discharge. Many factories, however, elect to pay the minimal fees rather than invest in costly treatment facilities. Moreover, one important study of local-level politics on water in China found that the local-level environmental protection bureaus had little incentive to close factories or enforce installation of pollution control equipment because the bureaus themselves were sustained financially by the fees.[42] A similar difficulty in ensuring that economic policies are implemented appropriately by the responsible agency is evident in Indonesia. During the late 1980s, the state raised reforestation taxes dramatically; however, the Indonesian minister of forestry admitted that less than 0.25 percent of the fees collected actually were being used in reforestation efforts.[43] Environmental officials in Asia also have begun to calculate the environmental externalities associated with various production processes and pollutants. For example, the National Environmental Protection Agency (NEPA) in the PRC called for revamping the structure of Chinese energy consumption patterns in order to prevent a 5 percent loss in agricultural productivity from climate change.[44]

Regionalization

The benefits of economic development in Asia are distributed unevenly among regions within states. In some cases, this has resulted in increased power for regional authorities, who may not share the same policy goals as national elites. In Malaysia, for example, regional authorities who receive revenues from timber royalties have hampered the efforts of the national government to curtail illegal logging. Moreover, each state has autonomy over its forests and is responsible for issuing its own forestry ordinances, for zoning forest areas, and for instituting the mechanisms to enforce the laws. Yet in one heavily logged area—Sarawak—there is only one forestry department official. In China, too, national officials have complained about the lack of progress in closing down new enterprises that use ozone-depleting substances because of resistance from local-level officials who derive substantial income from these firms.

In other cases, however, regions have led national governments in environmental protection efforts due to citizen interest or especially motivated local elites. In Japan, for instance, Kawasaki City approved a "basic environment plan" that was more stringent than the national government's plan to improve air, water, and soil quality as well as energy efficiency in its urban heating.

Nongovernmental Organizations and the Media

Asian nongovernmental organizations and media play important roles in raising the profile of the environment both among government elites and the general populace. They transmit information, educate, monitor the implementation of laws, and challenge official findings. Relative to those in the United States and Europe, however, Asian NGOs and media are less well institutionalized, although there is substantial variation among countries.

In the Philippines and Thailand NGOs and the press are frequent and vocal opponents of state policy. In Thailand NGOs are often an accepted part of the decision-making process for major development projects. Thai NGOs, for example, worked with the Electric Authority to reconfigure the Pak Mun hydropower project in order to minimize the number of people who would need to be relocated due to flooding. This process was facilitated by the fact that the government fully expected that its plans would undergo public review before the project was initiated.[45] In the Philippines in the late 1980s, local ethnic groups, provincial-level NGOs, the Roman Catholic Church, and the media all allied to launch a nationwide campaign and educational program against logging and poaching.

In Indonesia and Malaysia, the governments closely monitor and constrain the activities of the media and NGOs, often trying to co-opt them in support of government activities. The Indonesian Environment Ministry, for example, has called on NGOs to supplement its weak capacity and help mobilize public support for government programs such as its "Clean River Program," which worked to clean up twenty-four of the country's most polluted rivers. The Ministry of the Environment actively encouraged NGOs to ally with community groups and the media to monitor the progress of local industry efforts. By 1993 more than 2,000 enterprises had agreed to decrease their pollution loads, and the water quality of the rivers evidenced significant improvement.[46] However, grass-roots environmental movements without state support may be repressed. In the early 1990s local villages in Sumatra protested the deforestation and water pollution resulting from a rayon factory. In response, the government closed down an NGO and arrested and intimidated the protesters. Importantly, a national-level NGO (WALHI) filed the first-ever environmental court case challenging both government and industry compliance with environmental regulations, which it subsequently lost.[47] In general, watchdog organizations such as the press and NGOs are carefully monitored to prevent "all-out assault" on vested interests and government policy[48] Even the Indonesian environment minister, Sarwono Kusumaatmadja, has shown mixed feelings about his country's NGOs, commenting, "The judgmental attitude of the eco-lunatics is bad but I have no problem with most of the NGOs."[49] His perspective was echoed by the Malaysian energy minister, who stated, "Environmentalists are not qualified to make comments on the economic feasibility of such [Sarawak Dam] projects." The most important national newspaper in Malaysia rarely reports on NGO environmental activity, and in 1987 several environmentalists were arrested as subversives. Recently, however, with a new governmental focus on enforcing forestry regulations, NGOs such as Friends of the Earth have become more outspoken in their support of government efforts and their criticism of government failures.

Environmental NGOs have not been a major force in Japan since an initial burst of activity during the 1970s and early 1980s, which helped to spur environmental clean-up efforts. The domestic environmental legal structure does not offer a system for citizen review of government decisions or citizen access to government information. The new Environmental Basic Law invites public participation in the environmental impact assessment process; however, no procedures for involvement have been adopted yet.[50]

In China, the development of environmental NGOs is still in a nascent stage; organizations such as the Beijing Environment and Development Institute and Friends of Nature focus primarily on environmental education and environmental impact assessment projects. To some extent, however, the environment has become an acceptable outlet for citizen discontent. The government itself has initiated a highly popular investigative television program to report on environmental wrongdoings. It also conducts a weekly television talk show with the head of China's Convention in Trade in Endangered Species protection office. Local media also have become increasingly bold about reporting on environmental problems in their region. It remains to be seen, however, what will happen when these NGOs and the media pursue an issue that challenges the government position. Open media criticism of the Three Gorges Dam, for instance, has been severely constrained. Although the Chinese leadership commissioned environmental impact assessments during the initial stages of the planning process, the negative findings were largely ignored. Unlike the Thai hydropower project, there was no public review of the project, although a fierce debate took place in the National People's Congress, and the governor of Sichuan Province has voiced concern over the dam's impact on his province.[51]

International Intervention

While the primary response to environmental concerns in Asia must come from within Asia itself, the international community—including Japan within the Asia-Pacific region—has assisted in environmental protection efforts in Asia by accelerating domestic environmental awareness and enhancing state capacity through several means: Ideas and norms concerning the environment are transmitted among NGOs, local and national elites, the general populace, and multilateral institutions; technology and training are transferred; and international treaties or other multilateral fora serve to harmonize environmental laws among states.

The transmission of ideas and norms within the international community has had a profound effect on the evolution of institutions and policies in the Asia-Pacific region. In June 1992, the United Nations Conference on Environment and Development (UNCED), like the United Nations Conference on Human Environment twenty years earlier, spawned a wave of environmental legislation and new agencies and raised the environmental consciousness of the Asian populace.

The UNCED focused attention on issues and ideas of energy efficiency, sustainable development, and the link between poverty and the environment. The preparation for participating in the UNCED alone required countries to produce national environmental reports, which necessitated, in many cases, an unprecedented level of interministerial cooperation to collect data from various agencies, institutes, and regional actors. After the conference, a number of states initiated follow-up activities: The Philippine government established the first national commission on sustainable development to begin to implement Agenda 21, the global action plan to promote sustainable development that evolved out of the UNCED process; the Chinese drafted a national version of Agenda 21 that encompassed over seventy-five projects focused primarily on improving the domestic environment; and Japan passed a new environmental protection law and pledged to assume a leading role in fostering international cooperation on environmental issues and in providing aid to developing countries. In the wake of the UNCED, the Asian Development Bank also has been working with eight nations in Asia to integrate economic issues directly into national economic development agendas.

As a "consciousness-raising" exercise, the UNCED also may have inspired renewed efforts by states to take action on other international treaties. In 1992 Malaysia initiated a campaign to curb illegal logging; the state of Sarawak further decided to comply with the International Tropical Timber Organization's recommendations for reducing its logging activities by developing downstream timber industries and reducing log output. Some leading Asian diplomats such as Tommy Koh, Singapore's ambassador-at-large, have claimed that as a result of the conference, "Economic growth and environmental protection are no longer viewed as contradictory goals."[52]

Despite such optimism, the new ideological commitment to environmental protection voiced by many of Asia's political elites has not been matched by the financial commitment necessary to implement the new environmental projects. In general, the developing Asian nations have remained committed to the ideals espoused in the June 1991 Beijing Ministerial Declaration. The declaration, which was authored primarily by China but signed by forty-one developing states (including most Asia-Pacific nations with the exception of Japan, Taiwan, and Korea), asserted the primacy of development in the region and cited the responsibility borne by advanced industrialized nations for their historical contribution to the earth's environmental degradation. Ultimately, the Beijing Declaration called upon the advanced industrialized states to assume a much greater share of the financial burden of environmental protection in the developing states, for both domestic and global issues. Thus, the Chinese, for example, have stated that most of the project financing for their National Agenda 21 must come from international donors.

Despite inadequate financing, the mere establishment of new agencies and projects raises the profile of environmental thinking and begins to set the foundation for future activities and commitments. How well these commitments are fulfilled will depend substantially on the willingness of the advanced industrialized states to subsidize the efforts. If Asian countries are to respond systematically and effectively to the vast array of environmental problems that confront them, multilateral institutions and other international actors will have to expand their activities through the transfer of environmental technologies, training, and financial assistance. At the conclusion of the UNCED, Japan pledged to increase its assistance in the field of environmental protection to one trillion yen (U.S. $7.7 billion) during 1992–1997, an increase of 10 percent from the previous five-year period. Moreover, Japanese officials stated that separate funds would be made available specifically to respond to global environmental problems.[53] So far Japan has provided substantial financial support to Thailand to establish the Environmental Research and Training Center and to China to found the Sino-Japanese Friendship Environment Protection Center in Beijing. Korea has sent officials on environmental fact-finding trips to advanced industrialized nations and provided training programs for officials from China and Thailand on environmental technology. Both Korea and Japan have recognized the potential market for environmental technologies in Asia. An Organization for Economic Cooperation and Development report has stated that the market for environmental technologies is expected to grow at about 5.5 percent annually.[54]

Multilateral institutions such as the World Bank, the Global Environmental Facility, and the Asian Development Bank also will be critical to the future environmental situation in Asia by ensuring that regional infrastructure projects maintain high environmental standards and by establishing projects that are devoted primarily to environmental protection. In 1991 the World Bank loaned U.S. $1.6 billion for projects with primarily environmental objectives; in 1992 the Global Environmental Facility, with an operating budget of U.S. $1.3 billion, began supporting national-level responses to global environmental problems. As of July 1994, two of the six largest recipients of World Bank loans for environmental improvement were China and Indonesia. For pollution control in the urban areas, China received total commitments of U.S. $650 million out of a total U.S. $975 million allocated worldwide by the World Bank for this work. The World Bank also initiated a major new sanitation and sewage project in Indonesia. Both countries received loans for rural environmental projects.

The World Bank has begun to provide funds to nongovernmental actors to help implement the projects it has funded. In the past, the World Bank occasionally provided loans of such magnitude that the funds and managerial responsibilities overwhelmed the recipient's capacity for implementing the environmental protection programs. Moreover, the need to repay the loans created pressures to exploit further natural resources.[55] To prevent such difficulties with a grant it made to the Philippines, the World Bank provided a conservation grant of U.S. $2.9 million to traditional state agencies and a simultaneous grant of U.S. $1.9 million to an NGO consortium that will involve local communities as well as NGOs. This represents an explicit acknowledgment by the World Bank of the key role that NGOs and other local-level actors play in the implementation process. Fully 30 percent of the World Bank's new environmental projects now involve NGOs.

A second mechanism that the World Bank is using to enhance the environmental benefits of its infrastructure projects is development aid contingent on the gradual elimination of government subsidies for natural resource use. In China, for example, the decision by the World Bank to finance the development of the Sichuan natural gas reserves was predicated on China's agreement to phase in internationally competitive prices over a "reasonable" period. These conditions were designed in part to ensure that efforts to reduce methane emissions would be financially sustainable.[56]

The expansion of formal links between international trade regimes and environmental protection efforts is also likely to be the focus of future regional negotiations. In general, Asian countries—like the majority of those in the developing world—have resisted enforcing domestic environmental laws in the international arena, viewing such a linkage as an effort on the part of advanced industrialized states to prevent their goods from entering the international markets. Austria, in fact, abandoned plans to introduce a 70 percent tax on tropical timber when the Association of Southeast Asian Nations (ASEAN) complained that the law violated the General Agreement on Tariffs and Trade (GATT).

Although environmental concerns have been raised consistently at the Asia-Pacific Economic Cooperation (APEC) forum gatherings, adequate steps to incorporate environmental issues as an ongoing focus point have not occurred. APEC's stated goal of promoting sustainable development in the region contradicts its relative inaction in placing environmental issues on the same level as other issues.[57] Unlike the North American Free Trade Agreement (NAFTA), APEC has no regional environmental protection organization to monitor the implementation of its environmental provisions, "provide information on compliance with domestic laws, raise and harmonize environmental standards, levy fines or sanctions (including trade sanctions) for noncompliance, and serve as a source of information."[58] Thus far, there is little hope that such a group will emerge under the auspices of APEC.[59]

Transfer of Polluting Industries

Although the international community has helped states in the region to develop their capacities to protect the environment, in some ways it also has accelerated environmental degradation in the region. The transfer of high-polluting industries from industrialized states to developing states is only one example. In many cases, such transfer is welcomed by the host country. In Indonesia, for example, the government is establishing Batan Island as a free trade zone to support access to Malaysia and Singapore. To attract business investment, the government has let it be known that Indonesian environmental regulations will not be enforced. In the PRC in 1990, Prime Minster Li Peng personally managed a proposal from a Taiwan industrialist to construct a U.S. $7 billion petrochemical complex in Xiamen. The complex originally had been planned for southern Taiwan but Taiwanese environmentalists protested.[60]

Regional competition for foreign industry and joint venture opportunities increases the likelihood of such environmentally damaging development. In many cases, weak environmental legislation is seen as an attractive aspect of a bidding package from a particular nation. In some cases, however, the developing Asian nations simply may be too weak to take action against environmental offenders. As one environmentalist noted, "If a Korean developer decides to drop a wharf on a coral reef off the coast of Vietnam, Hanoi just doesn't have the capacity to stop it."[61]

International tourism also appears to be playing an important role in transforming the environment in Asia. Economic growth has provided many residents of the Asia-Pacific region with substantially more expendable income. This has produced a boom in Asian tourism, both intra- and interstate. Little thought, however, has been given as to how best to regulate the number of tourists to avoid despoiling cultural and scenic spots. One typical tourist pastime, which has received substantial media attention in recent times for its environmental ramifications, is the game of golf. Golf courses require extensive fertilizer and pesticide use, which pollutes the air and soil, is destructive to biodiversity, and uses vast amounts of scarce water resources. In Thailand one study estimated that one golf course consumes as much water as 6,000 city dwellers. However, golf brings billions of dollars to the tourism industry in Asia. Much of the initiative for the tremendous expansion in golf courses throughout Asia stems from the desire of Japanese golfers to find less expensive courses; Japanese investors have funded numerous courses in other Asian states. Domestic considerations also have driven the establishment of new courses. In Thailand the military and police have supported the construction of courses, some of which have been set in parks and wildlife sanctuaries. In Indonesia the state arrested farmers and environmentalists who were protesting the construction of new golf courses by members of President Suharto's government.[62]

U.S. Interests and Options

It is unlikely, although not impossible, that Asian environmental practices will pose a visible threat to the environmental and security interests of the United States prior to the year 2000. A relatively easy argument, therefore, can be made that the United States should concentrate its environmental efforts at home rather than in Asia. Political support in the United States for providing environmental assistance—and aid in general—abroad is low. The weak capacity in many developing Asian states to enforce environmental laws further suggests that U.S. resources would be utilized more effectively in the domestic arena. Finally, the United States itself is a leading contributor to several global environmental phenomena and could better spend its money addressing its own contribution to these problems.[63]

Such a perspective ignores several key issues that should form the basis for establishing U.S. priorities in the region. These issues further suggest that U.S. interests will be best served by an environmental policy that engages Asia rather than one that is primarily U.S.-centered.

First, over the next decade and beyond, the consequences of Asia's environmental policies will almost certainly challenge the environmental health of U.S. citizens and, potentially, U.S. economic and security interests. As rapid economic growth and consumption of energy-intensive goods in the region continue, China alone has the power to negate completely the efforts of the rest of the world to respond to ozone depletion and global climate change. These phenomena will subject the U.S. populace to negative health and economic costs, including increased occurrence of cancer, rising sea levels, and changing agricultural patterns due to climate change. The economic growth trends, patterns of energy consumption, and priorities of Asian elites further suggest that in most states, environmental degradation will continue to outpace the capacity to respond to the environmental consequences of this growth. Reform of the social and political context in which environmental decisions are made appears unlikely in most Asian-Pacific states within the next decade. Thus, a strategy to stave off the worst-case scenarios of continued ozone depletion and climate change will have to involve an expanded role for the international community.

Second, continued depletion of water resources or arable land in the region could induce a range of secondary policy challenges for the United States. These include large-scale migration, famine, and violent conflict—either inter- or more likely intrastate—over scarce resources. These secondary effects have not emerged as a sustained problem for international management, aside from periods of war or natural disasters. However, if loss of arable land and fresh water continues in the region, and is exacerbated by a global environmental phenomenon such as climate change, such crises may become a permanent part of the region's environmental landscape. In this case, there may be calls for U.S. involvement to help ensure regional stability. Dramatic increases in environmental refugees to the United States would also strain U.S. domestic welfare resources and potentially heighten domestic political tensions.

Third, the United States currently holds the largest market share in environmental technologies in the world, and the potential for increased sales is significant. However, in addition to traditional competitors such as Germany and Japan, the United States will increasingly face challenges from Korea, Taiwan, and even the PRC in its dominance of the market. Maintenance and further expansion of the U.S. market for environmental technologies is another important aspect of U.S. involvement in Asian environmental protection efforts.

These most immediate challenges suggest several courses of action for U.S. policymakers:

1. *The United States should link its infrastructure aid to projects that help limit Asian countries' role in global climate change and ozone depletion.* Japan has already taken the initiative in this area. Japanese officials announced that their 1996–98 aid package to the PRC (Japan's largest aid recipient) will emphasize environmental protection. Of the forty projects that Japan is funding, fifteen are related to the environment. Furthermore, Japan has stated that all Chinese thermal power plants funded with Japanese loans must include equipment to control SO_2 emissions.[64] The United States could similarly link its infrastructure aid to sound environmental practices. The development of Asia's energy infrastructure will have the most significant impact on U.S. environmental interests. The United States could rank the relative environmental consequences of each potential energy resource (e.g., fossil fuels, nuclear, natural gas, hydropower, renewables) available to Asian countries and offer financial support only to those less harmful to U.S. environmental interests. From such a ranking, for example, the benefits of hydropower for climate change would emerge; the United States might therefore reconsider its recent decision not to permit Export-Import Bank funding for the Three Gorges Dam in the PRC. Furthermore, the United States should use its influence within the World Bank and other major lending organizations to ensure that funding for new power plants or development of energy reserves is tied to the rationalization of energy prices within Asia.

2. *The United States should support the inclusion of environmental considerations within the context of APEC.* Many of the environmental con-

sequences of economic development within Asia will remain within the region. An established forum to discuss transboundary air pollution, polluted rivers and seas, and natural resource exploitation in shared or disputed territories would contribute to the peaceful resolution of regional environmental issues. Such a forum further offers the opportunity for information sharing, the harmonization of environmental legislation (with a phase-in period for the less-developed Asian nations), and the potential to levy sanctions or fees for transboundary pollution. Such activities would benefit directly the United States. As with NAFTA, trade agreements that emerge from APEC, in which environmental regulations are substantially more stringent in one state than in the other, will have negative environmental ramifications for all parties.[65] Moreover, the more advanced industrialized states will, in the end, bear a significant portion of the clean-up cost of the less-developed states' weak environmental protection practices. Such costs might appear in the form of U.S. contributions to World Bank and Asian Development Bank loans or in U.S. policies to address the domestic ramifications of global environmental change or ozone depletion. Finally, the argument could be made that countries with weak environmental protection regulations or lax enforcement or environmental laws are, in effect, levying a tax on goods imported from those states with stringently formulated and implemented environmental protection laws.

3. *The United States should support the expansion of the environmental technologies market in Asia.* University labs in the United States are at the forefront of environmental technological development, and Asian countries such as Korea and Taiwan are following the lead of Japan two decades ago and aggressively pursuing the licensing of these technologies. The United States could derive greater long-term benefits from technologies developed in the country by undertaking at least two strategies.[66]

    First, the United States should follow the Japanese lead and, where appropriate, link such technologies to U.S. development aid. For example, for the foreseeable future, China will be relying on coal as its primary energy source. Japan has linked its aid to the inclusion of desulfurization processes, which address Japan's primary environmental concern with the PRC, acid rain. Optimally, the United States should provide energy-efficient technologies and aid in the development of renewable energy alternatives. Given China's near-term reliance on coal, the United States also should promote technologies such as activated carbon fibers, which may be used as filters to trap carbon dioxide and carbon monoxide.[67] Doing so would not only further U.S. business interests but also would contribute to limiting China's contribution to global climate change, which is a U.S. environmental priority.[68]

Second, the United States should enhance the development of Asian domestic markets for the use of environmental technologies. While the United States cannot restructure the political relationships in China, Malaysia, or Indonesia that help sustain continued environmental degradation, it can take three steps to improve enforcement efforts and, at the same time, advance U.S. environmental technologies: a) identify key local, as opposed to national, officials and NGOs to establish direct links for joint research, training, and technology transfer; b) emphasize education for those elites who are not explicitly concerned with environmental protection but who may plan a critical role in policy planning; and c) develop innovative institutions such as Battelle Lab's Energy Efficiency Centers, which offer training in environmental and energy economics to mid-ranking energy officials, provide them with a modest budget, and establish a domestically managed and operated energy efficiency consulting firm to spread the use of efficient technologies. While this is a longer-term strategy, by contributing to the enhancement of Asian state capacity for environmental protection, the United States also sets in motion the expansion of the environmental technology market of U.S. goods.

4. *The United States should take the lead in global environmental affairs.* While the United States has taken the lead in responding to many international environmental problems, it has been slow to enact domestic legislation on some key issues, such as global climate change. The United States should align its domestic policies with global environmental objectives to establish the moral standing to encourage other countries to do the same. The United States also should exercise leadership in the governance and finance of multilateral institutions and agreements that promote environmental protection, including U.N. agencies, multilateral bodies, and conventions on biodiversity, climate change, and ozone depletion.[69]

Conclusions

There is substantial variation among the countries of the Asia-Pacific region, both in terms of their level of economic development and their commitment and capacity to care for their local environments. Overall, however, the picture for the immediate future—five to ten years—is fairly bleak. Continued rapid economic growth and patterns of energy consumption throughout the region will place increasing pressures on all elements of the environment, such as water, air, and forests. Similarly, the global and regional environments will be negatively affected by the region's economic and environmental practices. Ozone depletion, climate change, acid rain, and possibly increased localized conflict over scarce resources are all likely to draw heavily on already limited international financial reserves.

At the same time, in every country of the region, there are supporters of environmental protection within the government, the private sector, and, most important, the nongovernmental community. In many cases, NGOs have been responsible for the successes achieved thus far in pressuring more recalcitrant actors for stricter environmental laws and regulations. In addition, as the standard of living rises in each of the Asia-Pacific countries, there is a growing chorus of support for the political and economic reforms necessary for more effective implementation of these environmental laws and regulations. However, this is likely to be a long and tortuous process as various bureaucratic and other actors battle for development priorities based on traditional patterns of growth and consumption.

The role of the international community in determining how this process will evolve is a critical one. The international community and Japan within the Asia-Pacific region clearly can accelerate environmental awareness and enhance state capacity through technology transfer, investment, training, and joint research. The multilateral banks also can play a crucial part in ensuring that large infrastructure projects, such as hydropower plants, highways, and sewage systems, are undertaken in an environmentally sound manner. In all cases, the degree to which wealthier members of the international community, including those within the Asia-Pacific region such as Korea, Taiwan, Japan, and Singapore, elect to promote cooperation on environmental problems with those at earlier stages of economic development will be a defining factor in the future of the regional and global environment.

Notes

The author wishes to thank the members of the Asia Project Transnational Issues Group, especially Frances Seymour, for their suggestions and comments, and Nancy Yao for her research assistance.

1. This chapter focuses primarily on environmental degradation in urban areas.

2. Joseph Kahn, "Damned Yangtze," *Wall Street Journal* (April 18, 1994), p. A1.

3. Carter Brandon and Ramesh Ramankutty, *Toward an Environmental Strategy for Asia* (Washington, DC: International Bank for Reconstruction and Development, 1993), p. 21.

4. James Rush, *The Last Tree* (New York: The Asia Society, 1991), p. 4.

5. *World Development Report 1992* (New York: Oxford University Press, 1992), pp. 146–148.

6. Adam Schwarz, "Looking Back at Rio," *Far Eastern Economic Review* (Oct. 28, 1993), p. 48.

7. For example, in summer 1994 in the Huai River Valley and in September 1993 in Gansu Province.

8. Patrick E. Tyler, "A Tide of Pollution Threatens China's Prosperity," *New York Times* (Sep. 25, 1994), p. A3.

9. Vaclav Smil, "Environmental Problems in China: Estimates of Economic Costs," *East-West Center Special Reports* 5 (Apr. 1996), p. 54.

10. Chao-Chan Cheng, "A Comparative Study of the Formation and Development of Air and Water Pollution Control Laws in Taiwan and Japan," *Pacific Rim Law and Policy Journal* 3 (1993), p. S-62.

11. *Newsreview* (May 21,1994), p. 7.

12. World Resources Institute, *World Resources 1992–93* (New York: Basic Books, 1992), p. 317.

13 Tyler, "A Tide of Pollutions," p. A3.

14. In contrast, in the rest of the world only 25 percent of the energy needs are met by coal.

15. Gordon Fairclough, "Into Top Gear," *Far Eastern Economic Review* (Oct. 13, 1994), p. 58.

16. *World Resources 1992–93*, p. 317; World Resources Institute, *World Resources 1994–95* (New York: Basic Books, 1994), p. 334.

17. Brandon and Ramankutty, *Toward an Environmental Strategy for Asia*, p. 98.

18. Ibid., p. 89.

19. Hidefumi Imura, "Japan's Environmental Balancing Act," *Asian Survey* 34, no. 4 (Apr. 1994), p. 366.

20. S. Jayasankaran and John McBeth, "Hazy Days," *Far Eastern Economic Review* (Oct. 20 1994), pp. 66–67.

21. *World Resources 1994–94*, p. 198.

22. Author discussion with Japanese energy expert, October 1994, Council on Foreign Relations, New York.

23. Author discussion with National Environmental Protection Official, September 1994, Beijing, People's Republic of China.

24. *World Resources 1994–95*, p. 132.

25. Schwarz, "Looking Back at Rio," *Far Eastern Economic Review* (Oct. 28, 1993), p. 52.

26. Ibid., p. 58.

27. Almost 50 percent of Vietnam's forests were destroyed as a result of the Vietnam War.

28. *World Resources 1994–95*, p. 131.

29. Ibid.

30. Ibid., p. 79.

31. *State of the World 1994* (New York: W.W. Norton & Co., 1994), p. 17.

32. It is important to note that while industrialized countries have begun to employ environmental technologies to minimize the environmental impact of their development path, they have not fundamentally altered the development path.

33. This already is the case in Indonesia.

34. Ibid., p. 38.

35. *New Scientist* (Aug. 14, 1993), p. 2.

36. Michael Vatikiotis, "Clearcut Mandate," *Far Eastern Economic Review* (Oct. 24, 1994), pp. 66–67.

37. Paul Hardley, "Parks Under Seige," *Far Eastern Economic Review* (Jan. 20, 1994), pp. 36–37.

38. Imura, "Japan's Environmental Balancing Act," p. 362.

39. Author's discussion with Japanese energy expert Naito Masahisa, October 1994, Council on Foreign Relations, New York.

40. Imura, "Japan's Environmental Balancing Act," p. 376.

41. *Newsreview* (May 21, 1994), p. 7.

42. Abigail Jahiel, presentation at the Association for Asian Studies, Cambridge, MA (Apr. 14, 1994).

43. Rush, *The Last Tree*, p. 38.

44. Elizabeth Economy, "China and Global Climate Change," paper presented at Association for Asian Studies, Boston, MA (Mar. 1994).

45. *World Development Report 1992*, p. 88.

46. Colin MacAndrews, "Politics of the Environment in Indonesia," *Asian Survey* 34, no. 4 (Apr. 1994), p. 377.

47. Comments provided by Frances Seymour; on file with author.

48. Rush, *The Last Tree* (New York: Asia Society, 1991), p. 87.

49. Schwarz, "Looking ack at Rio," *Far Eastern Economic Review* (Oct. 28, 1993), p. 50.

50. Imura, "Japan's Environmental Balancing Act," p. 364.

51. Kari Huus, "More Dam Trouble," *Far Eastern Economic Review* (Oct. 24, 1994), pp. 66–67.

52. Schwarz, "Looking Back at Rio," *Far Eastern Economic Review* (Oct. 28, 1993), p. 48.

53. Imura, "Japan's Environmental Balancing Act," p. 360.

54. Candice Stevens, "The Greening of Trade," *OECD Observer* 187 (Apr./May 1994), p. 33. In 1990, the United States produced 40 percent of the world's environmental products and services, worth an estimated U.S. $80 billion.

55. Frances Korten, "The High Costs of Environmental Loans," *Asia Pacific Issues* 7 (Sept. 1993), p. 2.

56. The World Bank, *Making Development Sustainable* (1994), p. 141.

57. Stewart Hudson, "Fixing What's Broke with APEC: First Steps Toward a Sustainable Development Action Plan That Can Be Adopted at the November 1995 Osaka Ministers' Meeting" (Washington, DC: National Wildlife Federation Trade and Environment Program, 1995).

58. C. Ford Runge, *Freer Trade, Protected Environment* (New York: Council on Foreign Relations, 1994), pp. 66–68.

59. Author discussion with C. Fred Bergsten, October 26, 1994, Council on Foreign Relations, New York.

60. *New York Times* (Dec. 18, 1990), p. D7.

61. Schwarz, "Looking Back at Rio," *Far Eastern Economic Review* (Oct. 28, 1993), p. 50.

62. Philip Shenon, "Fore! Golf in Asia Hits Environmental Rough," *New York Times* (Oct. 22, 1994), p. A3.

63. Comments by a participant in the Asia Project Study Group on the Environment at the Council on Foreign Relations, Nov. 7, 1994.

64. Charles Smith, "Eager to Please," *Far Eastern Economic Review* (Jan. 26, 1995), p. 26.

65. This same weak enforcement capacity also entices high-polluting industries from the more advanced industrialized states.

66. There are many other steps that the United States could take, including the development of a domestic incentive structure more conducive to the research and development of environmental technologies and the incorporation of such technologies into U.S. consumption patterns, which would provide the nation with the "moral" standing to encourage Asian countries to reconfigure their energy structures or transportation models.

67. James Economy et al., "Tailoring Carbon Filters for Adsorbing Volatiles," *Chemtech* (October 1992), p. 597.

68. The economic rationale for such U.S. action is increased because Japan already has raised the costs of its power plant assistance for environmental reasons.

69. Comments provided by Frances Seymour.

Chapter 4

East Asia's Economic Transformation and Labor Migration

PAUL J. SMITH

The world is entering an era of unprecedented international migration. Millions of individuals are moving across national borders in search of jobs, higher wages, or simply a better life. Millions of others are forced involuntarily from their home countries by war, famine, environmental degradation, and other factors. As the scale of international migration grows throughout the world, immigration issues are becoming "high politics" in many countries' domestic and international affairs.[1] Debates are raging in many countries between restrictionists who want to limit the number of immigrants and admissionists who advocate free and liberal immigration policies.[2] In Asia—particularly East Asia—this phenomenon has reached a scale at which it can no longer be ignored by national leaders, both within the region and beyond.

International migration in East Asia is not a new phenomenon. Many of today's diaspora communities in Southeast Asia—particularly ethnic Chinese and Indian—are the products of migration waves that occurred decades or even centuries ago.[3] Astri Suhrke has identified four major migration phases that have influenced Southeast Asia: the ancient migrations (southward migration of the Mon, Khmer, and T'ai people, among others, beginning centuries before the Buddhist era); colonial period migration (from the mid-1800s to about the mid-1900s); refugee flows generated by wars in Indochina (1960–75); and labor migration (beginning in the late 1970s).[4] Labor migration—the subject of this chapter—is the current migration phase unfolding throughout East Asia; in light of present demographic realities, it may become the largest in scale and most far-reaching in its social and political consequences.

This chapter will explore the main forces driving Asian labor migration. First, it will address the socioeconomic causes and impact of migration. Rapid economic growth throughout the region is generating a growing wave of intraregional migration. Unemployment, poverty, and population pressures are spurring millions of people from East Asia's poorer countries to migrate to the region's wealthier nations, lured by the prospect of better jobs, higher wages, and a more attractive lifestyle. Today, over two million East Asians can be classified as intraregional migrants, compared with just 200,000 in 1980. Source countries, such as Indonesia, Bangladesh, and the Philippines, rely on this emigration as a safety valve against growing unemployment and low wages. Money sent home by migrant workers also provides a major source of foreign exchange. Host nations also benefit, as foreign laborers willingly take the "dirty, dangerous, and difficult" jobs shunned by local workers. Foreign workers frequently toil in Japan's construction industry, Malaysia's plantations, and Thailand's fishing industry, among others.

Second, the chapter will view the politics of Asian migration, particularly the response of national leaders to the consequences of mass migrations. Even when migrants provide economic benefits to the host country, their presence is not always welcomed. Many East Asian host states do not view themselves as "immigration countries" and regard the long-term presence of these foreigners as a cultural and economic threat. Some countries, particularly Malaysia and Thailand, treat illegal immigrants as a national security concern, and serious political disputes have erupted recently between countries in the region over immigration issues.

Third, it will look at the future of migration in Asia, taking special note of China's growing role as a source country. Political complications notwithstanding, the trend of intraregional migration in East Asia is likely to continue for the foreseeable future as the fundamental "push-pull" factors that drive migration become more intense. Traditional source countries are experiencing high rates of labor force growth and unemployment, and these trends are expected to continue well into the next century. Simultaneously, host countries continue to experience ever-worsening labor shortages as a result of rapid economic growth.

This chapter will conclude with an examination of the likely consequences of Asian migration for the United States, and will offer several policy recommendations for managing this phenomenon.

Economic Growth and its Migration Consequences

The rising tide of international migration in East Asia is uniquely linked to the region's phenomenal economic transformation. Fueled by unprecedented rates of economic growth, many East Asian countries have achieved remarkable levels of prosperity in a relatively short period of time. Despite the turmoil in Asian financial markets in the last quarter of 1997 and early 1998, most economists are optimistic that economic growth in East Asia will remain robust for the longterm.[5]

What is less well known, perhaps, is the fact that this prosperity is highly uneven. In East Asia extreme poverty exists side by side with conspicuous wealth.[6] Vast differences in wealth and income exist not only between countries in the region but also within individual countries—particularly between rural and urban populations. In some countries, this "wealth gap," or the perception of a wealth gap, is sparking social unrest and even threatening some governments.[7] Consequently, millions of Asia's poor—many having been exposed to video cassette recorders, satellite television, and other mass media conveying images of material abundance—are no longer content to sit idly by and wait for the region's wealth to trickle down. They are packing their bags and moving to the cities. If they cannot find work in the cities of their own country, they contact a friend or relative, a broker, or even a human smuggler and emigrate to a country where their labor is needed and where they can earn higher salaries. This pattern is repeated thousands of times every year, resulting in one of the most dramatic demographic shifts in modern East Asian history.

Today about two to three million East Asians work abroad as legal or illegal migrants in another Asian country, compared to about 200,000 in 1980.[8] Unemployment, poverty, and population pressures are the major

Table 4.1   Legal Versus Illegal Immigrants

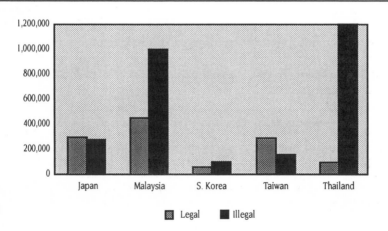

"push factors" spurring these migrants to leave their home countries. Labor shortages and jobs that offer higher wages act as important "pull factors" that draw migrants into their host country of choice.[9] Many of these migrants have decided to migrate even though they held (or could have held) a full-time job at home. Vast income differences among East Asian countries mean that even full-time employees in poorer countries have a great incentive to emigrate. Workers from the region's countries with low per-capita income realize that they can earn substantially greater incomes in those countries in which wage levels are higher, even if—as is often true—the salary they earn there is low by local standards. Additionally, the presence of ethnic networks throughout the region also influences and encourages international migration. In Japan, for example, relatives or compatriots of newly-arrived Bangladeshi immigrants often will help them find food, living quarters, and employment.[10]

Most of East Asia's immigrants are illegal, reflecting the policy of many host countries of discouraging the influx of large numbers of unskilled workers. Although many host governments issue a limited number of work permits and visas every year, or alternatively allow a limited number of workers to enter into job-training programs, these legal quotas cannot begin to satisfy the enormous demand for foreign workers in many of these host countries. Consequently, in many host countries the number of illegal workers may exceed the number of legal workers by two or three times.

The presence of a particular nationality of foreign workers in a host country often reflects geographic or cultural realities. For example, Indonesian migrants tend to be most common in Malaysia, reflecting cultural and geographic linkages between the two countries. Geography also plays a role in Thailand, where nationals from Burma and China are most common. Mainland Chinese travel to Taiwan because of obvious cultural and linguistic similarities between China and Taiwan.

Many East and Southeast Asian countries are both immigrant and emigrant countries. A country that attracts immigrant workers may see its own workers drawn to neighboring countries, where still higher wages can be obtained. For example, thousands of Burmese immigrants travel to Thailand every year looking for higher-paying jobs, while similar numbers of Thais look for still higher wages in Taiwan or Japan. Likewise, thousands of Indonesians are attracted to higher wages in Malaysia, whereas many Malaysians are drawn to higher wages in Singapore. A similar trend is occurring in China. While Chinese immigrants flow, legally and illegally, to jobs and other opportunities outside their country, other countries' immigrants—mostly from neighboring Pakistan, Vietnam, India, and Sri Lanka—are flooding illegally into China's prosperous southern province of Guangdong to find employment.[11] In some cases, job seekers from the region's poorest countries may migrate direct-ly to the region's wealthiest countries. The presence of friends or connections in the destination country, distance from the home country, ease of trav-el, and severity of anti-immigrant restrictions are among the factors that may influence a migrant's decision to "leapfrog" directly to a high-wage country.

Finally, as countries attain higher levels of prosperity, their role as emi-grant (source) countries may diminish or perhaps even cease. Tradi-tional labor-exporting countries in the region are facing their own labor shortages. South Korea has traditionally served as a major labor exporter for Asia and the Middle East. In recent years, however, strong econom-ic growth has turned the country into a labor importer. Countries such as South Korea and Taiwan are even beginning to witness a reverse migration of some of their own nationals who had previously sought jobs in third countries. In 1994 nearly 1,000 Koreans living abroad sought to regain their South Korean citizenship primarily for economic reasons.[12] Many Taiwanese graduates of U.S. universities also are opting to return to Taiwan in search of economic opportunities. Between 1991 and 1993 the number of Taiwanese returning home rose from 2,885 to 5,459, although the number of Taiwanese emigrants—estimated at roughly 20,000 annually—continues to exceed the number of return-immigrants.[13]

Impact of Migration on Source Countries

For many source countries, emigration can ease the pressures caused by high rates of unemployment, low wages, and population growth.[14] Some source countries actually encourage emigration as a means of dealing with their domestic unemployment problems. Bangladesh, for example, has looked to emigration as a means of reducing its number of unemployed, recently estimated at twelve million.[15] Chronic unemployment in the Philip-pines also has led to an official encouragement of emigration.[16] Similar-ly, Vietnam has expressed interest in promoting emigration as a solution to its growing unemployment crisis.[17]

Emigration is not only a useful method for countering unemployment, it can be extremely lucrative for the source country as well. Hundreds of thousands of migrant workers in Asia's major host countries remit bil-lions of dollars back to their families every year. Filipinos alone remit between U.S. $2 to 6 billion home annually.[18] During 1993 and 1994 approxi-mately 240,000 Bangladeshi nationals working abroad wired home U.S. $1.05 billion.[19] Similarly, Indonesians working abroad have remitted more than U.S. $1 billion in foreign currency back to their homes in recent years.[20]

Some experts argue that this transfer of money greatly benefits the source country in that is may be used to stimulate indigenous industries.[21] Others counter that the money is merely spent on basic necessities, such as food, medical care, and education, thus having only negligible impact on the source country's economic development.[22] Despite this uncertainty, it is clear that foreign remittances constitute a major, if not the primary, source of foreign income for many source countries. Bangladesh, Pakistan, and the Philippines, for example, rely on remittances from overseas workers as their largest single source of export income.[23] Moreover, this income serves as yet another incentive for source country governments to promote emigration.

Source countries also may benefit from emigration to the extent that their nationals acquire useful skills in the host country that can be applied at home later. The basic rationale behind foreign labor training programs is that migrants will acquire skills in the host country (while providing that country with inexpensive labor) that can be transferred back home, at least in theory. In practice, it is not clear that labor migration results in any significant transfer of skills. Many migrants are used merely for unskilled jobs, whereas those fortunate enough to receive technological training often discover that their skills cannot be transferred home because of differences in technology and level of economic development between the source and host countries.[24]

Impact of Migration on Host Countries

For host countries, foreign workers provide cheap and generally efficient labor. Regardless of legal status, migrant workers in East Asia typically earn wages that are below—often substantially below—the prevailing wages of the host country. Moreover, employers of illegal workers generally do not provide medical or disability insurance, making the services of these migrants an even greater bargain.

Both legal and illegal migrants typically engage in occupations shunned by local workers. The type of job or industry depends on the country. For example, many foreign laborers in Thailand, Taiwan, or Hong Kong work in the fishing industry. In Malaysia, a foreign worker is more likely to work on a plantation or in a factory. In Japan, foreigners may find jobs as construction workers, waitresses, or "entertainment industry" workers. Whatever the job or industry, it is typically one that is plagued by chronic worker shortages largely due to the low wages offered, the perceived low social status associated with the job, or because of heightened social and economic expectations of native workers.[25]

Perhaps the most striking aspect of East Asian intraregional migration is that so much of it is illegal. Illegal, an observer will quickly learn, often does not mean unacknowledged. Many host countries recognize and benignly tolerate the presence of illegal workers, yet they are not inclined to legalize them. Malaysia, for example, calls publicly for immigration curbs while privately welcoming foreign workers.[26]

Although skilled or professional workers may have a number of options allowing them to work legally in the host country, unskilled workers often are limited by strict quotas or restrictive visas. An unskilled migrant who is fortunate may be recruited or "contracted out" as part of a group to work in the host country for a set period of time. During periods of acute labor shortages, host countries simply may grant limited numbers of visas or work permits for unskilled foreign workers. An alternative route may be for the migrant to enroll in a labor training program. Under this program, the host country recruits a migrant worker to serve as a "trainee" for two or three years. In theory, the migrants will learn valuable skills which can be transferred back to the home country. In practice, however, many foreign trainee programs have been criticized as "vehicle[s] to bring in low-wage foreign workers for unskilled routine jobs where little if any training is involved."[27] Some trainees reportedly have quit their programs prematurely after complaining of harsh working conditions and inadequate pay.[28] South Korean officials report that increasing numbers of "technical trainees" are abandoning their training jobs to find more lucrative work in the country as illegal immigrants.[29]

Although an enormous demand for unskilled or semiskilled labor exists throughout East Asia, most host governments insist on maintaining restrictive policies designed to limit the influx of this class of migrant. The rationale behind such restrictions probably can be attributed to the following factors. First, domestic trade unions in many host countries are often vocal in their opposition to the influx of unskilled foreign workers. They fear that importing foreign workers will depress wages and lead to high unemployment rates among the local working population. When Hong Kong, for example, decided to import 27,000 foreign workers for its new airport project, unions protested that the move would result in unemployment among Hong Kong workers.[30] Labor unions in Taiwan also blame migrant workers for taking jobs away from Taiwanese workers.[31] Similarly, when the Thai government proposed legalizing the presence of roughly 700,000 illegal immigrants in July 1996, Thai labor leaders protested that the action would hurt local workers by depressing wages.[32] (In contrast, many East Asian governments face exactly the opposite pressure from business groups and corporations that are keen on liberalizing immigration rules in order to gain access to inexpensive foreign labor).[33]

Second, host countries also fear that admitting large numbers of unskilled workers may delay or hinder the transition to more sophisticated technology (including robotics) that would lessen the need for human labor. They point to the tendency of many host country firms to choose cheap foreign labor instead of investing in costly yet labor-saving technology upgrades.[34] Malaysia, for example, hopes to reduce its dependence on foreign labor by discouraging investment in labor-intensive industries in favor of investments that are capital intensive and based on advanced technology.[35]

Third, many host countries believe there are viable alternatives to admitting large numbers of unskilled foreign workers. They are looking at possibilities such as increasing female labor participation rates and including other underutilized segments of society (such as the elderly) in the workforce. Malaysia is encouraging married women to reenter the work force as a means of alleviating the nation's chronic labor shortages.[36] Taiwan has considered allowing prisoners to join its labor force to help solve its own worker shortage problem.[37] In Thailand, officials even have pondered the possibility of recalling all of the 700,000 Thai nationals working abroad in an effort to tackle the country's labor shortages.[38]

Finally, most East Asian countries hope that intraregional migration will be a temporary phenomenon that will not lead to permanent settlement.[39] Some argue that East Asian governments prefer to "turn on labor flows like a tap and then turn them off again if the workers are no longer needed."[40] Liberalizing immigration rules might deprive host countries of their ability to deport immigrants once they are perceived as no longer necessary.

East Asia's Illegal Immigration Safety Valve

The practice in host countries of maintaining strict laws against immigration is spurring large numbers of migrants to enter those countries by illegal means. Probably the most popular method for working illegally in a host country is simply to acquire a visitor or student visa and enter the country legally, with the intention of overstaying and finding work. In South Korea, officials estimate that roughly 60,000 illegal workers have used this method to enter the country in recent years.[41] Similarly in Malaysia, many Filipinos and Indonesians enter the country as tourists and stay on after their visas expire.[42] Similar trends have been reported in Japan. Because this method is so common, many host countries are cracking down against it and are denying short-term transit visas to nationals from major source countries, even if their travel plans are legitimate.[43]

Another increasingly popular method for illegally entering a host country is to do so as part of a tour group or as a participant in an international conference or sporting event. Following a 1992 international conference held in Japan, twenty-seven foreign participants—the majority from the Philippines—overstayed their visas, allegedly to seek employment.[44] At the 1994 Asian Games held in Hiroshima, Japan, fifteen Burmese nationals attempted to enter Japan illegally while posing as soccer cheerleaders.[45] South Korea also has had to contend with Chinese tourists abandoning their tour groups to look for employment.[46]

In addition, would-be immigrants are relying on forged or faked passports and visas to enter their chosen country illegally. The practice of fabricating or forging passports and visas is rife throughout East Asia and often is controlled by organized crime syndicates. Thailand is considered one of East Asia's premier centers for immigration document forgery.[47] Criminal gangs located in Bangkok's Chinatown and its business district ply a lucrative trade in stealing and forging passports and visas.[48] In 1995 Malaysian police busted a multimillion-dollar operation that supplied forged travel and other documents to that country's large immigrant population.[49] Police in Hong Kong also have found evidence of international document forgery syndicates based in their territory.[50] Japanese immigration authorities, meanwhile, report that large numbers of Thai or Filipino workers are attempting to enter Japan illegally with forged documents.[51]

Participation in a fake or "sham" marriage provides still another avenue for illegal immigration. In Japan, for example, many rural Japanese men face difficulties in finding a wife and are looking for potential candidates among Japan's poorer Asian neighbors. But many of these men discover that their foreign wives "disappear" after their arrival in Japan. Chinese women in particular have been known to enter Japan with a spouse visa, flee their Japanese husband, and find lucrative work in another part of the country.[52] In Hong Kong, triads (Chinese organized crime groups) have cashed in on the growing demand for fake marriages from foreigners—primarily women from the Philippines and Thailand—seeking to overcome the former colony's increasingly restrictive immigration rules.[53] Many of the women discover, however, that they must work as prostitutes in Hong Kong in order to pay off debts incurred by the fake marriages.[54]

Finally, an increasingly popular and dangerous method of gaining illegal entry is to use the services of migrant traffickers. As East Asian governments tighten their immigration rules, many would-be migrants are turning to professional human smugglers to get them through.[55] Many experts consider Thailand the human smuggling epicenter of East Asia, since it serves as both a source country and a transit country for smuggled immigrants headed to destinations in East Asia and around the world.[56] American officials estimate that at least 2,000 people in Thailand attempt to emigrate illegally to the United States every month by using fraudulently obtained or fake travel documents or with the assistance of human smugglers.[57] The majority of these 2,000 would-be immigrants are non-

Thai nationals, mostly Chinese, Indians, and Bangladeshis.[58] In Malaysia, strict immigration laws combined with enormous emigration demand in neighboring Indonesia have spawned a lucrative human smuggling trade in the Strait of Malacca.[59] Japan also has emerged as a favored target in East Asia for smuggling syndicates, especially those based in China.[60] In recent years, Chinese smuggling ships, similar to those that have approached the United States, have delivered thousands of Chinese illegally into Japan. Japan's Maritime Safety Agency has called for international action to counter the growing threat of human smuggling operations directed at the country.[61] Human smuggling, and its projected growth in the future, will likely remain East Asia's "immigration wildcard," defying the laws and sovereignty of both source and host countries.

The Politics of Labor Migration

East Asia's Immigration Backlash

As the scale of intraregional migration grows in East Asia, so do concerns about its social and cultural consequences. Many East Asian host countries do not view themselves as "immigration countries" and are beginning to express anxiety about the long-term cultural, social, and racial effects of immigration on their societies. One of the consequences of this anxiety is growing anti-immigrant sentiment throughout much of the region. In Japan, for example, antiforeign posters have been reported in areas frequented by foreign workers.[62] Similarly, Malaysians are expressing resentment toward immigrants from Indonesia and other countries and are accusing them of contributing to crime and "squatter problems."[63] Some Malaysian leaders have described illegal migrants as "troublemakers" and are urging Malaysian women not to marry them.[64] Some Hong Kong residents have complained about the "litter and inconvenience" resulting from Filipino workers' weekly Sunday gatherings in the territory's business district.[65]

Some host countries have gone a step further and characterize the influx of illegal immigrants as a threat to their national security. For example, Thai officials claim that the huge numbers of illegal immigrants from Burma constitute such a potential threat.[66] The Malaysian government also has described the hundreds of thousands of illegal immigrants as a matter of national security[67] and has even dispatched military troops to the border with Thailand to prevent further immigration.[68] Host governments are concerned that foreign workers may pose a security threat in one of two ways: involvement in crime and other threats to public order and, less commonly, engaging in activities that threaten the political structure of the host country.

Foreign workers' involvement with crime, or the perception that they are connected with crime, is often the most common complaint lodged against them. Malaysian authorities complain about the high number of violent crimes—such as robbery and sexual assault—in those communities with large numbers of foreign workers.[69] Between 1985 and 1991 immigrants in Malaysia were reportedly responsible for at least 15 percent of that country's murders and about 33 percent of its "gang robberies."[70] Police in Hong Kong also have linked crime to illegal immigration, and in 1994 they nominated illegal immigration as the territory's top law enforcement priority.[71] In 1996 police officials in Hong Kong announced that illegal immigrants from central China were a "major factor" behind the explosion in violent crime in the northern New Territories.[72] A common scenario in Hong Kong was for local crime syndicates to recruit illegal immigrants from China to carry out robberies and other crimes in Hong Kong. Once the crime was completed, the illegal immigrants were whisked back across the border with China, which was beyond the jurisdiction of the Hong Kong police prior to June 30, 1997.[73] Japanese police are similarly alarmed by the growing number of crimes committed by non-Japanese nationals. Of all the felonies committed by non-Japanese residents in 1993, about 53 percent were committed by illegal foreign workers.[74] Japanese police are particularly concerned with the increase in violent crimes committed by Chinese gangs in the Tokyo district of Shinjuku.[75] (Ironically, Japanese organized crime has reportedly infiltrated southern China.)[76]

In some instances the "security threat" posed by illegal immigrants is to the host country's government or political structure. Four decades of political and military hostilities have made Taiwan suspicious of its illegal immigrants from China—their economic contributions notwithstanding. For several years Taiwan has accused mainland China of sending spies to the island under the guise of illegal immigrants.[77] Prior to its 1994 elections, Taiwan intensified its crackdown against illegal immigrants from the mainland out of fear that they would engage in "subversive activities."[78] Two years later, and prior to the island's March 1996 presidential election, Taiwanese authorities rounded up 250 illegal Chinese immigrants who were believed to be spies or saboteurs. In one incident, police captured 24 mainlanders on the island's northeast coast who were carrying two pistols, 100 bullets, and 2 kilograms of amphetamine.[79] The Taiwanese government is so concerned about the national security implications of immigration from neighboring China that it has urged its fishing industry—long faced with severe labor shortages—to hire Southeast Asians instead of mainland Chinese.[80]

The Politics of Immigration in East Asia

Responding to the alleged threat posed by illegal immigrants, many host countries are enacting strict laws or other measures designed either to limit their numbers or to expel them altogether. Singapore, for instance, uses caning to deter illegal immigration. Employers can be caned if they are caught hiring illegal immigrants, and, under a proposed amendment to the country's Immigration Act introduced in 1995, prosecutors would no longer have to prove that the employer had knowledge of the employee's illegal status.[81] A year later Malaysia followed Singapore's lead by announcing that it too would cane anyone employing illegal immigrants or assisting their entry into the country.[82] Thai officials launched a similar campaign against illegal immigrants in 1993, which featured increased police raids and tighter border restrictions. Thailand's Interior Ministry warned local officials in 1994 that they would be charged with negligence if illegal immigrants were found in their jurisdiction.[83] In the Philippines, immigration authorities in 1994 ordered the arrest of 100,000 foreigners—primarily Chinese and Indian nationals—residing illegally in the country for more than three years,[84] prompting allegations of harassment and ethnic persecution from immigrant communities.[85] Cambodia also recently adopted a strict and controversial immigration law thought to be aimed at ethnic Vietnamese residing in the country.[86] South Korea, Taiwan, and Japan have implemented a number of less severe crackdowns against illegal immigrants in recent years.

Although many of these "get-tough" measures satisfy the demands of domestic constituencies in the host countries, they often entail a high diplomatic price. Stiff anti-immigrant crackdowns and laws often offend the source country whose nationals are arrested or deported. As a result, tensions over immigration issues are beginning to emerge between host and source countries throughout East Asia. Host countries may accuse source countries of not taking adequate measures to stop illegal emigration, while source countries resent the harsh treatment meted out to their nationals.

Recent immigration disputes between Malaysia and the Philippines may signal a trend for the rest of East Asia. In 1994 Malaysia decided to round up 1,200 Philippine maids near a Catholic church for possible immigration violations. The raids, conducted on Palm Sunday, angered the Philippine government, which later summoned the Malaysian chargé d'affaires in the Philippines to offer an explanation.[87] Malaysian officials refused to issue an apology, arguing that the incident was part of Malaysia's overall crackdown against illegal immigration and was not directed against any particular ethnic group.[88] In an apparent response to the Malaysian action, Philippine immigration officials raided the Subic Bay free port in search of illegal Malaysian workers.[89] In a separate incident several months later, Malaysian authorities arrested an additional 358 Filipina maids, prompting a diplomatic protest from the Philippines.[90] Possibly in response to the Malaysian action, a Philippine senator publicly announced several months later that Malaysia was a "high-risk and dangerous" destination for Filipino workers, where they were likely to "suffer from unfair labor practices and abuse."[91] The remark angered Malaysian officials, who summoned the Philippine ambassador in Kuala Lumpur to explain why their country was "inaccurately and unfairly" portrayed by the senator's remarks.[92]

Nearly one year later the Philippines became entangled in another immigration dispute, this time with Singapore. On March 17, 1995, Singaporean authorities hanged Flor Contemplacion, a Filipina maid convicted of double murder. Many Filipinos believed that Mrs. Contemplacion was not only innocent but a victim of her status as an unprotected Filipina working abroad. Her execution sparked a tide of public anger throughout the Philippines directed at both Singapore and the Philippine government. Thousands of Filipinos protested by participating in rallies and burning Singaporean flags.[93] One group of protesters even hurled a grenade at a Singapore Airlines office in the Philippines.[94] Philippine president Fidel Ramos responded to the execution by banning Filipinos from going to Singapore on employment contracts. He later recalled his ambassador to Singapore and threatened to break relations with Singapore entirely if a subsequent investigation found that Mrs. Contemplacion had been hanged unjustly.[95]

A separate and potentially more serious long-term immigration dispute is brewing between China and Russia over the issue of Chinese migration into Russia's far east. Russian authorities fear that between 300,000 and two million Chinese traders, workers, and farmers have migrated to its eastern regions.[96] Russian security specialists have warned that uncontrolled Chinese migration into the region could lead to the "peaceful loss" of the Russian far east.[97] Acting on these concerns, Russia imposed travel restrictions against Chinese, an act that promptly led China to detain Russian traders for violating Chinese immigration laws.[98] Prior to his April 1996 visit to China, Russian president Boris Yeltsin delivered a speech in the Russian far eastern city of Khabarovsk in which he assured local leaders and businessmen that he would pay "special attention" to the problem of illegal Chinese immigration into the region in meetings with his Chinese hosts.[99]

In some cases immigration disputes erupt because of controversial methods used by host countries to discourage unwelcome immigrants. Malaysia's decision to build a wall along its border with Thailand to keep out illegal immigrants and smugglers recently sparked a major row with the Thai government, which has compared the barrier to the Great Wall of China and the Berlin Wall.[100] Malaysian leaders have insisted that the wall is "friendly" and is intended to keep out illegal immigrants who enter Malaysia through Thailand, and not necessarily Thai immigrants.[101] Following Thai foreign minister Kasem Kasemsri's announcement that there was "no valid reason" for the wall and that the International Court of Justice in The Hague should be asked to rule on border wall plans, Malaysia retorted that Thai officials should air their complaints through diplomatic channels and refrain from raising Malaysia-Thai border issues in the media.[102]

Immigration disputes also have erupted between source and host countries over the issue of repatriation. After rounding up and capturing illegal immigrants, some host countries have discovered that the source country often refuses to repatriate its nationals. When Malaysia sought to repatriate 2,000 illegal immigrants from Burma in 1993, the Burmese embassy described the immigrants as traitors and refused to accept them.[103] Taiwan also has had difficulties repatriating illegal mainland immigrants back to China, and the issue has emerged as a major political dispute between the two governments.[104] Among other things, Taiwan accuses Beijing of purposefully stalling the repatriation of illegal Chinese immigrants caught on Taiwan.[105] Taiwan claims that when it takes the initiative to send mainlanders back to China, Beijing responds that it is "too busy" to deal with the issue.[106] In April 1996 delays by the People's Republic of China in repatriating its nationals from Taiwan prompted a hunger strike by 400 mainland Chinese being held in a Taiwan detention center.[107]

As the number of migrants increases in East Asia, immigration disputes may become even more politicized and contentious in the future. The fact that most migration issues are handled bilaterally between host and source countries probably contributes to the emotionalism and nationalism that have tended to surround recent migration disputes.[108] Like many regions of the world, East Asia lacks an institutional mechanism that can regularly manage or mediate such disputes. Although human rights groups—as well as major immigrant-sending countries such as the Philippines—have long urged that such an institution be established and that the rights of migrant workers be formally recognized, few countries in the region have been willing to embrace such ideals, perhaps because many feel that intraregional migration pressures will dissipate in the near or medium-term future. Even in such regional organizations as the Asia-Pacific Economic Cooperation forum (APEC) or the Association of Southeast Asian Nations (ASEAN), the issue of labor migration has been viewed as "contentious" and has been given—with rare exceptions—a low priority in formal discussions.[109] This situation may change as APEC and ASEAN seek to liberalize travel and immigration restrictions for professional and skilled workers.[110] If established to deal with the issues or problems surrounding these "high-end" migrants, these regional institutions may be able to help address disputes or disagreements associated with East Asia's burgeoning population of unskilled legal and illegal immigrants.

Future Projections of Intraregional Migration in Asia

Current economic and demographic trends throughout Asia suggest that intraregional migration pressures will increase in the future. Worsening labor shortages in major host countries, fueled largely by rapid economic growth and demographic factors, are not expected to be alleviated anytime soon. Japan anticipates a labor shortage of one million workers by the year 2000,[111] while Malaysian officials predict a labor shortage of at least two million by the year 2020.[112] Similar trends are being predicted for other major host countries in the region.

Simultaneously, Asia's traditional source countries are experiencing rapid growth in their labor forces. Bangladesh, an increasingly important source country for Southeast Asia, expects to see its labor force increase from 35 million to 46.5 million by the end of this decade.[113] Between 2000 and 2010, Indonesia's workforce will increase by roughly 16 million, while Vietnam's workforce will increase by about 10 million.[114]

The significance of these trends becomes clearer when viewed in the context of Asia's other major economic phenomenon—rising unemployment within major source countries. In Vietnam, where about 1.1 million young people reach working age each year, about 10 percent of urban dwellers are unemployed, compared to roughly 50 percent of all rural inhabitants.[115] One reason for rising unemployment in Vietnam has been the government's policy of closing unprofitable state enterprises. Since the late 1980s, more than 800,000 workers have lost their jobs as a result of such closures.[116] Indonesia anticipates that roughly 32 million of its citizens will be unemployed by the year 2000.[117] Unemployment pressures also are increasing in Bangladesh and Pakistan, countries that are likely to rely increasingly on East and Southeast Asia as their unemployment "safety valves."

Population pressures and unemployment in many of Asia's rural areas are driving hundreds of thousands of internal migrants into cities to look for jobs or higher wages. Indonesian leaders anticipate that 40 percent of their entire population will live in cities by the year 2000, a trend that may result in "more slums, joblessness and higher crime rates."[118]

Jakarta expects to see its population rise to 18 million by the year 2005. Urbanization in major source countries such as Indonesia and Vietnam could increase emigration pressures, especially if internal migrants are unable to find employment in the major cities.

China's Growing Role as a Major Source Country

With roughly 1.2 billion inhabitants, China is looming as a major source country in the growing trend of intraregional East Asian migration. Fifteen years of economic and political reforms in China have weakened the government's ability to control and regulate population movement both within and out of the country. One result of this demographic shift has been an increase in illegal Chinese emigration. According to some estimates, as many as 700,000 Chinese have emigrated illegally since 1990, and about 200,000 of those have settled in Asia.[119] Due to cultural and geographical reasons, Hong Kong, Taiwan, and Thailand have been most directly affected by recent Chinese emigration.[120]

Ironically, the growth in Chinese emigration is occurring just as the country registers record levels of economic growth—estimated at roughly 11 percent per year. Yet this rapid growth has not kept pace with the rising expectations of many Chinese. Common throughout China is the perception that no matter how wealthy the country is becoming, greater opportunity and prosperity exist elsewhere. Wage disparities between China and its wealthier neighbors only exacerbate this belief. Many Chinese calculate that they can earn far more in the sweatshops of Taiwan or factories in Thailand—with their paltry and illegal salaries—than they can under present conditions in their homeland.

While "pull factors" appear to be driving Chinese emigration now, "push factors" may play a more important role in the future. China currently has a labor force of roughly 707 million, and every year the government must find work for an estimated 14 million new entrants into the job market.[121] Consequently, China's unemployment crisis—both urban and rural—is expected to worsen dramatically in the years ahead. A recent Chinese labor ministry report warns that up to 153 million people could be unemployed by the year 2000.[122] Unemployment or underemployment in China's agricultural sector is already severe and is partly responsible for driving tens of millions of rural inhabitants into cities in search of jobs, a trend that shows no sign of abating.[123]

As unemployment and internal migration grow in China, the pressures for emigration are likely to increase. If internal migrants cannot find jobs in the cities, they may view emigration as an increasingly viable option. Moreover, due to the weakening of central government power and widespread governmental corruption (especially at the local and provincial levels), emigration restrictions are unlikely to be effective in stemming this exodus. Even if such restrictions are strengthened and enforced, they probably would simply play into the hands of human smugglers, whose services migrants would be forced to use in order to reach their destination country of choice.

East Asian Intraregional Migration and Consequences for the United States

Historically, the United States has played an important role as a host country for Asian migration. America's ethnic Asian population has grown from around 255,000 in 1940 to roughly eight million today.[124] Approximately three million Asians have immigrated into the United States over the past twenty years. The largest source countries have been the Philippines, South Korea, India, and China. Current census reports and other data reveal that Asian Americans are the fastest-growing immigrant group in the United States.[125] About 323,000 Asians are expected to enter the United States every year, and by the year 2050, Asians will comprise roughly 10 percent of the total U.S. population.[126]

Given the diversity that exists within Asia, it is difficult to generalize about the social and economic impact of Asian immigration into the United States, but certain patterns can be discerned. First, Asian Americans are often viewed as the "model minority" because of the perception that they are more prosperous and hard working than their host population. This stereotype was bolstered recently by a study sponsored mainly by the Leadership Education for Asian Pacifics which asserted that Asian immigrants have provided the United States with an "economic shot in the arm" because of their tendency toward entrepreneurship and hard work.[127] Among other things, the study found that of an estimated 2,000 high-technology companies in California's Silicon Valley, roughly 500 were headed by Asian Americans.[128] Nevertheless, some Asian Americans have rejected this hard working "model minority" label by pointing to the fact that they are represented on all rungs of the economic ladder.[129]

Another characteristic of Asian Americans is that they tend to settle in the western regions of the United States. The three cities with the largest number of Asian Americans are (in descending order) Los Angeles, Honolulu, and Oakland. In recent years, however, this pattern has begun to change as Asian Americans move to other parts of the country. The number of Asian Americans in such cities as Dallas and Atlanta, for example, more than quadrupled during the 1980s.[130] Immigrants from East Asia also tend to be perceived as more willing or able to adopt the language and culture of the United States when compared to some other immigrant groups.[131] Nevertheless, anti-Asian sentiment and racial prejudice do exist in the United States and may grow as the numbers of Asian immigrants increase. The real test of American acceptance of Asian immigration may be yet to come, as immigrants move into parts of the country unaccustomed to the presence of large numbers of Asian Americans.

A more sinister dimension of East Asian immigration into the United States has emerged recently in the form of criminal syndicates that smuggle tens of thousands of Asian immigrants into the country every year. In July 1993 the human smuggling ship *Golden Venture* carrying nearly 300 Chinese émigrés ran aground near New York City. Nine of the Chinese passengers drowned as they tried to swim ashore. Although the trafficking of Chinese immigrants into the United States had been going on for years, the *Golden Venture* incident brought the reality of Chinese migrant smuggling into the living rooms of the American public. As one immigration attorney involved with the *Golden* Venture case reportedly stated: "Nobody in Washington paid attention until one of these ships practically landed in midtown Manhattan."[132] Almost immediately President Clinton declared human smuggling a national security concern and authorized the National Security Council to direct the U.S. response.[133]

Responding to the American crackdown, smugglers changed their routes and tactics by, among other things, shifting their human trafficking operations into such transit corridors as the Dominican Republic, the U.S. Virgin Islands, and various Central American countries.[134] According to the U.S. government, up to 50,000 Chinese may be smuggled into the country every year.[135] Upon arriving, many of the immigrants are kidnapped or assaulted and forced to work in low-wage "indentured" jobs in order to pay their transport fees.

Another dimension of Asian migrant trafficking into the United States emerged in August 1995 when federal authorities raided a garment "sweatshop" near El Monte, California, in which seventy-two illegal immigrants were found laboring in slave-like conditions. Agents arrested eight Thai nationals who were accused of beating their "employees" and threatening their families in Thailand.[136] According to federal and state officials, an organized crime gang was responsible for smuggling the workers into the United States and confiscating their passports and a portion of their earnings in order to pay the smuggling fees.[137]

Many legal experts and labor activists have argued that the sweatshops uncovered by the California raids are the tip of the iceberg and that sweatshops "flourish throughout the garment industry's underground economy."[138] A General Accounting Office report published in 1994 (prior to the El Monte raid) found that "the sweatshop problem in the garment industry has not improved over the last 5 years primarily because of legislative, resource, and economic factors."[139] Sweatshops, according to the report, regularly subject their workers to safety hazards such as exposed electrical wiring, blocked aisles, unsanitary bathrooms, poor lighting, poor temperature control, and poor ventilation.[140] Among other things, the report concluded that "in general, the description of today's sweatshops differs little from that at the turn of the century."[141]

Policy Recommendations

The United States is likely to continue to play a major role as a host country for immigration from East Asia. Certain events—the recent return of Hong Kong to China, for example—may accelerate this trend. A war on the Korean peninsula or a "political meltdown" in China could generate millions of refugees, many of whom probably would head for the United States. When China threatened Taiwan with missiles in the spring of 1996, for example, more than 30,000 Taiwanese flocked to immigration fairs held in the island's two largest cities.[142] Recent evidence suggests that instability in East Asia—or the perception of instability—likely will lead to increased migration from the region to the United States.

At the same time, however, it is clear that anti-immigrant sentiment is rising in the United States. The passage of California's Proposition 187 in 1994 helped catapult immigration—both legal and illegal—to the top of the nation's political agenda. In 1996 Congress passed some of the most restrictive immigration legislation in years. Moreover, immigration issues played a much more visible role in the 1996 presidential election than they had in the recent past. The following policy recommendations are made with these two opposing trends in mind.

1. The United States must maintain and strengthen its crackdown against migrant trafficking from East Asia. Migrant trafficking contributes to the growth of organized crime in the United States, fuels anti-immigrant sentiment, and results in severe human rights abuses for the migrants themselves. Because it continues to be a major problem in the United States, migrant trafficking should be viewed—as it was characterized by President Clinton in 1993—as a "national security" concern that warrants the use of intelligence and military assets wherever appropriate. In addition, the United States should increase its intelligence gathering with regard to the organized syndicates that engage in human smuggling, cooperate with source countries, and apply diplomatic pressure to transit countries in order to enlist their assistance in stopping the human smuggling trade.

2. The United States should strengthen its domestic crackdown against "sweatshops" such as the one discovered in 1995 in El Monte, California. The presence of this type of industry undermines the credibility of the

United States as it seeks to improve human rights around the world. As one *Los Angeles Times* columnist wrote, "President Clinton goes on about prison labor in China but has yet to say a word about slave labor in El Monte."[143] The apparent toleration of slavery (or slave-like working conditions) in the United States hurts not only the immigrant workers but also the plight of American workers who are forced to contend with declining wages and working conditions.[144] Moreover, because of the link—in many cases—to organized crime, sweatshops help fuel the growth of migrant trafficking into the United States.

3. The United States should clarify its apparently contradictory policy regarding Chinese emigration. On one hand, the United States, in accordance with the Jackson-Vanik amendment to the Trade Act of 1974, requires that nonmarket economies allow open and free emigration in order to receive most-favored-nation (MFN) trading status. The Jackson-Vanik amendment originally was intended to pressure the Soviet Union to allow Jewish emigration, but after the 1989 Chinese crackdown at Tiananmen Square, Congress began to use it to influence relations with China.[145] At the same time, however, the United States has urged Beijing to restrict illegal Chinese emigration to the United States and other countries. This contradictory policy has not gone unnoticed in Beijing. Qian Qichen, China's foreign minister, has stated that the only obstacle to Chinese emigration is the refusal of the U.S. government to relax its immigration restrictions against Chinese.[146] For this reason, the Chinese government demanded in 1995 that the United States repeal the Jackson-Vanik amendment.[147] The United States should consider "delinking" immigration issues from U.S.-China trade issues in order to prevent Beijing from developing an "immigration card" that would allow it to pressure the United States or its East Asian allies with the threat of mass migration.[148]

4. The United States should consider its policy objectives in Asia in light of their potential to either increase or decrease migration or refugee flows within and out of the region. Prior to President Clinton's decision to renew China's MFN trading status last summer, Singapore's senior minister Lee Kuan Yew stated that "continued U.S. pressure on human rights could contribute to a breakdown in order that would drive millions of Chinese to seek refuge overseas."[149] While Mr. Lee's assessment may be slightly exaggerated, it raises an important point. Foreign policy choices made in the economic, trade, or military realms can have profound migration consequences. If the United States had indeed denied China MFN status, it could have led to increased unemployment in China, greater rural-to-urban migration and, ultimately, more pressure for emigration. Current disputes

with China over issues such as intellectual property protection, market access, and human rights should be analyzed in the context of possible migration consequences.

Notes

1. Myron Weiner, "Security, Stability, and International Migration," *International Security* 17, no. 3 (Winter 1992/93), pp. 91–126.

2. I am borrowing the "restrictionist" versus "admissionist" terms from the introduction of an essay by Philip Martin and Elizabeth Midgley, *Immigration to the United States: Journey to an Uncertain Destination* (Population Reference Bureau, Sept. 1994), which is available from the Internet at http://migration.ucdavis.edu/.

3. Lynn Pan, *Sons of the Yellow Emperor: A History of the Chinese Diaspora* (New York: Kodansha, 1994).

4. Astri Suhrke, "The 'High Politics' of Population Movements: Migration, State and Civil Society in Southeast Asia," in Myron Weiner (ed.), *International Migration and Security* (Boulder, CO: Westview Press, 1993), pp. 179–200.

5. "The Rise of Asia and Structural Change in the World Economy," *London Business School Economic Outlook* (Aug. 1996), p. 4. Of course, there are some who are less enthusiastic about East Asia's future. In particular, see Paul Kennedy, "The Myth of a Rising Asia," *New Perspectives Quarterly* 13, no. 3 (June 22, 1996), p. 46.

6. The number of "absolute poor" in Asia is believed to be around 800 million. See Michael Richardson, "Q&A: A UN Aide on the Outlook for Asia's Poor," *International Herald Tribune* (Sept. 13, 1993).

7. "South-East Asia's Wealth Gap," *The Economist* (Apr. 13, 1996), p. 29.

8. Surya B. Prasai, "Asia's Labor Pains," *Far Eastern Economic Review* (Apr. 29, 1993), p. 23. Philip Martin estimates the number to be between three and four million. See Philip Martin, "Migrants on the Move in Asia," *Asia Pacific Issues*, no. 29 (Honolulu: East-West Center, Dec. 1996).

9. A good theoretical discussion of demand-pull migration and supply-push migration is provided by Klaus F. Zimmerman, "European Migration: Push and Pull," *World Bank Research Observer* (Annual Conference Supplement, 1994), pp. 313–342. See also Philip Martin and Jonas Widgren, "International Migration: A Global Challenge," *Population Bulletin* 51, no. 1 (Washington, DC: Population Reference Bureau, Inc., Apr. 1996).

10. Raisul Awal Mahmood, "Adaptation to a New World: Experience of Bangladeshis in Japan," *International Migration* 32, no. 4 (1994), p. 513.

11. Tan Tarn How, "Guangdong Attracting Illegal Aliens," *Straits Times* (Singapore, June 24, 1995), p. 16.

12. "Number of Overseas Koreans Regaining South Korean Citizenship Rises," *South Korean News Agency* (Jan. 3, 1995), reported in *BBC Summary of World Broadcasts* (Jan. 5, 1995), FE/2193/D.

13. Linda Feldmann, "Reverse Brain Drain, U.S. to Asia," *Christian Science Monitor* (June 2, 1994), 2; Alice Hung, "China Tensions Driving Taiwanese Overseas," *Reuters* (Mar. 17, 1996), p. 39.

14. Kimberly A. Hamilton and Kate Holder, "International Migration and Foreign Policy," *Washington Quarterly* 14, no. 2 (Spring 1991), p. 192.

15. Pan Xiaozhu, "Roundup: Manpower Export-Mainstay of Bangladesh's Economy," *Xinhua News Agency* (Dec. 5, 1994); Dafizeck Daud, "Malaysia: Inflow of Bangladeshis into Malaysia Surges," *Business Times* (Malaysia), June 17, 1994).

16. "Manila Won't Condone Abuse of Workers Abroad, Says Ramos," *Straits Times* (Singapore, Nov. 11, 1994), p. 19. See also Bernardo M. Villegas, "Implications of AFTA on Philippine Labor Export," *Asian and Pacific Migration Journal* 2, no. 3 (1993).

17. "Vu Oanh Says Unemployment 'Beyond the Limit for Public Security,'" *'Nhan Dan'* (Hanoi, May 9, 1994) reported in *BBC Summary of World Broadcasts* (May 23, 1994), FE/2004/B.

18. Karl Schoenberger, "Living Off Expatriate Labor," *Los Angeles Times* (Aug. 1, 1994), p. 1A.

19. Pan Xiaozhu, "Roundup."

20. "Jakarta's Jobless Rate Rises to 7.2%," *Straits Times* (Singapore, Mar. 13, 1994), p. 13.

21. Charles W. Stahl and Reginald T. Appleyard, "International Manpower Flows in Asia: An Overview," *Asian and Pacific Migration Journal* 1, no. 3–4, (1992), citing Stahl and Habib (1989).

22. Louise do Rosario and Gordon Fairclough, "Toilers of the East," *Far Eastern Economic Review* (Apr. 2, 1992), p. 20.

23. Lin Lean Lim, "International Labor Migration in Asia: Patterns, Implications, Policy," in Miroslav Macura and David Coleman (eds.), *International Migration: Regional Processes and Responses* (Geneva: United Nations, 1994), chapter 5.

24. Rosario and Fairclough, "Toilers of the East."

25. In many newly industrialized economies, the educational systems have geared students toward white-collar employment opportunities, thus generating a dearth of blue-collar workers. See Osman Tseng, "Taiwan: Rising Unemployment Among Higher Educated," *Business Taiwan* (Aug. 22, 1994).

26. "Malaysia: Demographic and Social Trends," *EIU Country Forecasts* (Economist Intelligence Unit) (July 21, 1995).

27. Kiriro Morita and Saskia Sassen, "The New Illegal Immigration into Japan, 1980–1992," *International Migration Review* 28, no. 1 (1994).

28. "Dissatisfied Farming Trainees Leave Japan Prematurely," *Japan Economic Newswire* (Dec. 27, 1993).

29. "Number of Illegal Workers Rising in S. Korea," *Reuter Asia-Pacific Business Report* (July 7, 1996).

30. Chris Yeung and Louis Won, "Hong Kong: Worker Import Scheme Draws Union Backlash," *South China Morning Post* (Nov. 23, 1994).

31. "Taiwan: Labor Council Sets New Policy to Reduce Foreign Work Force," *China Economic News Service* (Feb. 15, 1996).

32. "Thailand: Labour Vows Action Over Illegal Aliens Employment—Huge Rally Planned at Government House," *Bangkok Post* (July 12, 1996).

33. "Thailand Labor: Fast-Paced Growth Lures Illegal Migrant Workers," *EIU ViewsWire* (Economist Intelligence Unit) July 31, 1996.

34. Osman Tseng, "Taiwan: ROC Policy for Hiring Foreign Laborers Needs to be Reviewed," *Business Taiwan* (Sept. 26, 1994).

35. "Malaysia Discouraging Labor-Intensive Investment," *Reuters World Service* (Feb. 19, 1995).

36. "Steady Growth Strains Labor Pool in Malaysia," *EIU Business Asia* (Economist Intelligence Unit) (Apr. 20, 1992).

37. "Taiwan to Use Convicts to Ease Labor Shortage," *Reuter Library Report* (Oct. 20, 1993).

38. Temsak Traisophon, "Thailand: Foreign Workers 'May Have Serious Diseases,'" *Bangkok Post* (Aug. 24, 1996).

39. Johanna Son, "Asia-Labor: More Migrant Workers, Not Enough Rights," *Inter Press Service* (Apr. 25, 1995).

40. Leah Makabenta, "Asia Pacific-Labor: In Denial over Growing Migrant Labor," *Inter Press Service* (Dec. 8, 1994).

41. "South Korea: Kew Editorial-Migrant Foreign Workers," *Korea Economic Daily* (May 3, 1994); "Gov't Considering Suspending Visa Waiver Accords to Curb Illegal Foreign Workers," *Korea Times* (Nov. 25, 1995), p. 1.

42. P. Ramasamy, "Foreign Labour: Asset or Liability?" *Straits Times* (Singapore), (Nov. 27, 1995), p. 24.

43. "22 Malaysians Refused Entry into Japan During Transit," *Japan Economic Newswire* (Nov. 23, 1994). See also "Manila Demands Tokyo Explanation of Detained Filipinos," *Japan Economic Newswire* (Nov. 3, 1994).

44. "Foreigners Overstay in Japan After Int'l Confab," *Japan Economic Newswire* (Oct. 27, 1992).

45. "Myanmar 'Soccer Fans' Denied Entry at Airport," *Mainichi Daily News* (Oct. 10, 1994), p. 12.

46. "Firms Face Labor Squeeze," *South China Morning Post* (Nov. 18, 1993), p. 11.

47. Kim Gooi, "Bangkok Is Asia's Hub for the Illegal Travel Business," *Deutsche Presse-Agentur* (Sept. 23, 1996).

48. Robert Horn, "Thailand a Key Crossroads in International People Smuggling," *Associated Press* (Jan. 8, 1996).

49. "Syndicates Dealing in Fake Documents Smashed," *Straits Times* (Singapore) (Mar. 9, 1995), p. 17.

50. "Police Bust Major Philippine Counterfeit ID Syndicate," *Japan Economic Newswire* (Oct. 24, 1994).

51. "Countermeasures Against Illicit Trafficking in Migrants in Japan," background paper of the government of Japan submitted to the eleventh International Organization for Migration seminar on migration, Oct. 26–28, 1994, Geneva.

52. "Japanese Men Losing Foreign Brides," *Asahi News Service* (June 6, 1994); Peter Kenny, "Japan Police Probe Marriage Racket," *United Press International* (June 16, 1994).

53. Scott McKenzie, "New Move to Combat Marriage Racketeers," *South China Morning Post* (Apr. 2, 1994), p. 4.

54. Ibid.

55. "Trafficking in Migrants: Characteristics and Trends in Different Regions of the World," discussion paper submitted by the International Organization for Migration to the eleventh IOM Seminar on Migration.

56. "Thailand Haven for Illegal Workers, Gangsters," *Straits Times* (Singapore, Mar. 17, 1994), p. 13.

57. John-Thor Dahlburg, "Smuggling People to U.S. Is Big Business in Thailand," *Los Angeles Times* (Sept. 5 1995), p. A1.

58. Ibid.

59. *Trafficking in Migrants Quarterly Bulletin* (International Organization for Migration), no. 5 (Dec. 1994); "KL, Jakarta Plan More Sea and Air Patrols Against Illegal Immigrants," *Straits Times* (Singapore, July 27, 1994), p. 14; "Malaysia Finds 24 Bodies from Capsized Boat," *United Press International* (Nov. 15, 1994).

60. "China: Stowaway Traffic to Japan Increases," *South China Morning Post,* May 9, 1994.

61. "Japan Warns of Upsurge of Illegal Immigrants," *Reuters World Service* (Oct. 28, 1994).

62. Kunda Dixit, "Japan: Land of the Rising Swastika," *Inter Press Service* (Apr. 29, 1993).

63. Surya B. Prasai, "Intra-Asian Labor Migration," *Asian Survey* 33, no. 11 (Nov. 1993).

64. "Local Women Urged Not to Marry Illegal Immigrants," *Straits Times* (Singapore; Apr. 7, 1994), p. 15.

65. "Never Sunday," *South China Morning Post* (Aug. 28, 1994), p. 14.

66. "Thailand to Get Tough on Myanmar Illegal Aliens," *Straits Times* (Singapore; Feb. 26, 1994), p. 19. The deputy secretary-general of Thailand's National Security Council has expressed his concern that illegal Burmese immigrants will become a significant minority group in ten or fifteen years if their current influx is not halted. See "Thailand: Rising Burmese Influx Causes Alarm," *Bangkok Post* (Jan. 9, 1994).

67. "Caning, Stiffer Fines to Stop Influx of Illegal Immigrants," *Straits Times* (Singapore; Mar. 18, 1994), p. 23.

68. "Troops to Remain at 'Sensitive' Points Along Thai Border," *Radio Malaysia* (Nov. 7, 1994) reported in *BBC Summary of World Broadcasts* (Nov. 11, 1994), FE/2150/B.

69. "Up to One Million Illegal Aliens May Be Working, Hiding in Malaysia," *Straits Times* (Singapore; Aug. 15, 1994), p. 21. Immigrants reportedly have taken over certain parts of Kuala Lumpur; see Lokman Mansor, "Malaysia: Consistent Efforts Needed to Curb Influx of Foreign Workers," *Business Times* (Malaysia, Feb. 23, 1995; Kampung Gajah, "Immigrants at Illegal Settlements Involved in Crime," *New Straits Times* (Malaysia; Mar. 22, 1996).

70. Muharyani Othman, "Labour Pains of Migrant Workers," *New Straits Times* (Malaysia; Apr. 5, 1996).

71. Darren Goodsir, "Hong Kong: Police Link Illegal Immigration to Crime," *South China Morning Post* (May 9, 1994).

72. John Flint, "Immigrant Influx Blamed for Crime Explosion," *South China Morning Post* (Mar. 26, 1996).

73. Peter Lim, "Rising Crime Rate Swells Ranks of Private Security Guards," *Agence France Presse* (Sept. 25, 1995).

74. Mitsuo Arai, "Illegal Foreigners—A Problem That Won't Go Away," *Daily Yomiuri* (Feb. 28, 1995), p. 9.

75. "Chinese Lead Increase in Foreign Crimes in Japan," *Reuter Library Report* (Sept. 2, 1994).

76. "Japan's Organized Crime Infiltrating South China," *Japan Economic Newswire* (Aug. 12, 1994).

77. "Chinese Communists Infiltration into Taiwan," *Central News Agency* (Mar. 20, 1993).

78. "Taiwan to Enforce Illegal Chinese Crackdown," *Reuters World Service* (Oct. 3, 1994).

79. "Taiwan Has Nabbed 250 Chinese Illegal Immigrants," *Deutsche Presse-Agentur* (Feb. 6, 1996); Vyacheslav Tomilin, "Illegal Immigrants Arrested on Taiwan," *ITAR-TASS* (Feb. 8, 1996).

80. "Boats Discouraged from Hiring Mainland Chinese 'For Reasons of National Security,'" *Central News Agency* (Nov. 7, 1994), reported in *BBC Summary of World Broadcasts* (Nov. 9, 1994).

81. "Singapore Labour: Government Clamps Down on Illegal Foreign Workers," *EIU ViewsWire* (Economist Intelligence Unit) (Dec. 6, 1995).

82. Michael Richardson, "Malaysia: Caning for Illegals' Bosses," *International Herald Tribune* (Oct. 21, 1996).

83. "Thailand: Officials to Face Wrath Over Illegal Immigrants," *Bangkok Post* (Oct. 9, 1994).

84. "Manila Out to Nab Illegal Immigrants," *Straits Times* (Singapore; Mar. 14, 1994), p. 17.

85. "Philippines: Indians Cite Bias in Immigration Crackdown," *Inter Press Service* (Mar. 15, 1994).

86. Leah Makabenta, "Cambodia: Only for Khmers?" *Inter Press Service* (Aug. 25, 1994).

87. "Malaysia Denies Discrimination in Roundup of Filipinos," *Japan Economic Newswire* (Apr. 5, 1994).

88. Lokman Mansor, "Malaysia: No Reason to Apologize for Rounding Up Immigrants—PM," *Business Times* (Malaysia; Apr. 7, 1994).

89. Alec Almazan, "Officials Raid Subic Bay for Illegal M'sian Workers," *Business Times* (Apr. 25, 1994), p. 3.

90. "Philippines Protests at Maids' Arrest in Malaysia," *Reuters World Service* (Nov. 2, 1994).

91. "Malaysia Protests Philippine Senator's Remarks," *Reuter Library Report* (Jan. 16, 1995).

92. Ibid.

93. "Mindanao Offficials Rally for Boycott of Singapore Products," *GMA-7 Television* (Quezon City; Mar. 20, 1995), reported in *BBC Summary of World Broadcasts* (Mar. 22, 1995), FE/2258/B; Rene Pastor, "Filipinos Burn Singapore Flag as Protests Mount," *Reuters World Service* (Mar. 25, 1995).

94. "Bomb Blasts at Singapore Airlines, Foreign Ministry," *GMA-7 Television* (Quezon City; Mar. 26, 1995), reported in *BBC Summary of World Broadcasts* (Mar. 28, 1995), FE/2263/B.

95. Martin Abbugao, "Manila Recalls Ambassador, Threatens to Cut Singapore Ties," *Agence France Presse* (Mar. 22, 1995); Robert H. Reid, "Ramos Threatens to Cut Ties with Singapore," *Associated Press* (Mar. 22, 1995).

96. Zhores Medvedev, "Keeping Russia's Far East," *Moscow Times* (Jan. 6, 1995).

97. "Migration Could See 'Peaceful Loss' of Far East and Kaliningrad Region," *'Novaya Yezhednevnaya Gazeta'* (July 27, 1994), reported in *BBC Summary of World Broadcasts* (July 30, 1994), SU/2061/B.

98. Sheila Tefft, "Chinese Leader's Visit to Russia Will Boost Military, Economic Ties," *Christian Science Monitor* (Sept. 2, 1994), p. 3.

99. "Yeltsin to Raise Issue of Illegal Chinese Immigration into Russia," *RIA News Agency* (Moscow; Apr. 24, 1996), reported in *BBC Summary of World Broadcasts* (Apr. 24, 1996), EE/D2595/B; Carol J. Williams and Rone Tempest, "Yeltsin Talks Tough Before Arrival in China," *Los Angeles Times* (Apr. 25, 1996).

100. "Malaysia Tells Thailand Border Wall is Friendly," *Reuters World Service* (Apr. 12, 1996); "Work on 27km Border Wall Progressing Well," *New Straits Times* (Malaysia; Mar. 7, 1996).

101. "Thailand: Border Wall Is on Malay Land, Insists Mahathir," *Bangkok Post* (Mar. 3, 1996).

102. "Thais Told: Leave Border Issues Out of Media," *New Straits Times* (Malaysia; Feb. 28, 1996), 8; "Malaysia 'Willing to Resolve' Border Wall Issue with Thailand," *Voice of Malaysia External Service* (Kuala Lumpur; Feb. 21, 1996), reported in *BBC Summary of World Broadcasts* (Feb. 22, 1996), EE/D2542/B; K.P. Waran, "Border Wall Issue to Be Resolved via Diplomatic Channels," *New Straits Times* (Malaysia; Feb. 22, 1996), p. 1.

103. Leah Makabenta, "Malaysia: Feeling the Strain of Migrant Worker Influx," *Inter Press Service* (Nov. 25, 1993).

104. "China Accused of Stalling Immigrant Repatriation," *Voice of Free China External Service* (Jan. 27, 1994), reported in *BBC Summary of World Broadcasts* (Feb. 2, 1994), FE/1911/4; Julian Baum, "Cross-Strait Purposes," *Far Eastern Economic Review* (Apr. 14, 1994); "'Failure' of Cross-Straits Talks Analyzed," *Zhongguo Tongxun She* (Nov. 27, 1994), reported in *BBC Summary of World Broadcasts* (Dec. 1, 1994), FE/2167/G.

105. "Illegal China Immigrants on Taiwan Hunger Strike," *Reuters World Service* (Apr. 12, 1996), (U4-F).

106. "Taiwan: MAC Urges Beijing to Take Back Illegal Immigrants Held Here," *China Economic News Service* (Apr. 13, 1996).

107. Ibid.

108. Johanna Son, "Asia-Labor: Filipino Maid's Hanging Sends Wake-Up Call to Region," *Inter Press Service* (Mar. 27, 1995).

109. "APEC Economic Committee Meets in Manila," *United Press International* (Feb. 10, 1996).

110. Johanna Son, "Asia-Pacific: Freer Labor Market, but Only for Some," *Inter Press Service* (Jan. 12, 1996).

111. Reginald Dale, "Now the Foreign Tide Laps at Japan," *International Herald Tribune* (Oct. 25, 1994).

112. Kalimullah Hassan, "Malaysia Faces Acute Labor Shortage by the Year 2020," *Straits Times* (Singapore; Aug. 18, 1994), p. 3.

113. Charles W. Stahl and Reginald T. Appleyard, "International Manpower Flows in Asia: An Overview," *Asian and Pacific Migration Journal* 1, no. 3–4, (1992).

114. Jerrold W. Huguet, "The Future of International Migration Within Asia," *Asian and Pacific Migration Journal* 1, no. 2 (1992).

115. "Vu Oanh Says Unemployment 'Beyond Limit for Public Security,'" *'Nhan Dan'* (Hanoi, May 9, 1994), reported in *BBC Summary of World Broadcasts* (May 23, 1994), FE/2004/B.

116. Satyanarayan Sivaraman, "Labor-Vietnam: In a Dilemma Over Rising Worker Militancy," *Inter Press Service* (Nov. 22, 1994).

117. Paul Jacob, "A Time Bomb?" *Straits Times* (Singapore; Jan. 2, 1994), p. 14.

118. "Soeharto on Issue of Urbanization," *Xinhua News Agency* (July 15, 1994).

119. "Global Chinese Migrants Top 700,000," *Reuters World Service* (Mar. 16, 1994).

120. Roughly 30,000 Chinese illegally cross the border into Hong Kong every year. See Marcus Eliason, "Chinese Illegals: Richer Asian Countries Also Have Problems," *Associated Press* (June 11, 1993). In Taiwan, authorities estimate that about 30,000 illegal mainland immigrants have sneaked onto the island since the lifting of martial law in 1987. See "Taiwan to Enforce Illegal Chinese Crackdown," *Reuters World Service*, October 3, 1994. An estimated 100,000 Chinese illegally reside in Thailand; see "Thailand Haven for Illegal Workers, Gangsters," p. 13.

121. "China-Basic Data," *EIU China Hand* (Economist Intelligence Unit), (May 1, 1996).

122. "China Labor: Unemployment Rises; Workers Leave State Enterprises," *EIU ViewsWire* (Economist Intelligence Unit) (Aug. 29, 1996).

123. "China Labor: State to Address Massive Migrant Worker Problem," *EIU ViewsWire* (Economist Intelligence Unit), (June 26, 1996).

124. John Miller, "Impact of Asians Growing in US Politics," *Straits Times* (Singapore; Mar. 12, 1995), p. 9.

125. Carey Goldberg, "Asian Immigrants Help Bolster U.S. Economy, New Report Says," *New York Times* (Mar. 31, 1996), p. A32.

126. "Demographic Futures: Immigration Impacting Projected Population," *Minority Markets Alert* (Mar. 1993).

127. Goldberg, "Asian Immigrants Held Bolster U.S. Economy.

128. Ibid.

129. Ann Scott Tyson, "Asian Americans Spurn Image as Model Minority," *Christian Science Monitor* (Aug. 26, 1994) p. 6.

130. William P. O'Hare et al., "Asians in the Suburbs," *American Demographics* (May 1994), p. 32.

131. Robert W. Gardner, "Asian Immigration: The View from the United States," *Asian and Pacific Migration Journal* 1, no. 1 (1992).

132. Marlowe Hood, "Clinton Acts on Ships of Shame," *South China Morning Post* (June 13, 1993), p. 1.

133. Ibid.

134. Ashley Dunn, "After Crackdown, Smugglers of Chinese Find New Routes," *New York Times* (Nov. 1, 1994), p. A1.

135. *Presidential Initiative to Deter Alien Smuggling: Report of the Interagency Working Group* (Washington D.C., 1995).

136. "The Profits of Sin: Immigration," *Economist* (Aug. 12, 1995).

137. James Sterngold, "Agency Missteps Put Illegal Aliens at Mercy of Sweat-shops," *New York Times* (Sept. 21, 1995), p. A16.

138. Lora Jo Fo, Laura L. Ho and Leti Volpp, "Manufacturers and Retailers Must be Liable," *Los Angeles Times* (Aug. 24, 1995), p. 9.

139. "Garment Industry—Efforts to Address the Prevalence and Conditions of Sweatshops," *GAO Reports,* GAO/HEHS-95-29, (Nov. 10, 1994).

140. Ibid.

141. Ibid.

142. Alice Hung, "China Tensions Driving Taiwanese Overseas," *Reuters* (Mar. 17, 1996).

143. Robert Scheer, "Where's Clinton on Slave Labor Here at Home," *Los Angeles Times* (Aug. 11, 1995).

144. Roy Beck, "The Wages of Immigration; Liberals Won't Face the Real Cost of Foreign Workers," *Washington Post* (Apr. 21, 1996), p. C1.

145. Gerrit W. Gong, *Developing a Consensus for the Future: A Report of the CSIS U.S. China Policy Task Force* (Washington, DC; Center for Strategic and International Studies, 1996), p. 21.

146. "Qian Qichen on China-U.S. Relations," *Central People's Broadcasting Station* (Beijing; Nov. 9, 1993), reported in *BBC Summary of World Broadcasts* (Nov. 12, 1993), FE/1844/G.

147. "China Demands U.S. Repeal of Emigration Law," *Agence France Presse* (Apr. 27, 1995).

148. Su Xiaokang, "Playing Politics with Population in China," *Los Angeles Times* (Dec. 11, 1995).

149. Michael Richardson, "Singapore Fears a Chinese Upheaval," *International Herald Tribune* (May 27, 1994).

Chapter 5

Forced Displacement in Asia: New Challenges and New Strategies

SADAKO OGATA AND JOHAN CELS

The end of the Cold War created not only new opportunities to bring to a close long-standing refugee crises but also new uncertainties and conflicts. Intrastate conflicts have replaced interstate wars as the major cause of large-scale forced population movements. Since 1991 the international community has had to respond to four refugee emergencies involving the displacement of more than one million persons—namely, northern Iraq, Somalia, Rwanda, and the former Yugoslavia.

As a consequence of these intrastate conflicts, the number of persons falling within the responsibility of the United Nations High Commissioner for Refugees (UNHCR) continued to rise, from 17 million in 1991, to 23 million in 1993, and to more than 27 million at the beginning of 1995. As of January 1996, however, a small but significant decrease had taken place—to 26.1 million persons—due to the absence of new refugee emergencies and the progress toward solutions made in 1995. Still, the magnitude of this transnational problem and the need to identify solutions early on has forced the refugee issue high on the international agenda.

Although it has fewer refugees than Africa or Europe, Asia's refugee problem is large in scale. As of January 1, 1996, some 1.5 million persons are of concern to UNHCR in South and Southeast Asia.[1] This population is comprised of 887,800 refugees, 357,500 returnees, 249,700 internally displaced persons, and nearly 47,000 asylum seekers.[2] Of the refugees, the largest caseloads in 1995 were in China (288,300), India (274,100), Nepal (126,100), and Thailand (101,550). Among the assisted returnees, the largest caseloads are in Myanmar (196,300), Sri Lanka (54,000), and Vietnam (18,200). In comparison with Africa (9 million) and Europe (7.7 million), the number of persons in Asia of concern to UNHCR has declined in recent years.

No country in the region has been immune to the problem of forced population movements, and policy responses have varied considerably between South and Southeast Asia. Although the solutions of the Indochinese and Cambodian refugee problems are acknowledged as major successes of the international community and the UNHCR, the conflict in northern Sri Lanka, the outflows from Bhutan and Tibet, and the presence of Myanmar refugees in Bangladesh and Thailand are all examples of the ongoing nature of refugee problems in Asia. As elsewhere, Asia's refugee problems are closely linked to political, security, and humanitarian issues. Economic growth has contributed to the relative peace and stability in the region, but new issues such as human rights, internally displaced persons, transition from authoritarian to democratic regimes, and migration are gaining prominence. Each of these issues has the potential to contribute toward forced human displacement.

The growing interdependence among states has led to increasing pressure to respond to forced human displacement on a regional and multilateral basis. It is unlikely, however, that the international community will respond as generously as it did in Cambodia and Vietnam. Since many of the intrastate conflicts do not affect the immediate strategic interests of the major international and regional powers, less external intervention may be a direct consequence.

On the one hand, this may have the beneficial effect that intrastate conflicts will no longer have the added dimension of a proxy confrontation between major powers or neighbors. On the other hand, the declining role of outside actors may reduce their stabilizing influence, which may well give free hand to a proliferation of "teacup" or "orphan" conflicts.[3] An effective post–Cold War strategy addressing forced human displacement in Asia and elsewhere must be based on a new policy paradigm— a comprehensive strategy emphasizing protection, solutions, and prevention.

This chapter reviews the refugee problem in Asia to illustrate how past legacies have led to different approaches within the region and how they continue to shape current developments, and then draws attention to emerging issues that may lead to large-scale forced displacements in the future. On the basis of this analysis, the final part of this chapter outlines a new policy paradigm to deal with the transnational issue of forced population displacement. Before discussing the refugee problem in Asia, the next section reviews the basic elements of the international refugee regime, including the various legal instruments and institutions created to respond to forced population displacements.

Yesterday's Legacy

The International Refugee Regime

In 1950 UNHCR was established to provide international protection and to promote durable solutions for refugees. These solutions have been interpreted as voluntary repatriation, integration into the host community, or resettlement to a third country.[4] In 1951 the Convention Relating to the Status of Refugees was adopted to complement the statute of UNHCR, and formed the basis on which the international post–World War II refugee regime has been established.[5] Today the 1951 Refugee Convention binds 131 signatory nations to internationally agreed standards for the admission, protection, and treatment of refugees. It defines refugees as persons fleeing their country from persecution for reasons of race, nationality, political opinion, or religious beliefs, and the principle of nonrefoulement prohibits states from returning a refugee to a country where his life or her freedom could be threatened.[6]

The international refugee regime has been greatly influenced by the surrounding political context. In the 1950s the ideological and strategic interests of Western states coincided with the granting of asylum to those fleeing Communist repression from East and Central Europe, and refugees were either integrated in the country of asylum or resettled elsewhere in the West—primarily the United States. Neither prevention nor voluntary repatriation was considered a feasible policy option during that time.

From the outset, developments in Asia had a fundamental impact on the extension of UNHCR's mandate and activities. The scope of the 1951 Refugee Convention initially was limited "to events occurring in Europe before 1 January 1951" and was aimed exclusively at dealing with persons fleeing Communist rule in Europe.[7] In the immediate postwar period, the defeat of Japan and its withdrawal from occupied territories in East Asia and the subsequent struggles between national independence movements and former colonial powers led to large-scale forced population movements. Moreover, these refugee crises often were exacerbated by violent struggles between nationalist and Communist parties, which broke out shortly after achieving independence. Containment of communism was the driving force of Western policies in Asia and greatly determined the response toward refugee movements. The Chinese civil war between 1945 and 1949 ended with hundreds of thousands of Chinese fleeing to Formosa. The Korean War resulted in the displacement of millions of Koreans in 1950 and 1951, and the United Nations Korean Reconstruction Agency (UNKRA) was established to assist, as part of the overall U.N. effort, in the relocation of Koreans in the south and their repatriation from Japan.[8]

The exodus of Chinese and European refugees—primarily White Russians who fled the Bolshevik revolution in the early 1920s—to Hong Kong created urgent humanitarian needs in the early 1950s.[9] Because of the existence of "two Chinas," these refugees could not be deemed to have lost protection of their country of nationality, and thus they fell outside the U.N. high commissioner's mandate. The problem was solved when the General Assembly authorized the high commissioner to use his or her "good offices" to help this group of refugees.[10] The concept of "good offices" gave the high commissioner the flexibility to assist specified groups of persons without having to pronounce on their legal status as refugees. This proved to be an important development, and subsequent resolutions by the General Assembly gradually extended UNHCR's mandate to include other persons of concern, such as returnees and specific groups of internally displaced persons.[11] These gradual extensions of UNHCR's mandate have allowed the high commissioner's office to respond to different types of forced displacement, both outside and inside countries.

The decolonization movement and state-building process in Asia and Africa during the 1950s and 1960s led to large-scale displacements of people seeking protection from generalized violence rather than individual persecution. Proxy wars between the major powers were waged in newly independent countries such as Afghanistan, Angola, Cambodia, the Horn of Africa, and Mozambique, among others. In recognition of the changing circumstances, the 1967 "Protocol Relating the Status of Refugees" was adopted by the United Nations, which dropped the geographical and time limitations from the refugee definition, and thus transformed the refugee problem into a truly global issue.[12] Although receiving countries generously provided protection, local integration often was not considered desirable, nor was resettlement deemed viable. Instead, the emphasis was placed on the temporary nature of asylum and repatriation as a solution.

Specific developments in Africa and Central America also led to the adoption of regional refugee instruments that complemented the universal ones.[13] However, little or no progress has been made toward developing the regional tools and instruments in Asia necessary to deal effectively with complex forced population movements.[14] Instead, Asian governments have sought to deal with refugee movements on a bilateral basis and to minimize international or multilateral involvement. Despite the recurrent refugee crises and the significance of the 1951 Convention only a few Asian states have acceded to it, namely Cambodia, China, Japan, Korea, Papua New Guinea, and Philippines, and even fewer have adopted legislation and procedures to implement its provisions.

Many times political and security considerations take precedence over humanitarian concerns. The early return of refugees often has been the immediate aim, to the detriment of their protection needs. The responses of third countries and international organizations were largely determined by Cold War politics and superpower rivalry; consequently, preventing forced displacement received scant attention. In turn, however, developments in Asia also have greatly influenced the development of UNHCR's mandate and operations, and led to several innovative responses, such as the comprehensive policy toward the Vietnamese boat people and the establishment of open relief centers in Sri Lanka.

Refugee Movements in South Asia

The causes of the large-scale forced population movements have been closely related to the postcolonial nation-state building processes. In turn, the East–West confrontation, particularly in East Asia, has affected these processes. Consequently, the responses have been different between South and Southeast Asia. Whereas the countries of South Asia have sought to deal with these movements on a bilateral level, the countries of Southeast Asia have turned to the international community—in particular Western governments—to take responsibility. The interests, or the lack thereof, of the major powers in the region also have greatly influenced the responses to these crises. In South Asia, refugee movements have not been perceived as fundamentally affecting the security interests of states beyond the countries immediately involved. In Southeast Asia, on the contrary, the politicization of the refugee crises has greatly determined their outcome.

Since 1947 an estimated 35 million to 40 million people have been forced to leave their homelands in South Asia. Refugee movements have been not only a consequence of interstate tensions or internal conflicts but also a cause of war and intervention.[15] The largest movements occurred immediately after the end of World War II and were linked to the establishment of new states. The partition of British India led to one of the greatest population exchanges in recent history. In 1947 and 1948 some six to seven million Muslims fled from India to Pakistan, and after the outbreak of intercommunal fighting, some eight million Hindus and Sikhs left Pakistan for India. The independence of Burma in 1948 also caused most of the 900,000 Indians there to flee that country.

Following independence, efforts to build a common national, cultural, religious, or social identity often contributed to the expulsion of minority groups. Often they were viewed as illegal migrants who—even after several generations—did not have a right to residence or citizenship. Moreover, the fear that minority groups would demand a growing share of the political and economic power has been a common theme throughout the region. This has resulted in strict citizenship laws and even exclusion policies.

Refugees in South Asia have not only been the product of conflict or human rights abuses; they have also contributed to strife, war, and military intervention. Following the internal conflict in East Pakistan, some eight to nine million Bengali Hindus fled to India. India considered the influx as a threat to its national security and invaded East Pakistan in 1971. Likewise in Sri Lanka, the outbreak of the ethnic conflict caused the flight of hundreds of thousands of Tamils to southern India in the early 1980s. Although the Tamils were generously received in India, they posed increasing security and political concerns for their host, as dramatically illustrated by the assassination of Rajiv Gandhi on May 21, 1991. In 1987 India had sent a peacekeeping operation to Sri Lanka but withdrew its forces following a number of security incidents.

Due to these security concerns, states in South Asia have increasingly emphasized the early return of the refugees, under often less than ideal circumstances, rather than allowing them to stay, as was the case right after national independence. After Bangladesh achieved independence in 1971, India repatriated the refugees over a short period of time. India also increased pressure upon Sri Lanka to accept the return of Tamils in 1987 and 1991. It was only in 1992 that India accepted UNHCR's involvement, and a Memorandum of Understanding was signed in which UNHCR agreed to monitor the voluntary repatriation movements. In 1993 Bangladesh also started to repatriate 250,000 Burmese Muslims who had fled Arakan in Myanmar in 1991. The repatriation initially was considered a bilateral issue between Bangladesh and Myanmar, but after the refugees expressed unwillingness to return in the absence of oversight, and certain nongovernmental organizations (NGOs) questioned the voluntariness of the return, a Memorandum of Understanding was signed with UNHCR covering the terms of repatriation. UNHCR sought, and was given, assured presence and unimpeded access to the returnees.

Refugee Movements in Southeast Asia

Unlike the refugee crises in South Asia, the decolonization process in Southeast Asia was heavily affected by communist insurgencies and prolonged conflicts. Humanitarian considerations often were subjugated to political and security concerns. As long as geopolitics dominated the Indochinese refugee problem, solutions other than resettlement were considered politically inopportune. Hence the heavy international involvement in regional refugee crises.

Following the fall of the South Vietnamese government and the withdrawal of U.S. forces, the flow of refugees was minimal and no cause for alarm.[16] Between April and May 1975 the United States resettled some 134,000 Vietnamese who had either been evacuated from South Vietnam or picked up from boats. Not until 1978, due to the deteriorating relationship between Vietnam and China that led Vietnam to adopt discriminatory measures directed primarily at the Chinese community, did a large-scale exodus from Vietnam begin, consisting largely of ethnic Chinese. Consequently, between 1978 and 1980 some 250,000 ethnic Chinese fled to China and were settled in the south. By 1979 more than 200,000 Vietnamese refugees had arrived in Southeast Asia.

The response of the neighboring countries was less than hospitable on occasion, and the right of asylum was challenged from the outset. When the first boatloads of refugees started to arrive in 1978, countries feared that the "boat people" would be stranded there, causing anxieties about historic animosities and ethnic tensions. Moreover, the Association of Southeast Asian Nations (ASEAN) viewed the refugee outflow as a deliberate effort of the Vietnamese government to destabilize the region. Consequently, Thailand and Malaysia started to prevent boats from landing on their shores. These policies caused a major international outcry following the push-off of some 386 boats carrying more than 50,000 refugees.[17]

In June 1979 the five member states of ASEAN agreed in principle not to accept any further boat people. In July 1979 the crisis prompted the largest intergovernmental meeting on refugees since the inception of UNHCR.[18] For Western countries the preservation of asylum was the principal objective, whereas ASEAN states argued that protection could be provided only on a temporary basis and if linked to the automatic resettlement of the refugees. The ASEAN nations also emphasized Vietnam's responsibility in resolving the crisis.[19] An important aspect of the resulting agreement was Vietnam's commitment to adopt measures to stop illegal departures. Prior to that, UNHCR had negotiated the Orderly Departure Program (ODP), which has allowed Vietnamese eligible for family reunification or other humanitarian reasons to leave directly to resettlement countries. Although the success of the 1979 agreement was relatively short-lived, it was of major significance as it aimed to "manage" the refugee outflow by specifying the responsibilities of the different countries involved. Its major shortcomings were that it did not deal with the underlying causes of the refugee problem or address the responsibility of Vietnam toward its own citizens.

Following the 1979 conference, the renewed commitment of Western states to resettle the Vietnamese boat people kept pace with the rate of new arrivals, and the number of refugees present in Southeast Asian countries diminished significantly. A new crisis, however, occurred in the late 1980s when Western countries reduced their resettlement quotas while the rate of arrivals surged anew, leading once again to push-offs, detentions, and piracy attacks. In addition, the nature of the refugee flow changed significantly. Most of the new arrivals originated from northern Vietnam, and many of them were suspected of migrating in search of economic betterment, not out of fear of persecution. The automatic linkage between granting refugee status to all new arrivals and resettlement was thought to have created a pull effect, attracting people to risk their lives in rickety boats in search of golden opportunities—preferably in the United States.

The renewed challenge to the principle of first asylum, the changes in the international political climate, and the improving relations between Vietnam and its neighbors provided the opportunity to revisit the regional arrangements. ASEAN played a critical role during the negotiations leading up to the Comprehensive Plan of Action (CPA), adopted at the International Conference on Indochinese Refugees in 1989.[20] The main objectives of the CPA were twofold: to protect genuine refugees from Vietnam and to prevent the further outflow of nonrefugees. The agreement placed interlocking and mutually reinforcing obligations on the countries of origin and of first asylum, and the major donor and resettlement states.

Under the CPA, countries of asylum in the region agreed to admit the asylum seekers and to establish screening procedures, with UNHCR's assistance, to identify refugees according to international standards. Only those recognized as refugees would be guaranteed resettlement by Western countries. In turn, Vietnam acknowledged its responsibility toward its own citizens by agreeing to take back refugees whose asylum claim had been rejected and by committing itself to observe scrupulously the safety of the returnees, while the UNHCR agreed to monitor returnees' safety and to help create a climate conducive to their return.[21] The Vietnamese government also committed itself to expand the ODP. More than 600,000 Vietnamese have benefited from this program since its inception, including 436,000 who have resettled in the United States.

The CPA has been a major success. In 1995 only 227 persons newly arrived in the region. Twenty years after the start of the Vietnamese refugee crisis, 754,842 Vietnamese have been resettled and more than 74,000 have repatriated voluntarily to Vietnam. The prospect of joining ASEAN and linking its economy with the growing regional economy proved an attractive incentive for Vietnam to normalize its relations with neighboring states (or, as characterized by Thai policy thinking, "from the battlefield to the marketplace").[22] The official close of the CPA on June 30, 1996, marked the end of the Vietnamese boat people problem. The major outstanding issue is the return of the nonrefugees to Vietnam.

The role of the media in the Indochinese refugee crisis was critical, especially in galvanizing U.S. public opinion. For example, dramatic reports of pirate attacks on the high seas mobilized support for the unique antipiracy program. The media, in cooperation with NGOs, also helped build a strong U.S. constituency in support of continuing resettlement quotas for Vietnamese boat people. Uninformed media reports, however, also contributed to the high expectations and false hopes among the screened-out camp population in Southeast Asia about alleged policy reversals.

Progress on the Vietnamese refugee problem was closely linked to the settlement of the Cambodian question. The Cambodian conflict comprised the second major regional refugee crisis in 1975. When the Khmer Rouge took power in Cambodia in 1975, some 30,000 Cambodians fled to neighboring Thailand, where they were assisted by UNHCR. Vietnam's invasion of Cambodia in December 1978 caused an additional 350,000 Cambodians to flee. The Thai government viewed the Cambodian problem as a threat to its national security and classified these Cambodians as "illegal immigrants," instead of refugees. To deter the arrival of more refugees, a policy of "humane deterrence" was adopted that included closing the border between Thailand and Cambodia; the establishment of closed camps, except for those managed by UNHCR; and the refoulement of some 40,000 Cambodians in 1979.[23] The international response was subject to competing superpower politics, with the refugees being used as pawns.[24] Assistance to the Cambodian refugees was supplied mainly by Western nations with NGOs providing essential services in the camps.[25] The United Nations Border Relief Operation (UNBRO) was created in 1982 to help channel aid to the refugee camps. The security of the Cambodian refugees became a major concern, as UNBRO did not have a protection mandate and camps were situated near the border, vulnerable to indiscriminate shelling from the Cambodian factions.

Between 1987 and 1988 the improving relations between the Soviet Union and China created new opportunities for a negotiated settlement of the Cambodian crisis. Following the withdrawal of its forces from Cambodia in 1990, Vietnam's relations with ASEAN and Western states improved significantly and culminated in Vietnam joining the regional organization and normalizing its relations with the United States in July 1995.[26]

A major breakthrough was achieved during the Paris peace negotiations, which took place between 1989 and 1991. Agreement was reached on the repatriation of the refugees at the end of the first Paris International Conference on Cambodia, incorporated as Annex 3 of the 1991 Comprehensive Political Settlement of the Cambodian Conflict.[27] The United Nations Transitional Authority for Cambodia (UNTAC) was set up with a mandate extending beyond traditional peacekeeping.[28] UNTAC contained a strong civilian component focusing on institution-building, including civil administration and a police force, reconstruction, and the organization of elections. Humanitarian issues and human rights were an essential part of UNTAC's mandate to implement a political and peaceful solution.[29] UNHCR was assigned the responsibility for the repatriation of 370,000 refugees. The repatriation was completed by the spring of 1993, well before the elections, which were held in May. Throughout the operation and despite the continuing conflicts with the Khmer Rouge, UNHCR was perceived by the various factions as neutral and impartial, enabling it to complete the repatriation program successfully.

UNTAC's success was due largely to the fact that it aimed to resolve conflict through negotiations instead of enforcement. Progress toward national reconciliation and the establishment of democratic institutions were linked to obtaining international assistance and development aid. UNTAC sought actively to support Cambodia's social, political, and economic institutions as part of the transition to peace.[30] The return of the refugees was not only dependent on but also instrumental to national reconciliation. Although the main objectives were met, the sustainability of the achievements must still be tested fully.[31] Despite the development of small-scale projects, the reintegration of the returnees has proceeded slowly, and the lack of available arable land has proven to be a constraining factor. Moreover, continuing military skirmishes have led to internal displacement and further refugee outflows into Thailand at regular intervals.[32] Landmines pose a deadly threat to farmers, and thousands of Cambodians have fallen victim to the eight to ten million uncleared mines across the country.[33] Although rehabilitation efforts have been an essential element to consolidate the peace process and to facilitate progress toward the reintegration of the refugees, sustainable development projects have been hampered by the absence of lasting military and political stability.

Responses to the Laotian refugee problem in Thailand have been dominated by international concerns, as was the case with the Vietnamese and Cambodian refugees. Since 1975 nearly 360,000 Laotian refugees arrived in Thailand, of whom 320,000 were resettled (primarily in the United States), and some 24,000 repatriated.[34] In 1986 Thailand introduced a screening procedure for Laotian refugees, and those who were not considered refugees were returned. Within the context of the CPA, the Laotian refugee question also has been addressed along lines similar to those dealing with the Vietnamese boat people.

Today's Issues, Tomorrow's Problems

Contrary to developments in Africa and Europe, the end of the superpower rivalry did not unleash repressed internal conflicts in South and Southeast Asia. Asia's economic miracle has contributed to the political and social stability in the region and has, in turn, improved interstate relations. Economic development in the region has led to significant growth in income, education, and social services, but new problems have appeared. Land scarcity, environmental degradation, and income inequalities can contribute to forced population displacement, but they are not the primary causes.[35] Political behavior of governments and lack of respect for human and minority rights—exploiting ethnic, religious, or social differences—are often the direct factors causing conflict and resulting in forced population movements.[36]

In this section we will consider four issues—namely, human rights, internally displaced persons, transition of authoritarian political regimes to democracy, and migration—that may affect relations among and within states in the region and beyond, and may contribute to large-scale forced population displacements in the future.[37]

Human Rights

Human rights in Asia, and minority rights in particular, have attracted increasing interest.[38] Nationalism based on common religious, cultural, or ethnic traditions has been a key rallying force in many Asian countries. On occasion, minorities have been portrayed as a threat to national security, which has led to their exclusion and even expulsion. The long-standing Tibetan issue has caused a steady flow of Tibetan refugees—now more than 100,000—to India. Karen, Mon, and Karenni minorities from Myanmar have fled to Thailand, which in turn led to military engagements between Thai and Myanmar forces. Borders in Asia, as elsewhere, often were drawn artificially, separating communities from their common heritage.

High birth rates among minority groups also have been viewed as potentially upsetting delicate ethnic balances and as a threat to the political and economic power of the majority group. On occasion, Chinese minorities throughout Southeast Asia have been treated as scapegoats for the various countries' ills. The Khmer Rouge has especially targeted the Chinese community in Cambodia. The traditional animosity between Vietnamese and Cambodians has led to regular attacks upon Vietnamese fishermen on the Mekong River and the Tonle Sap Lake.[39] From July 1992 to August 1993 UNTAC reported the killings of 116 ethnic Vietnamese.[40] Radio broadcasts incited ethnic hatred and violence, and some 30,000 ethnic Vietnamese fled Cambodia following attacks attributed to the Khmer Rouge in 1993.[41] When they sought to return to their villages, they were prevented from doing so by the Cambodian authorities. Some 3,000 continue to wait in their boats near Chrey Thom for official permission to return home despite repeated interventions by UNHCR.

Related to the question of minority rights are issues of citizenship, which can result in statelessness. Although a minority group may have resided in a country for several generations, its members still may not be considered residents or citizens, as is the case with the ethnic Vietnamese in Cambodia.[42] After fleeing, it may be difficult for the refugees to establish citizenship, due to a lack of supporting documents. The country of origin may refuse to repatriate, absolving itself of responsibility toward its own population. In some instances, refugees who leave their countries out of fear of persecution are deemed to have renounced, or are being deprived of, their citizens' or residents' rights. Consequently, this may give rise to de facto statelessness, further complicating the problem of finding solutions by leaving people in a legal limbo.

Internally Displaced Persons

Although the issue of internally displaced persons is interrelated with the respect for human rights, it has attracted relatively little attention in Asia.[43] Governments in the region have tended to consider this issue as an exclusive prerogative of sovereign states, not recognizing the potential impact on interstate relations and regional security. Recently, however, there has been growing recognition that human rights violations resulting in large-scale human displacement inside countries may constitute a threat to regional and international security.

UNHCR activities on behalf of internally displaced persons include providing life-saving relief assistance, monitoring the treatment of minority or majority groups, facilitating the evacuation of civilians in life-threatening situations, identifying solutions and facilitating their return home, and undertaking steps toward reconciliation and rehabilitation. Some 30 million persons are thought to be displaced internally worldwide, including six to seven million persons in Asia alone.[44]

Democratization

The third issue relates to the growing demands for political openness and democratization by the emerging urban middle class and political groups in Asia. The transition from an authoritarian political regime—often dominated by the military—to a democratic government has not always proven to be trouble-free. The uneven distribution of economic wealth and political power has helped radicalize sections of society and led to political violence and internal conflicts. In Pakistan, the Mohajirs (refugees from India) and the Bihari Muslims (repatriated from Bangladesh) have sought to protect their interests by negotiating fixed quotas for federal government employment and access to educational facilities, calculated on the basis of their percentage in the total population.[45] The famine in North Korea following the floods in August 1995 reportedly left hundreds of thousands persons homeless and has fueled reports of political instability.[46] A sudden political transition in North Korea may lead to destabilization and unmanaged population movements.

One of the principal challenges confronting Asia is how to ease communal tensions in multiethnic or multireligious societies to prevent them from degenerating into mass violence. Cultural or ethnic differences have become far more divisive factors than ideological differences, just as in many states fragmentation has been a much stronger drive than integration. Claims for political and territorial self-determination are prevalent, and, more often than not, they are accompanied by violent attempts to create ethnic and/or religious homogeneity. Pakistan and India have clashed regularly over Kashmir. In Sri Lanka, despite the proposed establishment of autonomous regions in which the Tamils would enjoy considerable political and administrative authority, fighting continues.[47] These examples dramatically illustrate the difficulties encountered in finding political solutions to long-standing conflicts.

Migration

As Paul Smith argues in the previous chapter, migration is a growing problem in Asia today.[48] Rising unemployment, poverty, population pressures, and the uneven distribution of wealth within and among countries will lead to even greater migratory pressures. Three of the top five countries with the highest population growth are in Asia, namely China, India, and Indonesia.

On the one hand, migration has been viewed positively by both the receiving and the sending countries in the region. Migrants contribute to the economic growth and development of receiving countries, while emigration can act as a pressure release for countries with high rates of unemployment, poverty, or other population pressures. As in the case of the Philippines, remittances sent home by migrants constitute a significant source of foreign exchange earnings.

On the other hand, some states view the size and composition of migratory movements as potential threats to the political, ethnic, or religious balances within their borders. To limit migration, states may seek to adopt stringent entry regulations and polices, but their effectiveness may be limited given the porous borders and the limited capacity to control them. Instead, governments may seek to influence the exit rules of other states.

Both China and North Korea pose potential significant problems in this area. Both countries apply stringent exit rules, making it difficult to leave and seek employment abroad. Nevertheless, pressures from citizens within each country to leave are expected to increase. Following the economic and political reforms in China, a large-scale "peasant flood" is taking place, which already amounts to an estimated 50 million long-term and approximately 100 million short-term migrants.[49] The scope of this internal movement has created serious political, administrative, and social problems as the migrants converge on the urban-industrial centers.

As in Western Europe and North America, the problem of mixed migratory movements also arises in Asia. Many of the migrants are refugees in need of international protection. Since few states have acceded to the international refugee instruments, no mechanisms are available to distinguish refugees from migrants. States in the region often designate refugees as migrants, denying them the protection they require, as Thailand did in response to the influx of Cambodian refugees.

The effects of human rights violations, internally displaced persons, nondemocratic policies, and migration go beyond the region. Improved communications and the ease of international travel have made the world a global neighborhood, affecting not only intra- but also interregional relations. The arrival of the *Golden Venture* ship in New York in June 1993, carrying nearly 300 Chinese migrants applying for refugee status, dramatically illustrated this interrelationship and fueled the debate over immigration in the United States. Australia and New Zealand are becoming countries of first asylum instead of traditional countries of resettlement. To address the issue of forced population displacement in the world today, bilateral approaches are no longer adequate given the growing interdependence among states and regions in the world.

A New Policy Paradigm for Tomorrow

A comprehensive strategy is required to deal with the complexities of forced displacement today and in the future. Such a strategy should consist of complementary measures that aim to break the vicious circle of internal displacement, exile, return, internal displacement, and renewed exile typical of many refugee crises. Such a comprehensive strategy also must promote the overall stability of the affected countries and regions—a strategy in which respect for human rights, the promotion of economic and social development, and the maintenance of peace and security are the key elements. To implement this strategy, the concerted efforts of governmental, intergovernmental, and nongovernmental actors are essential.

The CPA and the repatriation of Cambodian refugees as part of the 1991 Paris peace settlement represent some of the first attempts to develop such a framework for international cooperation. Although from a conceptual and legal point of view clear distinctions exist among refugees, internally displaced persons, returnees, and war-affected civilians, such distinctions often are less apparent from an operational and protection point of view. In many humanitarian emergencies, the reasons why people flee are often similar for refugees and internally displaced persons, the only distinction being that the latter have not crossed an international border. In the pursuit of solutions, returning refugees are mingled and often indistinguishable from internally displaced and war-affected civilians. In practice, therefore, policies and programs must examine the needs of the afflicted communities as a whole, taking into account the requirements of the host population receiving the returnees. Instead of a country-based strategy, from the perspective of either countries of origin or asylum, a situational approach should be key to a comprehensive strategy.

The key components of such a comprehensive strategy are protection, solutions, and prevention. These components are closely linked. Protection in countries of asylum depends on the progress toward solutions in countries of origin. In turn, durable solutions must address the underlying causes forcing people to flee and aim toward preventing new humanitarian emergencies from occurring. Such a strategy might take the following form in South and Southeast Asia.[50]

Protection

This component of a comprehensive strategy should—as a minimum—include admission, respect for the principle of nonrefoulement, and repatriation where conditions in the country of origin permit. Norms and mechanisms for the protection of internally displaced persons should be developed to avert people in refugeelike situations from moving abroad unnecessarily. Steps toward improving the scope and quality of refugee protection in Asia could be undertaken. Asian states should consider acceding to the 1951 Convention and the 1967 Protocol relating to the Status of Refugees.[51]

In addition, the adoption of national refugee legislation and procedures is necessary. In Southeast Asia, a post-CPA policy must be developed to build on recent achievements in refugee protection. The adoption of inclusive citizenship laws will improve the protection offered to minority groups and prevent statelessness. Also, the humanitarian character of refugee protection should be reinforced in the region, as refugees should not serve as a foreign policy instrument by supporting armed insurgent movements.

Solution

Voluntary repatriation is, in most instances, the most appropriate solution to large forced population movements. The right of refugees to return to their homes must be respected; the responsibility of states toward their own citizens, which is concomitant to this right, needs to be underlined.

However, repatriation can be successful only if the conditions exist in the country of origin for the successful economic, social, and political reintegration of returnees. In countries ravaged by conflict or war, the gaps between the delivery of short-term humanitarian assistance and the implementation of longer-term rehabilitation and development programs should be bridged. The return of refugees is not only an essential element toward solving humanitarian crises but also contributes toward national reconciliation.

Although increasing emphasis has been placed on voluntary repatriation in recent years, resettlement must remain an option for refugees without a solution in sight in either the country of asylum or origin. In some situations, neither repatriation nor resettlement may be feasible; therefore, local integration should be considered as a viable solution instead of maintaining squalid refugee camps over long periods of time. Humanitarian action can lessen human suffering and save lives, but the solutions to crises are predominantly political ones. Relief cannot substitute political will and action to identify and implement solutions.

Prevention

Preventive measures should be directed toward tackling the reasons that force people to move. In Asia, a wide variety of activities could be adopted, such as the promotion of human, citizenship, and minority rights; prevention of statelessness; ethnic and religious tolerance; economic and social sustainable development; conflict resolution and negotiation; and accountable governance. Likewise, national institution and capacity building through government and nongovernmental agencies will give states the means to respond effectively to humanitarian emergencies. Particular attention may be given to the development of a strong civil society.

Implementing such a comprehensive strategy will require the close coordination of national, regional, and international actors, and goes beyond the capacity of any single one. The resurgence of Asian states on the international political and economic scene also implies that their roles and responsibilities—like those of the international community at large—toward conflicts and forced displacement in the region have evolved. It is unlikely that external intervention in the region on a scale similar to that in the past will take place, unless the strategic interests of major regional and/or international powers are directly affected (such as fighting on the Korean peninsula or over Taiwan). Developments in South Asia are more worrisome given the lack of immediate solutions to several long-standing conflicts, the ongoing ethnic and religious tensions, and the emergence of new potential conflict zones.[52]

Therefore, countries and intergovernmental structures in the region are expected to play an increasing leadership role in preventing and identifying solutions to forced displacement. As forced displacement is a transnational issue, regional and subregional organizations, such as ASEAN and the South Asian Association for Regional Cooperation (SAARC), have an important role to fulfill by providing a forum for early warning, conflict resolution, and identifying solutions to humanitarian crises.[53] Regional intergovernmental agencies may provide a mechanism to muster the political will to stop the fighting and address the underlying causes of conflicts. In this context, the development of common norms, and rules and mechanisms for crisis prevention, refugee protection and problem solving are invaluable. With respect to internal conflicts and internally displaced persons, they also provide a framework to assess and mitigate the consequences upon neighboring states. It is essential that regional approaches not be limited to broad, formal agreements but include clearly defined implementation and follow-up mechanisms, including a balanced assignment of responsibilities.

Given their strategic interests and close economic linkages with countries in Asia, extraregional actors will continue to play a significant, albeit diminished, role. The United States in particular will continue to have a leadership role. The growing Asian community in the United States forms an effective lobby, linking respect for human rights to assistance programs. Vietnamese groups in the United States have played an important role in building support for the resettlement of Vietnamese asylum seekers and the Orderly Departure Program over the years. Likewise, human rights organizations are closely monitoring government policies and exercising pressures to ensure that returnees' rights are respected, as in Myanmar and Vietnam.

Several of the other transnational issues analyzed in this book, such as environmental damage, drugs, human rights, and population growth, have a direct or indirect bearing on forced population movements. These relationships should be examined and clarified further. For example, economic actors, such as the Asian Development Bank and the international financial institutions, may play a key role in facilitating the reintegration of displaced persons into their communities as an integral part of any rehabilitation plan for conflict-torn states or by assessing the potential impact of stringent financial requirements upon population movements.

Conclusion

Despite the optimism about Asia's future, new challenges on the horizon will need to be addressed with some urgency. Asia should abide by and strengthen the rules of the refugee protection regime. In the future, it will be highly unlikely that the international community will launch generous assistance and resettlement programs similar to those that favored the Vietnamese and Cambodian refugees. Instead, more emphasis will be placed on regional solutions and protection strategies. Therefore, Asia, with the support of the international community, should consider developing a comprehensive refugee policy focusing on prevention, protection, and solutions and build the capacity through its regional and national governmental and nongovernmental organizations to implement such a policy.

As a leading Asia-Pacific power, the United States can contribute by strengthening its collaborative efforts toward prevention and solution of refugee and migration-related crises in the region. Not only at the bilateral but also at the multilateral level, the United States will remain crucial. Active participation in and financial and human support of the United Nations and regional organizations will be required. During this period of transition, enhanced efforts by Asian countries, supported by the continuing commitments of the United States, can lead to the consolidation of the refugee protection regime in the region.

Notes

1.   These numbers include 53,000 persons of concern to UNHCR in Australia and New Zealand, the majority of whom are of Asian origin.

2.   The latter group consists largely of Vietnamese asylum seekers in the Association of Southeast Asian Nations (ASEAN) and Hong Kong, whose claim to refugee status has been rejected and who are expected to return during 1996.

3. Leslie H. Gelb, "Quelling the Teacup Wars: The New World's Constant Challenge," *Foreign Affairs* 73, no. 6 (Nov.–Dec. 1994), pp. 2–6.

4. General Assembly Resolution 428 (V) of December 14, 1950, on the Statute of the Office of the United Nations High Commissioner for Refugees.

5. United Nations Treaty Series, No. 2545, Vol. 189, p. 137.

6. "Convention Relating to the Status of Refugees, "Art. 1 and p. 33.

7. Ibid., Art. 1.

8. Gil Loescher, *Beyond Charity: International Cooperation and the Global Refugee Crisis* (New York: Oxford University Press, 1993) p. 62.

9. Louise W. Holborn, *Refugees: A Problem of Our Time: The Work of the United Nations High Commissioner for Refugees*, Vol. 1 and 2 (Metuchen, NJ: Scarecrow Press, 1975), pp. 657–702.

10. General Assembly Resolution 1167 (XII), 1957; and Resolution 1388 (XIV), 1959.

11. Only upon request of the secretary-general or the General Assembly has UNHCR a mandate to deal with specific caseloads of internally displaced persons, such as the Kurds in northern Iraq, the displaced persons and affected civilians in Bosnia and Herzegovina, and the displaced persons in Sri Lanka. For an overview see Office of the United Nations High Commissioner for Refugees, *UNHCR's Operational Experience with Internally Displaced Persons* (Geneva: UNHCR, 1994).

12. "Protocol Relating to the Status of Refugees" of January 31, 1967, United Nations Treaty Series, No. 8791, Vol. 606, p. 267.

13. Organization for African Unity, "Convention Governing the Specific Aspects of Refugee Problems in Africa," United Nations Treaty Series, No. 14 691; "Cartagena Declaration on Refugees," adopted by the Colloquium on the International Protection of Refugees in Central America, Mexico, and Panama, held in Cartagena on November 19–22, 1984.

14. "Principles Concerning Treatment of Refugees," adopted by the Asian-African Legal Consultative Committee, Eighth Session, Bangkok, 1966.

15. Myron Weiner, "Rejected Peoples and Unwanted Migrants in South Asia," in Myron Weiner (ed.), *International Migration and Security* (Boulder, CO: Westview Press, 1993), pp. 150–178.

16. For an overview of the initial response to the Indochinese refugee crises, see Barry Wain, *The Refused: The Agony of the Indochinese Refugees* (Hong Kong: Dow Jones Publishing Co., 1981).

17. For an overview, see Alan Simmance, "The International Response to the Indo-Chinese Refugee Crisis," Paper submitted to the International Seminar on the Indochinese Exodus and the International Response, UNHCR and Ministry of Foreign Affairs of Japan, Tokyo, October 27–28, 1995.

18. "Report of the United Nations Secretary-General," Meeting on Refugees and Displaced Persons in South East Asia, Geneva, July 20 and 21, 1979, A/34/627.

19. ASEAN Foreign Ministers meeting, Bali, June 28–30, 1979.

20. United Nations, General Assembly, International Conference on Indo-Chinese-Chinese Refugees, "Draft Declaration and Comprehensive Plan of Action," Approved by the Preparatory Meeting for the International Conference on Indo-Chinese Refugees on March 8, 1989, A/Conf. 148/2, April 26, 1989.

21. In 1988 Vietnam and UNHCR signed a revised Memorandum of Understanding on Voluntary Return. The memorandum committed both parties to expand and accelerate the Orderly Departure Program.

22. Quoted in Takashi Inoguchi, "The Indochina Vortex in Historical Context," Paper presented at the International Seminar on the Indo-Chinese Exodus and the International Response, October 27-28, 1995, United Nations University, Tokyo.

23. Dennis McNamara, "The Origins and Effects of 'Humane Deterrence' Policies in South-East Asia" in Gil Loescher, and Leila Monahan (eds.), *Refugees and International Relations* (New York: Oxford University Press: 1989), pp. 123–134.

24. William Shawcross, *The Quality of Mercy: Cambodia, the Holocaust and Modern Conscience* (New York: Simon and Schuster, 1984).

25. For a detailed discussion, see Simmance, "International Response"; and Zia Rizvi, "Indo-Chinese Refugee Exodus: Comments on Some Specific Aspects," Paper presented at the International seminar on the Indo-Chinese Exodus; UNHCR took over the activities of UNBRO in 1991.

26. Muthiah Alagappa, "Regionalism and the Quest for Security: ASEAN and the Cambodian Conflict," *Journal of International Affairs* 46, no. 2 (Winter 1993), pp. 439–467.

27. Sergio Vieira de Mello, "Humanitarian Issues in Conflict-Resolution: The Cambodian Example," Paper presented at the Conference on Conflict and Humanitarian Action, Princeton, October 22–23, 1993; and Yukio Imagawa, "The Cambodian Exodus, Its Background and Solution," Paper presented at the International Seminar on the Indo-Chinese Exodus.

28. United Nations, *The United Nations and Cambodia: 1991–1995,* The United Nations Blue Books Series, Volume 2 (New York: United Nations Department of Public Information, 1995); Security Council Resolution 745 (1992) on UNTAC and implementation of the Paris Agreements, February 28, 1992.

29. Dennis McNamara, "UN Human Rights Activities in Cambodia: An Evaluation," in Alice Henkin, *Honoring Human Rights and Keeping the Peace: Lessons from El Salvador, Cambodia, and Haiti* (Washington, DC: The Aspen Institute, 1995), pp. 57–82.

30. The media also played an important role in the process leading up to the elections. The regular radio broadcasts organized by UNTAC mobilized and informed the population about the latest developments and countered false information.

31. For a detailed evaluation of UNTAC, UNIDIR and the Institute of Policy Studies, see "Report and Recommendations: IPS/UNITAR International Conference on the United Nations Transitional Authority in Cambodia: Debriefing and Lessons," Singapore, August 2–4, 1994.

32. In the provinces of Seam Reap, Bantaey Meanchey, and Battambang, an estimated 20 percent of the internally displaced are refugees repatriated from camps in Thailand.

33. United Nations, "Assistance in Mine Clearance: Report of the Secretary-General," A/49/357, 1994.

34. UNHCR, *Statistics Concerning Indo-Chinese in East and South-East Asia*, (Geneva: UNHCR, January 1996).

35. This point is made in Astri Suhrke, "Environmental Change, Migration, and Conflict" in Chester A. Crocker; Fen Osler Hampson with Pamela Aall (eds.), *Managing Global Chaos: Sources and Responses to International Conflict* (Washington, DC: United States Institute of Peace Press, 1996).

36. Myron Weiner, "Bad Neighbors, Bad Neighborhoods: An Inquiry into the Causes of Refugee Flows," *International Security* 21, no. 1 (Summer 1996), pp. 5–42.

37. Also see Trevor Findlay, "Turning the Corner in Southeast Asia" in Michael E. Brown (ed.), *The International Dimensions of Internal Conflict* (Cambridge, MA.: The MIT Press, 1996), pp. 173–204.

38. David A. Bell, "The East Asian Challenge to Human Rights: Reflections on an East West Dialogue" *Human Rights Quarterly* 18 (1996), pp. 641–667.

39. Minority Rights Group, *Minorities in Cambodia*, 1995, pp. 17–25.

40. United Nations Transitional Authority for Cambodia, *Human Rights Component Final Report*, Phnom Penh, September 1993, p. 31.

41. United Nations, *Report of the Special Representative of the Secretary General on the Situation of Human Rights in Cambodia*, E/CN.4/1994/73, February 24, 1994, p. 49.

42. The draft Cambodian immigration law caused considerable concern as it led to the deportation and expulsion of aliens. Thus minority groups, such as the Vietnamese, could be defined as aliens, in the absence of a citizenship law, and expelled even if they had resided in the country for generations.

43. United Nations, Commission on Human Rights, "Report of the Representative of the Secretary-General," Mr. Francis Deng, Submitted Pursuant to Commission on Human Rights Resolution 1993/95. Addendum: "Profiles in Displacement Sri Lanka," E/CN.4/1994/44/Add.1, 1994.

44. Francis M. Deng, *Internally Displaced Persons: An Interim Report to the United Nations Secretary-General on Protection and Assistance* (New York: Refugee Policy Group and United Nations Department of Humanitarian Affairs, 1994), p. 9. At the beginning of 1995, approximately two million internally displaced persons in Asia were of concern to UNHCR.

45. Shelton O. Kodikara, "Ethnonationalism in South Asia: A Comparative Regional Perspective," in Muni and Baral (eds.), *Refugees and Regional Security*, pp. 61–62.

46. Nayan Chanda, "Help Wanted," *Far Eastern Economic Review* (Dec. 14, 1995), p. 20.

47. Manik DeSilva, "Cornered in Colombo," *Far Eastern Economic Review* (Feb. 15, 1996), p. 14.

48. For an overview of the literature, see: Paul J. Smith, *East Asia's Economic Transformation and Its Impact on Intraregional Labor Migration* in This volume; Peter Stalker, *The Work of Strangers: A Survey of International Labour Migration* (Geneva: International Labour Office, 1994), pp. 247–270; Linda Low, "Population Movement in the Asia Pacific Region: Singapore Perspective," *International Migration Review* 29, no. 3 (Fall 1995), pp. 745–764; Myron Weiner, *The Global Migration Crisis: Challenge to States and Human Rights* (New York, NY: HarperCollins, 1995).

49. Guang Hua Wan, "Peasant Flood in China: Internal Migration and Its Policy Determinants," *Third World Quarterly* 16, no. 2 (1995), pp. 173–196.

50. In addition to the CPA and the Cambodian peace settlement, comprehensive approaches have been used in Central America, within the context of CIREFCA as an integral part of the peace settlements, and the CIS. The latter is of particular interest as it is geared toward preventive action, instead of responding to the consequences of humanitarian emergencies as part of a solutions oriented strategy. See UNHCR, IOM, OSCE, *Report of the Regional Conference to Address the Problems of Refugees, Displaced Persons, Other Forms of Involuntary Displacement and Returnees in the Countries of the Commonwealth of Independent States and Relevant Neighbouring States*, Geneva, May 30–31, 1996, CISCONF/1996/6, July 4, 1996.

51. In recent years, India, Pakistan and Bangladesh have become members of UNHCR's Executive Committee; this should considerably contribute to a fruitful dialogue.

52. The dissolution of the Soviet Union has created new areas of tensions and conflict, the potential implications of which are not yet clearly understood. Reportedly, the fighting and Islamic revival in Tajikistan has had an impact on China's western provinces, where tensions between Muslim and Chinese populations have grown.

53. The member states of SAARC are India, Pakistan, Sri Lanka, Bangladesh, Maldives, Bhutan, and Nepal.

Chapter 6

The Impact of Asian Economic Growth on Human Rights

SIDNEY JONES

The protection of human rights, like the protection of the environment, can be achieved only through concerted international action, and like environmental degradation, human rights violations in one country have implications far beyond that country's borders.[1]

In Asia, abuses against ethnic minorities or nationalist insurgents have led to refugee outflows from Burma to Thailand, from Indonesia to Papua New Guinea, from Tibet to Nepal, and from East Timor to Australia. More generally, the pattern of systematic human rights violations in Burma triggered Western sanctions and was a factor leading Burma's military rulers to seek help from China, which in turn exacerbated regional fears of Chinese expansionism. Failure of the Cambodian government to protect ethnic Vietnamese, or, worse, active involvement in assault against them, has caused tensions with Vietnam. Treatment of migrant workers from the Philippines and Insonesia in Singapore and Malaysia has caused serious diplomatic rifts among these nations. The July 1996 assault by Indonesian security forces on the democratic opposition headquarters and the subsequent riot in Jakarta has increased the potential for instability in the largest country in Southeast Asia, as long as the government continues to meet demands for change with repression rather than acknowledging the legitimacy of the grievances.

Even if international law did not treat human rights as an issue transcending national boundaries, the impact of domestic repression still would be felt across those borders. An important question, therefore, is not whether human rights violations are an appropriate concern of the international community—they are—but whether the economic dynamism of East and Southeast Asia in particular necessitates a different response than would be the case elsewhere.

The debate in the United States in the early 1990s over rescinding China's most-favored-nation (MFN) status brought the issue of the relationship between economic growth and human rights to the forefront. In particular, it raised the question of whether the rapid growth of the so-called miracle economies of East Asia—Japan, Korea, Taiwan, Singapore, Hong Kong, China, Indonesia, Thailand, and Malaysia—had affected human rights practices in the region and whether the newfound economic strength and self-confidence of these countries required a rethinking of strategies to address human rights violations.

The MFN debate effectively ended in 1994,[2] but the underlying dilemma of using economic sanctions with Asian trading partners continues. How can the United States exert pressure on human rights issues without damaging its economic interests? China's economic clout, including its enormous purchasing power as well as its capacity to use business deals to persuade other Western governments to downplay human rights criticism, seemed to make any U.S. policy based on economic sanctions self-defeating.

But the debate has ramifications that go far beyond the utility of sanctions. It raises questions in this country about whether economic reforms and freer markets lead inexorably to democratization and respect for human rights; whether Western countries have any right to impose their values on Asia; whether existing Asian governments represented generally held Asian public views; and whether Asia's growing economic power is sapping the will of developed countries not just to use sanctions but to take any concrete action against serious human rights violations.

In this chapter I will argue four main points:

- The much-touted "Asian concept of human rights" masks not only important differences among Asians but important commonalties between Asian and Western countries. The governments of China and Indonesia take a different, and in some ways contradictory, stance from that of Singapore and Malaysia, and major differences exist between governments and nongovernmental organizations in the region. At the same time, all governments of the region accept the principle of international law that there are particularly egregious human rights abuses that can never be tolerated, including torture and political murder.

- No obvious relationship exists among economic growth, level of economic development, and overall protection of human rights in Asia. In many East Asian countries some social and economic rights, such as the right to education, have been enhanced by economic development, but other rights have been ignored or actively violated, such as the right to take part in trade unions or to enjoy "just and favorable" working conditions. Likewise, in terms of political and civil rights, some rights, such as freedom of expression, appear to be enhanced in some countries by economic development; on other rights, such as the right not to be subjected to torture, level of economic development has little bearing.

- Rapid economic growth has produced new kinds of abuses that are challenging East Asian governments' claim to deliver "growth with equity." Squatters are forcibly, and often violently, evicted to make way for new development projects, or tribal peoples are tricked into signing over ancestral land for commercial operations. Workers are locked into unsafe buildings and forced to work under Dickensian conditions to ensure maximum profits for Asian business owners. And corruption combined with conspicuous consumption has increased social tensions between the very rich and the very poor in many Asian towns and cities.

- "Commercial diplomacy," or the assumption that economic development will improve human rights protection, is not in itself a substitute for a human rights policy that addresses both short- and long-term human rights problems. At the same time, the importance of U.S. trade and business interests in the region means both that a human rights policy not linked in some way to trade policy will rapidly become irrelevant and that the leverage brought about by increased economic interests must be used in pursuit of human rights goals.

The "Asian Concept of Rights"

Beginning about 1990 but gathering force as the 1993 Vienna World Conference on Human Rights approached, several Asian governments—notably Singapore, China, Indonesia, and Malaysia—set forth an "Asian concept of human rights," which in its most basic version argues that economic development has to precede the full flowering of political and civil rights, that Asians place greater value on the harmony of the community than on individual freedoms, and that interpretation of international standards on human rights should be left up to individual states to determine, in accordance with their history, culture, political system, and level of economic development.[3]

The first two premises of the Asian concept of human rights may be contradictory. The first suggests that exercise of individual rights will emerge naturally from economic development; the second suggests that even in developed Asian societies, stability and order will be more highly valued than protection of individual rights.

China and Indonesia have been the most vocal proponents of the first premise. Few would argue with China's statement in its White Paper on human rights that "for any country or nation, the right to subsistence is the most important of all human rights, without which the other rights are out of the question."[4] But some scholars, such as the economist and philosopher Amartya Sen, point out that guaranteeing subsistence depends on some freedom of expression and government accountability. The classic example is the Great Leap Forward in China: Had Chinese felt free to tell the truth about agricultural production, a famine that killed as many as 30 million between 1959 and 1961 could have been avoided. Many have suggested that the Three Gorges Dam project in China, in which an estimated one million people may have to be resettled, is a catastrophe in the making, but the absence of public debate will prevent the project from being stopped or its flaws corrected. The famine in East Timor in 1976–77 also was caused more by Indonesia's controls on population movement and access to the territory than it was by a food shortage—which could have been easily rectified.

An Indonesian official echoes the Chinese position:

> Most of the Asian countries also happen to be at the level of development which necessitates the accordance of priority to the fulfillment of the most basic rights of peoples, such as the eradication of illiteracy, the alleviation of poverty, the improvement of health and the creation of employment opportunities.
>
> After all, how can one express one's opinions freely if one is illiterate; how can one really enjoy the right to property if one lives well below the poverty line; and how can one join in labor associations if one is unemployed?[5]

There are two flaws to the argument. The first is the notion that the ability to exercise or enjoy basic civil rights depends on economic status or level of education (implying illiterate farmers can have no opinion on government actions that directly affect their lives). The second is the suggestion that governments will be able to alleviate poverty and uphold other economic rights most effectively without a free flow of ideas or public participation in the decision-making process.

Senior minister of Singapore Lee Kuan Yew and Malaysian Prime Minister Mahathir bin Mohamad take a different stance than leaders of their larger, and poorer, neighbors. Both argue that even if everyone were highly educated, some curbs on freedom of expression would still be necessary for the good of society. According to Lee:

> I find parts of [the American system] totally unacceptable: guns, drugs, violent crime, vagrancy, unbecoming behavior in public—in sum, the breakdown of civil society. The expansion of the right of the individual to

behave or misbehave as he pleases has come at the expense of orderly society. In the East the main object is to have a well-ordered society so that every-
body can have maximum enjoyment of his freedoms. This freedom can only
exist in an ordered state and not in a natural state of contention and
anarchy.[6]

If carried to a logical conclusion, this argument suggests that economic
growth without strong state intervention and, by extension, restrictions
on certain rights can lead to a breakdown of society with all the evils apparent in the West. Such a premise runs counter to the argument often
made from the South Korean and Taiwan experiences that economic
development will lead to a progressively more open society. The Singaporean stance may stem from the fact that Singapore is already wealthy
enough that the rationale of authoritarian controls to produce economic growth no longer applies. If the Indonesian-Chinese argument held that
economic development would lead to enhanced political freedoms, Singapore should be the freest state in Asia.

Bilahari Kausikan, another Singaporean government official, argues
that "good government," even in a developed society, requires certain
restrictions on rights to preserve order. Arbitrary detention is acceptable
in order to deal with military rebels or religious and other extremists. Curbs
on freedom of expression are allowable to avoid fanning racial tensions
or exacerbating social divisions. "Draconian laws" can be used to
break up the power of entrenched interests, to carry out land reform, for
example.[7]

Kausikan's view is antithetical to the idea that individual civil and political rights will expand naturally as economic development proceeds; the
curbs he suggests have little to do with economic status. This also illustrates the problem with an authoritarian government making decisions
about what rights to restrict and why. Who is to say when arbitrary
detention becomes "necessary" or whether the label "extremist" will be
applied indiscriminately to those who oppose the government, as was
the case with the social workers and church figures arrested in Singapore
in 1987 and 1988? Who will judge whether a newspaper article or speech
incites racial violence or merely calls for an end to government discrimination against an ethnic group? Who is to say whether "draconian
laws" serve to substitute one set of entrenched interests for another? This
was the case in the Philippines, where martial law decrees helped enrich
former president Ferdinand Marcos and his cronies. In Indonesia, controls on freedom of expression and laws against defaming the head of state
make serious investigation of the Suharto family's business interests all
but impossible.

Many scholars of Asia have argued for a variant on the "development first" proposition: that a certain degree of authoritarianism—suppression of political parties and protection of the state from the pressures of competing interest groups—was necessary to take the hard political and economic decisions that produced the region's spectacular growth. Certainly there were many in Korea who believed that economic development required political stability, and the only guarantee of that stability was a strong central government with the ability to take coercive measures against the political opposition and the business community. Columbia University professor John Bresnan has made a similar case for Indonesia, that strong central control, which protected decision makers from competing interest groups, combined with continuity of basic economic policies, enabled the Suharto government to adopt long-term policies that protected the rural sector, increased educational opportunities, and facilitated the broadening of the industrial base beyond oil and oil-based products.[8]

It would be hard, however, to argue that the suppression of political rights necessitated the violations of civil rights that occurred under these authoritarian administrations, such as the widespread political arrests, torture, and summary executions of the Park Chung-hee and Chun Doo-hwan years in South Korea or the first two decades of the New Order in Indonesia.[9] But without channels to criticize the government and hold police and military accountable for abuse, there is no check on excesses save the innate benevolence of the government in power.

A little authoritarianism can soon turn into a lot. This is why martial law or emergency regulations that temporarily deprive citizens of rights in the name of national security or public order can be so dangerous; once extra powers have been granted security forces, they often become institutionalized. For example, a state of emergency has been in effect in Brunei since 1962, and in Indonesia, the Operational Command to Restore Order and Security (KOPKAMTIB) was in operation from late 1965 to the end of 1988 (and continues under another name to this day).

Another flaw in the argument that authoritarianism may be essential to growth is that it ignores the possibility that factors other than authoritarianism may have been equally important in producing economic achievements. As a 1994 issue of the *Economist* points out, "If dictators made countries rich, Africa would be an economic colossus."[10] It may well be that earlier democratization would have produced greater economic gains for Taiwan and South Korea, or that Singapore and Indonesia could grant a greater measure of political and civil rights without doing any damage—and perhaps even enhancing—their ability to guarantee social and economic rights.

Equating Growth of the Middle Class with Improved Human Rights

As for the future, many U.S. and international policymakers suggest that if economic growth is allowed to continue unhampered, human rights protection will take care of itself; a growing middle class will demand democratization. Because the argument is so pervasive, especially as the "commercial diplomacy" of many Western countries in Asia intensifies, it is worth examining in more detail.

The growth-equals-democracy argument is the classic "modernization" theory of the late 1950s, posited by, among others, Daniel Lerner in *The Passing of Traditional Society*. According to Lerner, increasing urbanization leads to rising literacy, literacy to increased media exposure and then to participation in the political process. "The model evolved in the West is a historical fact," says Lerner. "That same basic model appears in virtually all modernizing societies on all continents of the world regardless of variations in race, color [or] creed."[11] Events in Thailand in May 1992 seemed to support Lerner—it was middle-class professionals in the streets with their cellular phones who gave a major boost to democratization by forcing the ouster of an unpopular general who had come to power in a coup. The middle class as a catalyst for change also has been used to explain the rising pressure for democratization and the lifting of some controls on freedom of expression and association in Taiwan and Korea.

Lerner's theory has been challenged repeatedly by dependency theorists, by cultural determinists, by Marxists, and by Lee Kuan Yew—and other Singaporean officials—who argued that what Asians care about is efficiency, not democracy, and that order and development are more important than freedom. Bilahari Kausikan has argued that "popular pressures against East and Southeast Asian governments may not be so much for human rights or democracy but for good government: effective, efficient, and honest administrations able to provide security and basic needs with good opportunities for an improved standard of living."[12]

The problems with such simplistic correlations are evident in Indonesia, Malaysia, and China. In Indonesia, business interests that might otherwise have been a force for democratization are either too closely linked to patronage structures of the central government, such as the enormous conglomerates of the Suharto family, or to the ethnic Chinese, who for the most part do not see their interests served by democratization, despite the political and social discrimination they have endured under the New Order government. A government by a democratically elected Muslim majority could institute a policy akin to the New Economic Policy of Malaysia whereby *pribumi*, or indigenous entrepreneurs, would be deliberately favored and the discrimination against the Chinese could intensify. Moreover, regionalism in Indonesia militates against democratization. As one observer has noted, "While Filipino landlords and Indian businessmen and landlords demand representative institutions through which the political parties they control can participate, the interests of military and bureaucratic regional elites in Indonesia are better served by their links with the center than through elected representative institutions."[13]

Malaysia experienced dramatic growth in its middle class between 1970 and 1990, which transformed the composition of that group from overwhelmingly Chinese to about one third Malay. This transformation came less as a natural result of economic growth than as a result of deliberate state intervention after severe racial riots in 1969 to have what amounted to an affirmative action policy in favor of Malays. The end result politically was to strengthen the state rather than have the new middle class become a check on state power.

Finally, there is the complex situation in China. During the China visit of Ron Brown, the late U.S. Secretary of Commerce, in August 1994, spokespersons for the U.S. Department of Commerce extolled the virtues of increased trade and foreign investment in China, including the growth of the purchasing power of the average Chinese, the growth of the middle class, and eventual demands for democratization. Perhaps—but in the short run, Chinese citizens who demand political change face arrest as "counterrevolutionaries." A new set of security laws, promulgated in June 1994, has narrowed the boundaries for lawful dissent and increased the penalties on those who venture beyond them. Moreover, many China specialists argue that the economic reforms were designed from the outset to preserve the party's power, giving it a new legitimacy in the context of a changed international environment. While the reforms may mean some redistribution of power and the emergence of new groups and organizations, the latter will be dependent for the near term on party patronage, and the end result is to bolster the status quo rather than to democratize.[14] The social changes wrought by reform therefore do not guarantee enhanced protection of human rights, and those who are concerned about ongoing abuses must find ways to address them now, rather than wait for the middle-class millennium.

The Notion of Basic Rights

Even government officials in Asia who support an "Asian" concept of rights acknowledge that there are certain violations of political and civil rights that no Asian government would countenance, no matter what the stage of economic development. The list varies, depending on which official is speaking. Kausikan lists genocide, murder, torture, and slavery; his colleague, Kishore Mahbubani, has a slight variant: "torture, slavery, arbitrary killings, 'disappearances,' or shooting of innocent demonstrators."[15]

These lists are instructive, because they include precisely the abuses around which much Western criticism is centered. They are also the abuses that may be the least subject to change with economic development. Examples include:

- massacres in Cambodia (1975–79);
- killings in East Timor (1975–84, 1991);
- Kwangju killings, Korea (1980);
- Beijing killings (June 1989);
- Rangoon killings, Burma (September 1988);
- political killings and disappearances in the Philippines (1972–88);
- killings in Aceh, North Sumatra (1989–91);
- killings in Bangkok (1976, 1992);
- torture in South Korea, China/Tibet, Indonesia/East Timor, Cambodia, Burma, the Philippines;
- slavery of commercial sex workers in Thailand and elsewhere in Asia and compensation for "comfort women" from Asia enslaved by Japan during World War II.

Political imprisonment also has been a major concern of Western countries, but it is worth noting that international concern about arbitrary detention in China largely grew out of attention to the killings in Tiananmen Square. To the extent political imprisonment has become a major human rights issue in South Korea, Taiwan, Indonesia, the Philippines, and Vietnam, it is because elites and human rights organizations from those countries made it one.

In terms of the *principle* of what constitutes "hard-core" human rights violations, there does not seem to be enough difference between East and West to warrant a separate "Asian concept of human rights." The concern of some Asian officials about economic development notwithstanding, it is protection of individuals against torture and arbitrary killing that they hold to be most fundamental, even if they are no more consistent about addressing abuses than their Western counterparts. On closer examination, the major argument that some Asian governments have with the West is not over different principles of human rights. It is over the tone, style, and means used to address political and civil human rights violations; the use of aid and trade conditions in the battle for human rights; and the tendency to equate human rights with democracy, with the implicit attacks on the legitimacy of some political systems that equation entails.

Economic and Social Rights

Where do economic, social, and cultural rights fit into the debate? For the most part, they are ignored. None of the defenders of the "Asian concept" of rights, such as Malaysia, China, Indonesia, and Singapore, has ratified the ICESCR; nor, for that matter, has the United States. The United States and other countries rarely challenge Asian governments over protection of these rights for several reasons. First, and most important, there is very little understanding of social and economic rights as human rights and very little pressure on Western governments from their own constituencies to address them. Major international human rights organizations, such as Amnesty International and Human Rights Watch, have not yet fully embraced social, economic, and cultural rights in their mandates. U.S. legislation with human rights language, from the 502(b) section of the Foreign Assistance Act to several sections of the Trade Act, deny U.S. aid and trade to countries that engage in gross violations, defined as executions, disappearances, widespread arbitrary arrests—all of which are violations of civil and political, not social and economic, rights. Indeed, it is precisely because the violations of political and civil rights so often lead to immediate physical suffering and death that they arouse international attention—whereas denials of education, health care, employment, and trade union rights do not.

Many also assume that the impressive economic performance of most East Asian countries automatically entails protection of internationally recognized rights to health, education, employment, and an "adequate standard of living." For the majority of the population, this is undoubtedly true. But Asian nongovernmental organizations (NGOs) are increasingly attacking their governments on violations of these rights as they apply to specific groups: indigenous peoples, migrant workers, ethnic minorities, and women, for example. Many Asian NGOs also are increasingly concerned that development policies that have brought about short-term gains in living standards may not be sustainable and will have long-term negative consequences for large numbers of people through pollution, environmental degradation, or reduced access to land and water resources. Some Asian NGOs also are concerned that economic models that emphasize free markets, unrestricted foreign investment, and dismantling of state controls serve to increase the gap between rich and poor, increase regional economic disparities, reduce social welfare measures designed to help the urban and rural poor, and result in restrictions on worker rights.[16]

Asian governments have brought social and economic rights into the debate over human rights in three ways. As noted, the governments of China and Indonesia argue that protecting the right to economic subsistence must precede the granting of all other rights. They, and many of their Western admirers, have sought to have their economic achievements given more attention in assessment of their human rights record, and object to trade conditions as undermining their ability to protect the economic rights of their citizens. Just as sanctions in Iraq and Haiti resulted in a declining living standard for those the sanctions were designed to help, they argue, U.S. revocation of MFN status in China or of tariff benefits under the Generalized System of Preferences program in Indonesia would set back economic development. As Kishore Mahbubani put it, "If current Western policies had been in force in the 1950s and '60s, the dynamic economic growth and gradual democratization of Taiwan and South Korea could have been cut off before they had a chance to develop, by the demand that authoritarian governments be dismantled."[17]

The Impact of Growth on Human Rights in Practice

If the relationship between growth and protection of human rights is difficult to sort out in theory, it does not become much clearer by examining actual practices in East Asian countries. In most East Asian countries, the ability of governments to protect some of the economic and social rights outlined in the ICESCR has improved over the last two decades for a majority of the population. If the right to an adequate standard of living (Article 11) can be roughly assessed by reduction in the number of people living below the poverty line, then Indonesia, Malaysia, Singapore, and Thailand made significant progress, according to the World Bank, between the early 1970s and the mid-1980s.[18]

But in Thailand, according to an International Monetary Fund report, "the incidence of poverty was actually higher in 1991, on the heels of years of tremendous export-based growth, than 10 years earlier, prior to both the adjustment process and the economic boom."[19] Looking at aggregate national figures, life expectancy in all East Asian countries increased substantially between 1960 and 1990, suggesting improved capacity to protect the right of citizens to enjoy "the highest attainable standard of physical and mental health" (Article 12), and school enrollment figures rose substantially for most countries—Burma is a notable exception—in the region between 1970 and 1990.

East Asian countries performed far worse—in some cases abysmally—with regard to other provisions of the ICESCR, and in some cases economic growth exacerbated the problem. Violations of Articles 7 and 8—the enjoyment of just and favorable conditions of work and the right to form and join the trade unions—were rampant throughout the region. The creation of special economic zones where unionization is effectively banned and where workers are forced to work excessively long hours in fire-prone factories characterized many parts of East Asia. Worker unrest, focused in part on demands for independent unions, plagued both China and Indonesia in the same period.

The right to social security, guaranteed by Article 9 of the ICESCR, is becoming a major issue in China due to the unprecedented flow of millions of rural migrants attracted by economic opportunities in the southern coastal provinces. The lack of a social safety net, combined with the perception—often a reality—of an increasing gulf between rich and poor in countries such as Indonesia and Thailand, suggests a more widespread problem. The right of peoples (not governments) to freely dispose of their natural wealth and resources, as provided for in Article 1, implies a guarantee of ancestral land and resource rights. Asian NGOs believe that right has been eroded steadily throughout large parts of East Asia, land-titling programs in the Philippines and some parts of Indonesia notwithstanding. Finally, despite their claims to the contrary, both Indonesia and China have violated another right guaranteed by Article 1—the right of all peoples to self-determination and the ability to "freely determine their political status and freely pursue their economic, social and cultural development"—with regard to East Timor and Tibet.

If the relationship between economic growth and the protection of economic, social, and cultural rights is uneven, the link between growth and the improvement of political and civil rights is even less apparent. We can start with the "hard-core" violations listed by the two Singaporean officials—summary executions, shooting of innocent demonstrators, torture, and disappearances—and look at three countries, China, Indonesia, and South Korea, over the twenty years between 1974 and 1994. While hard data on these violations are not available (they are not published by national statistic bureaus, and human rights organizations cannot know what goes on in police lockups), the broad outlines can be ascertained. They show no obvious correlations between growth and protection of human rights.

In all three countries, economic growth shot upward, albeit with setbacks and at different rates. China, in the final throes of the Cultural Revolution, experienced a slight downturn in growth between 1974 and 1976, but even at the height of the political upheaval in 1969–70, the economy still grew at a healthy rate. In fact, in the immediate aftermath of the Great Leap Forward, between 1960 and 1962, China's economic growth had been steady. Yet that growth did not prevent a major political disaster from taking place.

When Deng Xiaoping entered upon his economic reform program, a period of even more rapid economic growth began. From 1980 to 1988, China's gross domestic product (GDP) gradually increased to 11 percent. It fell back to 3.9 and 4.5 percent respectively in 1989 and 1990, began booming again in 1991–92, then shot up to an extraordinary 13.4 percent in 1993. Although the savage state-sponsored violence of the Cultural Revolution ended in 1976, it would be foolish to argue that economic growth had anything to do with the cessation of Red Guard atrocities. As far as can be ascertained, the use of torture has continued since 1978. The Tiananmen Square crackdown of June 1989 illustrated that a steadily growing economy did not guarantee restraint on the part of security forces when the legitimacy of the party appeared to be at stake. In Tibet, the shooting of unarmed demonstrators on October 1, 1987, came seven years after economic and political reforms had begun following the visit of Chinese Communist Party Secretary-General Hu Yaobang's visit in 1980. After the Cultural Revolution, "disappearances"—in which government security forces take a person into custody and then refuse to acknowledge the detention or disclose his or her whereabouts—were not a problem until 1994, when activists were secretly detained and held incommunicado.[20]

In Indonesia, the rate of growth between 1974 and 1978 was 6.9 percent. Between 1979 and 1981 it averaged 7.7 percent. In the period between 1982 and 1988, it declined to 3.3 percent with the drop in oil prices, then shot up again to 7.1 percent between 1988 and 1991.[21] In 1992 and 1993 growth continued at about 6.2 percent. Again, no correlation exists between economic growth and a reduction in the most severe human rights abuses. Indonesia invaded East Timor in 1975, with a huge death toll from a combination of direct killings and war-related famine over the next three years—probably upward of 100,000, with some sources putting the toll at twice that figure. As many as 2,000 people, most of them civilians, are believed to have been killed during the Indonesian army's counterinsurgency operations in Aceh from 1989 to 1991. Incidents of the army firing on peaceful demonstrators showed no decrease, with the September 1984 Tanjung Priok incident in Jakarta followed seven years later by the November 1991 massacre in Dili, East Timor. In both cases, the death toll is believed to be around 100, but no systematic, independent investigation was carried out in either case.[22] Torture continued unchecked, from Medan to Jakarta, as late as 1994, and there was every indication that police and army officials believed that torturing prisoners was part of standard interrogation procedure.[23]

GDP grew in South Korea at a rate of 9.5 percent from 1965 to 1980 and at about 8.6 percent from 1980 to 1987. The growth rate was 12 percent between 1987 and 1988, then decreased from 9.6 percent in 1990 to 9.1 percent in 1991 to 5.1 in 1993, and finally to 4.9 percent in 1993.[24] The worst crackdown of the period took place during the Kwangju massacre in May 1980; anywhere from 1,000 to 2,000 people are believed to have died when riot police and paratroopers used rifles and fixed bayonets against student demonstrators and others. While no killings approaching the scale of the Kwangju massacre followed, other abuses, particularly torture, continued to be pervasive. It took widespread public concern about the torture-related death of a student named Park Chong-chol in January 1987 to bring about a change. The reforms initiated by President Roh Tae-woo in 1987 encouraged greater discussion about the case in the National Assembly and led to its reinvestigation. The combination of outcry and public discussion was undoubtedly a factor in the gradual diminution of reports of torture from 1988 on, although the problem has by no means been eradicated.

Little evidence exists that the abuses in these countries were affected one way or another by economic growth per se. The exception would be the two years following the Tiananmen crackdown in China, when it could be argued that abuses led to a deterioration in economic growth. Likewise, the reduced incidence of torture in Korea had more to do with democratization than with economic growth, although the two are not unrelated.

If we look at arbitrary detention in the same countries over the same period, China's spectacular growth does not appear to have resulted in any lessening of this practice. Clearly, there has been no return to the scale of detention that characterized the Cultural Revolution, nor is there likely to be. But if we consider the period between 1979 and 1994, the waves of political imprisonment that would be defined as arbitrary detention by the United Nations have not lessened with continued growth. If anything, the reverse seems to have been the case since 1989, as the government appears determined not to let the economic reforms lead to challenges to party rule. In Tibet as well, from 1987 onward, detention increased as public demonstrations of support for the Dalai Lama took place.

In Indonesia, as the period 1974 to 1994 began, tens of thousands of suspected supporters of the Indonesian Communist Party who had been detained without charge or trial between 1965 and 1967 following Sukarno's overthrow remained imprisoned; most of those people had been released by 1981 after intensive international pressure. Thousands were also detained on Atauro island off the coast of East Timor following the Indonesian invasion in 1975; most were released by 1987, although some were transferred to regular prisons. The use of the draconian antisubversion law to punish nonviolent critics and opponents of President Suharto's New Order was common through the late 1980s. While that law, which makes subversion a capital offense, is still on the books, the tendency over the last five years has been to use political charges under the Criminal Code, which carry lesser penalties, to arrest outspoken critics. An apparent trend downward in the number of arrests of Suharto critics for nonviolent expression and association was reversed in 1995 and 1996 as the president's own vulnerability, intolerance of criticism, and determination to resist demands for political change increased.

In South Korea there is little obvious correlation between arbitrary detention and economic growth over the last twenty years. The Chun Doo-hwan government, from 1979 (after the assassination of Park Chung-hee) to 1987, was worse than its immediate predecessor in terms of sheer numbers of political arrests, most of them under the repressive National Security Law (NSL), which criminalizes the act of belonging to or supporting "anti-state" (that is, pro–North Korea) organizations. Despite South Korea's impressive gains in terms of democratization since 1987, there were more arrests under the NSL in 1990, 1991, and 1992 than in any year of the Chun government except 1987.[25] That fact, in and of itself, should be a reminder of the dangers of equating democracy and human rights.

In terms of freedom of expression, Korea has shown the most visible progress since 1987. In Indonesia, freedom of expression increased steadily from about 1990 until 1994—when three news publications were arbitrarily closed down; a chill has descended over the media since. In China, while many observers point to the increasing frankness and willingness to speak out against their Chinese colleagues, public discourse on political and economic issues is still tightly controlled, with increasing attention to the dangers—from the government's perspective—of the Internet.

Rights Unrelated to Development

Obviously, there are problems with using simple growth statistics. Even if the statistics are reliable, which is not always the case, there would almost certainly be a time lag between certain kinds of economic development and improvement in human rights. It is also true, however, that many human rights issues in East Asia are not directly affected by economic growth. Issues linked to nationalism confound traditional stereotypes. An improvement in the standard of living of Tibetans or East Timorese does not buy loyalty toward Beijing or Jakarta respectively. Indeed, improved educational opportunities can have the opposite effect. As people who believe themselves under occupation have more opportunity to understand the nature of the economic and political relationship with the colonizing power, they may become more, not less, determined in their opposition. Economic reforms and greater access to Tibet followed

Hu Yaobang's visit there in 1980, but the largest political demonstrations against Chinese rule that Lhasa had seen since the 1950s took place in September and October 1987, seven years after the reforms had taken root. A July 1994 policy conference on Tibet in Beijing, designed to promote economic development of the Tibetan Autonomous Region, resulted in tighter controls over monasteries, increased surveillance of Tibetan cadres suspected of harboring nationalist sympathies, and a dramatic increase in political imprisonment.[26]

An analogous situation prevails in East Timor. The large pro-independence demonstration on November 12, 1991, in Dili on which Indonesian forces opened fire was led largely by young people who were children at the time of the Indonesian invasion and who grew up better off economically than their parents had been under the Portuguese. The notion of human dignity is critical here—economic advances, if accompanied by second-class status or racial or ethnic discrimination, rarely lead to improvements in human rights.

Likewise, human rights problems linked to specific political situations are also unlikely to be changed dramatically by economic growth. One result of North Korean leader Kim Il-sung's death in August 1994, for example, was an outbreak of demonstrations in the South demanding reunification with the North, and South Korea's then-President Kim Young-sam's use of the NSL to arrest thousands of students, academics, and other political protesters who joined in. Some suggested the crackdown came as a result of the South Korean president's need to bolster support among conservatives for his Democratic Liberal Party after by-election losses the previous May.[27]

The lack of basic civil rights for the people of Hong Kong is a legacy of British colonial control. However, clear evidence of compilation of dossiers on residents whom China considers politically suspect, a denial of visas to those active in the Chinese dissident movement, and a crackdown on the press clearly had nothing to do with patterns of economic development in Hong Kong and everything to do with the political dynamics of the recent 1997 takeover.

Finally, the use of torture is more clear-cut, if no less problematic. Even those who argue that economic growth requires some degree of authoritarianism do not suggest that it necessitates brutality. China has ratified the U.N. Convention Against Torture and Other Forms of Cruel, Inhuman or Degrading Treatment or Punishment, and Indonesia has signed it. Yet economic growth has not stopped the continued use of torture as a routine form of interrogation to obtain "confessions" and inflict summary punishment. Nor does torture disappear with rising income levels of police. Rather, it is an abuse that can be curbed only by a systematic effort by senior government officials to denounce it and severely punish those who use it or by free public debate that can shed light on practices that a government may like to keep hidden, as in the Philippines after 1986, when a key intelligence agency was disbanded and secret detentions all but ended.

The Underside of Development

The notion that development automatically brings human rights improvements is questionable in the case of industrial and service workers. Worker rights soon may become the most divisive human rights issue in Asia. It symbolizes the social transformation and dislocations taking place in Asia: the flow of workers from rural areas into cities; the declining place of agriculture in the GNP of many countries; and the changing role of women, especially with the importance of female workers in key export-oriented industries such as garments, shoes, toys, and electronics.

The issue of worker rights is also highly charged politically. Asian governments see it as a disguised protectionist tool used by the North against the South. At the same time, many NGOs in the region see inattention to worker rights as symbolic of the collusion between their governments and the West in the interests of more profits. Concern over worker rights in Asia has become a major issue for labor lobbies in developed countries, and in the United States more economic sanctions are written into law for violation of labor rights than for any other single kind of abuse.

The internationalization of labor flows has meant that the lack of worker rights in host countries has led to serious diplomatic tensions in the region. These tensions have erupted as an issue between the Philippines and Malaysia, for example, over the treatment of Filipino domestic workers in Malaysia. It is also a source of tension between Indonesia and Malaysia over Indonesian guest workers in the latter, and between Thailand and Japan over the treatment of Thai women illegally recruited to work in Japanese brothels.

Worker rights is not only a question of wages and working conditions, although those are the key issues that led to an estimated 10,000 strikes and work stoppages in China in 1993, or the 15,000 to 20,000 workers out on the streets of Medan, North Sumatra, in April 1994. Some degree of freedom of association is essential, so that workers have some ability to negotiate the terms of their employment. As long as government regulation and official "unions" fail to function, workers are going to continue to get hurt—or killed—as the result of unsafe working conditions. The fire at the Kader toy factory in Thailand in May 1993, or at a toy factory in Shenzhen, China, that killed 84 women in November 1993, or at the textile factory in Fuzhou, China, that killed 61 the following December might all have been prevented had the workers had some ability to organize and present grievances. One hardware factory in Shenzhen reportedly had five separate accidents in one week where workers' fingers were severed.[28]

The tight controls on freedom of association, combined with mounting citizen grievances, also mean that Asian governments are in many cases creating a pressure cooker with the potential to cause far greater future damage than relaxing controls would do now. Deng Xiaoping and the rest of the Chinese leadership fear nothing more than the "Polish disease"—the emergence of a politically sophisticated workers' movement backed by the country's intellectuals. The Chinese government has tried to nip any such alliance in the bud, as with the arrests in mid-1994 of intellectuals and labor rights activists who had established the League for the Protection of the Rights of the Working People of the People's Republic of China.[29] The message of the league, which stated explicitly that it did not challenge the principles of the Chinese Communist Party and was not a union but merely an interest group, was that inflation, corruption, large-scale unemployment, and decreasing public safety were becoming such serious issues that workers were likely to rebel in large numbers unless their rights were respected.

In Medan, North Sumatra—a province of Indonesia—on April 14–15, 1994, the lack of any outlet to address mounting grievances over wage levels and benefits led thousands of workers to take to the streets, where their anger was easily manipulated by other political forces and led to an outbreak of anti-Chinese violence in which one Chinese businessman was killed and hundreds of Chinese-owned stores vandalized. The major issues of the massed workers could have been addressed in a more responsible fashion had the workers been able to organize legally; instead, the Indonesian authorities had a major public order problem on their hands. Another major issue in the Medan riots was the "invisible costs" of production in Indonesia in the form of corruption and illegal levies. The labor leaders claimed that if employers could reduce their pay offs to local officials, civilian and military, they would have more to pay their workers without affecting overall profitability.

Forced labor—particularly in the form of debt bondage—is another increasingly important issue across East Asia. If wages, working conditions, and the right to organize are the salient issues of urban Asia, forced labor is an issue on the plantations, mines, and timber concessions of the region, often involving upland indigenous peoples and migrant workers. In Irian Jaya, a Korean-owned plywood company hired ethnic Asmat loggers. In the remote camp where the loggers lived and worked, the only source of basic foodstuffs was the company store. There the workers were allowed to buy on credit, but no accounts were kept. At the end of the month, the workers would be told that their credit purchases exceeded their wages, and they were not paid—even though the workers had no way of verifying the company's statements.

The increase in human trafficking that has followed trading routes in Asia leads to another form of forced labor. Burmese and Chinese women and girls who are recruited to work in brothels by cash payments—usually to their parents—and the promise of good jobs in restaurants or hotels. With the young women ensconced in brothels, the owners withhold the cash payment as a debt that the women must work off. They are kept in virtual slavery until the owner arbitrarily decides that the debt is paid or a woman is no longer wanted. If a woman tries to escape, she faces arrest in Thailand as an illegal immigrant. The same is true for Indonesian women trafficked to Malaysia, and Thai and Filipina women trafficked to Japan. Such trafficking also contributes to the spread of human immunodeficiency virus (HIV) and acquired immunodeficiency syndrome (AIDS)—a phenomenon that is as much a rights issue as it is a public health problem. Even if many countries now recognize that AIDS must be addressed as an issue that transcends national boundaries, there is no such real recognition about worker rights.

Nonetheless, growing regional ties have given labor issues a higher profile for several reasons. Many Asian and international observers acknowledge that some of the worst working conditions in Asia are in plants set up with Asian capital, from Singapore, Hong Kong, Taiwan, or Korea in particular. The disastrous fire in China's Fujian Province in December 1993, which killed sixty-one workers, took place at a Taiwanese-owned firm, and one of the big strikes in Indonesia in 1993 was at a Korean-owned electronics firm. Such occurrences raise the question as to whether Asian governments with an explicit commitment to uphold human rights across borders—such as Japan and Korea—have the will or influence to dictate the practices of their own investors. This situation also gives rise to complacency among U.S. corporations, which can point with pride to the relatively favorable workplace conditions in their own joint ventures and plants versus those of their Asian counterparts. But growing worker discontent is likely to have effects that go beyond a single plant.

If the worker rights issue, from the perspective of Asian governments, points out the ulterior motives of the industrialized countries in taking up human rights issues for their own economic purposes, to local NGOs it illustrates the hypocrisy of their own governments in stressing social and economic rights issues. Trade union rights—the right to organize and bargain collectively—form a key plank of the International Covenant on Economic, Social, and Cultural Rights. Article 8 of that treaty recognizes "the right of everyone to form trade unions and join the trade union of his choice, subject only to the rules of the organization concerned, for the promotion and protection of his economic and social interests." Few countries in East and Southeast Asia fully respect that right, and even in countries that do—the Philippines and Malaysia—exceptions have been made for free trade zones as a way of attracting more investment.

Economic growth in Asia clearly has raised the importance of worker rights, and it has become a major policy issue for the United States in Thailand, Indonesia, and Malaysia. Violations of labor rights practices are particularly susceptible to American economic sanctions, under Section 301 of the Trade Act, the Generalized System of Preferences Program, and legislation relating to the Overseas Private Investment Corporation (OPIC). The worker rights provisions of Section 301 have never been invoked, but some activists have urged that these provisions be explored as an alternative means of exerting economic pressure on China. The U.S. government has taken a prominent role in support of a "social clause" in the World Trade Organization that would require all WTO members to meet basic labor rights standards in order to take advantage of tariff benefits. While the countries in the Association of Southeast Asian Nations (ASEAN) in particular have dismissed the "social clause" as yet another form of protectionism, many NGOs in the region support the idea as a way of preventing labor practices from sinking to the lowest common denominator. For example, if wages in South Korea go up as a result of pressure from unions, foreign businesses simply will move to China or Burma where restrictions are tighter and labor is cheaper.

Asian Responses to Human Rights

In part because of the issues development has raised, in part because of the political consequences of not addressing them, and in part because of the international attention to human rights, there is a growing constituency for human rights issues within East Asia, both nongovernmental and governmental. The strength of that constituency, however, does not always correlate with level of economic development. The government of the Philippines is more committed to the notion of universal human rights than is Singapore, for example, and the NGO movement that has become an important voice for human rights improvements is stronger in Southeast Asia than in Japan or Korea.

The rise in importance of the NGO movement throughout East Asia is linked to economic growth, but the linkage is not always direct. The emergence of quasi-NGOs in China—many of them associated with academic institutions or think tanks—may be the result of both the positive and negative effects of economic growth: positive, with regard to the exposure to ideas that economic reforms have brought, negative in that there is a growing awareness of the need to deal with problems, such as environmental degradation, that development has caused.

There are no human rights NGOs to speak of in Singapore, Brunei, Vietnam, Burma, or North Korea. The reasons for this have more to do with political systems than with economic development. NGOs in Japan are much weaker than Japan's economic strength would suggest. A 1992 directory lists 173 Japanese NGOs, about 80 of which are human rights or environmental in orientation. (NGOs in the Philippines number in the tens of thousands, by contrast.) One reason for the weakness of Japanese NGOs is their historical ties to the political left. Many members of the political elite consider NGOs to be part of the radical fringe, and it is only in the last decade that their work has been taken more seriously. Another factor is that NGOs in Asia have thrived especially in areas where government services are inadequate, and human rights concerns often have emerged from grass-roots development activities. By the time donor countries saw support for NGOs as a useful tool for development, not only Japan but South Korea and Taiwan were already economically advanced.

While the huge expansion of NGOs in the 1980s in East and Southeast Asia—particularly the latter—can be traced in part to the availability of funds from donor countries, the roots of the NGO movement in Asia are deep. The largest human rights organizations in the region emerged in response to political crackdowns in their own countries, when their colleagues were subject to arrest and detention. The West did not prompt these NGOs in terms of the issues that were given priority—getting friends and associates out of prison was paramount. This was true in Indonesia with the formation of the Legal Aid Institute in 1971, in the Philippines after Marcos declared martial law in 1972, in Thailand with the emergence of human rights organizations after the 1973 coup, and in Korea in the mid-1970s. The first—short-lived—human rights organization appeared in China in 1979, at the beginning of the Democracy Wall period, a two-year span of political breathing space made possible by the death of Mao and the arrest of the Gang of Four. A wall in central Beijing became a forum for discussion of political ideas through the posting of large posters. Founder Ren Wanding, who was arrested then, was rearrested after the events of June 1989 and remains in prison today. To claim that concern for political and civil rights is a Western conceit is to do an enormous disservice to the efforts of many Asians to oppose abuse of state power in a period before support for NGOs became a Western vogue.[30]

The accusation by Asian governments that NGOs are a channel for introducing foreign values because of their reliance on foreign funds is a case of the pot calling the kettle black. It is true that indigenous funding for NGOs is almost nonexistent. However, the economic growth of East Asia has been due in part, according to the World Bank, to its openness to foreign ideas and technology—and foreign financing.[31] Their countries have shown no objection to Western aid or development experts, and many of their government institutes receive generous grants from the same donors who fund the NGOs. Why funding for NGOs should be subversive when grants to government agencies and academic institutions are not is a mystery.

A positive consequence of economic growth in Asia is that the NGOs, like their governments, are building regional ties and common interests. The communications revolution has been critical in this regard. For example, when anti-Chinese flyers began circulating in Medan on April 14, one reason NGOs were convinced they were written by the military or its hired thugs was because they were typed, and all self-respecting labor activists had computers.

The recognition of shared interests was instrumental in producing the Bangkok NGO Declaration of March 1993, which effectively rebutted the notion of an "Asian concept of human rights."[32] It became clear at the Bangkok NGO meeting that strong bonds had been established among NGOs within Southeast Asia—especially among Thais, Filipinos, Indonesians, and Malaysians—and between Southeast and South Asia. Korean, Japanese, and Taiwanese organizations, for the most part, were less well-attuned to international debates on human rights and more inward-looking in terms of their own priorities and concerns; Japanese environmental organizations were the exception. By 1996, however, more common ground had been established, with Japanese organizations galvanized by the 1995 Asia-Pacific Economic Cooperation (APEC) summit and parallel NGO conference in Osaka, and several Korean rights groups taking an interest in the practices of Korean companies operating in Southeast Asia.

Perhaps the most important effect of the growth of NGOs is that the demand for human rights, as defined by international law, is becoming more vocal in every East Asian country, including Singapore. This underscores the fact that concern over human rights is not a creation of the West, as some Asian governments would like to depict it. It means that the human rights policies of Western governments have a receptive public audience in Asia.

Many Asian governments have been responsive, at some level, to domestic and/or international pressure on human rights. None of these governments is a monolith, and many officials genuinely support a greater degree of openness. Even some of the governments that are considered hard-liners on human rights have developed mechanisms for responding to criticism, which serve to acknowledge the legitimacy of the issue.

China formed the Chinese Society for the Study of Human Rights, a putative NGO that it sends to international conferences to promote the government viewpoint. It also issued a White Paper on Human Rights in October 1991 as a direct response to criticism of the Tiananmen Square crackdown, as well as a subsequent paper in 1992 on the criminal justice system and the rights of prisoners. There are serious efforts under way in the Institute of Law of the Chinese Academy of Social Sciences to understand international human rights law and how it applies to China and some lively debates on constitutionalism taking place within the academic legal community. Many scholars give credit to that community and to international pressure for the legal reforms passed by the National People's Congress in March 1996.

In June 1993 President Suharto of Indonesia formed a national human rights commission, which proved to be more independent than expected. Three years later it had become a lightning rod for complaints of abuse from all over Indonesia and had succeeded in prosecuting military personnel for human rights abuses in Irian Jaya and East Timor, among other places. As 1996 drew to a close, the commission was facing the toughest challenge of its short life in the face of strong pressure from the president and senior officers to downplay human rights violations in the investigation into the causes and aftermath of the July 1996 riots.

The ASEAN countries have been discussing establishing either a bureau of human rights within the ASEAN secretariat or an Eminent Persons Delegation that would be able to take quick action—of a quiet, diplomatic sort—in case of a major human rights violation in a member country. The problems of any such initiative, however, were demonstrated by the Indonesian response to the conferences on East Timor held in Manila and Bangkok respectively in 1994. Following the conference held in Manila, Indonesia canceled twelve joint ventures worth over $200 million as an expression of displeasure with the Ramos government and arrested 250 Filipino fishermen for allegedly fishing in Indonesian waters. Ramos tried to explain that he could not stop the conference, but he did refuse to issue visas to foreigners—including one to Danielle Mitterand, wife of the French president. Most of the foreign delegates turned up anyway, but the incident was a good illustration of the lengths to which Indonesia was willing to go to prevent discussion of its most serious human rights issue. It was also a good indication of why any ASEAN human rights body was doomed. After a similar conference was held in Thailand, the Indonesian foreign minister, Ali Alatas, said that the "ASEAN spirit included not allowing one country to be used as a platform to discredit another."[33]

Japan's response to the human rights debate has been different. Its human rights practices have not, for the most part, been the subject of much international scrutiny, although human rights groups within Japan and abroad have raised concerns about its treatment of the Korean minority and the *burakumin* or *dowa* (sometimes referred to as the Japanese "untouchables"). Compared to the rest of the region, however, Japan has had a relatively good record on human rights since the end of World War II.

That record, combined with its economic clout as the largest donor in the region, should make Japan a logical partner of the United States in a campaign for human rights improvements in Asia, even given the sensitivities of wartime abuses by Japanese forces. It is true that revelations over the last few years about Japan's use of Asian "comfort women" for its military during World War II have generated more international attention than any abuse taking place in Japan today. Even so, concern that Japan cannot be an effective human rights advocate because of the legacy of the war is voiced more often by Japanese officials than by human rights activists and victims in the region, many of whom would welcome greater Japanese pressure on their governments.

In fact, Japan has played a positive, if low-profile, role in support of human rights. At international meetings, including the 1993 World Conference on Human Rights in Vienna and the annual meetings of the U.N. Commission on Human Rights, Japan usually speaks and votes with the United States, supporting universalism over Asian particularism, rejecting the economic development first argument, and affirming that aid and trade can be used in support of human rights ends. (South Korea takes a similar public stance.)

Japan also has taken concrete steps on a few major human rights issues in the region. Following the Dili massacre in Indonesia in 1991, a letter from the Japanese government was reportedly a critical factor behind President Suharto's decision to set up a national commission of inquiry. Japanese diplomats were also prominent among the observers at the trials of East Timorese in 1992 and 1993. In Burma, Japanese intervention was largely responsible for securing access of the U.N. High Commissioner for Refugees (UNHCR) in 1993 to Arakan, the northwestern state where military atrocities had led to the exodus of some 300,000 refugees to Bangladesh in 1991–92. Japanese efforts also helped obtain family visits for opposition leader Aung San Suu Kyi when she was under house arrest and were responsible in part for bringing about her conditional release in July 1995.

In addition, since 1991 Japan has formally incorporated human rights concerns into its policies on Official Development Assistance (ODA). The relevant principle states that "full attention should be paid to efforts for promoting democratization and introduction of a market-oriented economy and the situation regarding the securing of basic human rights and freedoms in the recipient country."[34] The government has invoked this principle in explaining—after the fact—its cut-off of new aid to Burma after 1988 and the ending of aid programs in Haiti, Zaire, and the Sudan. Japan also has invoked ODA to support democratization in Mongolia and the former Soviet republics of Central Asia.

At the same time, Japan has been critical of what it sees as an over-reliance by the United States on economic sanctions. Tokyo criticized the U.S. stance on Burma, saying that Western isolation of Burma and the de facto trade embargo had pushed Burma's ruling State Law and Order Restoration Council (SLORC) into the arms of China, and objected to American threats to revoke most-favored-nation (MFN) status for China unless human rights improved.

In its 1993 report on ODA, Japan's Ministry of Foreign Affairs noted:

> Where democratization is concerned, each developing country faces economic conditions and social needs unique to it and widely different from other developing countries. Therefore, it is not proper to unilaterally and hastily impose the political system or institutions of Western countries on developing countries. One must view the efforts of democratization of developing countries as a trend. Therefore, it is impractical and improper, for instance, to cut aid immediately after the recipient country exceeds its military spending over a certain limit or it veers away from a democratic model set arbitrarily by the donor country.[35]

On the other hand, where there are clear problems, such as reversals to democratic process, flagrant violations of human rights, or continuing excessive military spending from the perspective of Japan and the international community, Japan has to reconsider its aid policy toward such country. In certain past cases, Japan and/or the international community have been successful in urging a recipient country to remedy an unacceptable situation, obviating the necessity for Japan to alter its aid policy. These cases served to underscore the importance of quiet and continuous demarches to the developing countries.[36]

The influence of Japanese business interests is another major factor in preventing more frequent official resort to economic pressure as a tool of human rights policy. On the other hand, Japan's desire for a greater international role commensurate with its economic power, such as permanent membership in the U.N. Security Council, suggests that the country may be willing to take part in international coalitions to press for human rights improvements through U.N. agencies or through international bodies such as the International Committee of the Red Cross.

U.S. Policy Options

Where does all this leave U.S. policy? Growth has altered the human rights agenda of NGOs and governments, but the impact of growth on human rights practices has not always been positive. Likewise, there is no single set of policy tools that the United States or other developed countries can bring to bear to address human rights abuses in the region.

The tools available to any country to try to curb human rights abuses in another are limited. On the incentive side, they can include long-term programs in support of the rule of law, training of legal scholars and practitioners, educational exchanges, and other development programs. They can include support for NGOs and, in some cases, facilitation of trade and investment. They also can eliminate whatever punitive measures may have previously been imposed.

On the punitive side, they can use stigmatization such as public condemnation, publication of reports, or participation in U.N. resolutions. Other punitive measures include diplomatic demarches, such as delivering a letter from the head of state, refusing to engage in high-level visits, calling in another country's ambassador to express concern, recalling one's own ambassador (or, as in the case of Burma, failing to appoint one), or breaking off diplomatic relations altogether. The threat of economic sanctions is the most obvious—if the most problematic—punitive measure. Sanctions can include withholding loans at international financial institutions, withholding aid, banning commercial sales of certain products, or imposing selective or total embargoes.

Many onlookers assume that East Asia's growing economic strength has affected the utility of some of these tools, since the countries are no longer dependent on the United States for aid, and their economies are resilient enough to withstand other forms of sanctions. In early 1992 the Indonesian government rejected Dutch aid and sent all Dutch development workers packing in response to Dutch criticism of the November 1991 massacre in East Timor. Likewise, China faced down the United States over MFN. And after British newspapers revealed that Margaret Thatcher's government had provided aid to a major hydroelectric project in Malaysia in exchange for that country's purchases of British arms, against the advice from economists, development specialists, and environmentalists, the Malaysian government banned all trade with British companies for seven months. "Why let British companies make money out of Malaysia . . . if we are going to be vilified?" Prime Minister Mahathir Mohamad asked.[37] Former president of Indonesia Sukarno reacted the same way to the United States from a position of total economic collapse in 1964, and we can find similar examples of nationalist reactions from Japan and China in the nineteenth century.

But Asian countries have also responded positively to economic pressure on human rights in the last three years. When threatened by the United States with the revocation of tariff benefits under the Generalized System of Preferences (GSP) program because of violation of worker rights in 1993, the Indonesian government did not reject the pressure—it responded with a series of legal reforms, as yet unenforced, and a significant rise in the minimum wage. As long as it believed the threat from the United States was credible, China responded to the pressure exerted by the MFN debate by releasing some prisoners and entering into negotiations with the International Committee of the Red Cross over access to its prisons.

On balance, however, one effect of Asia's economic power has been to strengthen the will of Asian governments to withstand the West and undermine the will of the West to exert human rights pressure in the first place. "Commercial diplomacy" from the Commerce Department and the U.S. trade representative has to a large extent supplanted the human rights diplomacy of the State Department. Fear of losing out to European and Japanese investors has caused the American corporate community to urge that human rights be soft-pedaled in U.S. policy. At the same time, a strengthened emphasis on security concerns in East and Southeast Asia, stemming both from concern about China's growing military capacity and potential flashpoints involving Asian countries in the Spratly Islands, Taiwan Straits, and the Korean peninsula, have led many policymakers to conclude that U.S. engagement with China must be strengthened and major irritants in the U.S.-China relationship smoothed over. Human rights is one of the chief areas where some policymakers see it expedient to turn a blind eye.

The desire to strengthen economic and security ties at the expense of human rights ignores the extent to which China, and to some degree other East Asian governments, link the three issues. Many Chinese officials see the United States as bent on containment of China, using trade, security, and human rights as cudgels. In 1996 China's efforts to "punish" the United States by giving contracts to Airbus instead of Boeing was a response not just to the demand for release of political prisoners but to U.S. pressure over intellectual property rights, missile technology transfers to Pakistan, and because the United States granted a visa to Taiwan's president and deployed a warship to the Taiwan Straits in March. No evidence suggests that downplaying human rights issues would diminish the Chinese government's belief in a U.S. containment strategy.

It is clear that any effective human rights policy must be linked to trade.

This approach might entail using major government-sponsored corporate visits, such as those of Ron Brown, late secretary of commerce, to Beijing in 1994 and New Delhi in 1995 as a vehicle for broaching human rights issues, or building human rights provisions, such as a "social clause," into major trade agreements. The human rights–trade linkage does not necessarily mean economic sanctions. Many policy analysts—including members of the corporate community, the Clinton administration, many members of the U.S. Congress, and many in the human rights community—increasingly see unilateral sanctions as counterproductive, except in rare circumstances.

Asian governments perceive (correctly) that there is a lack of a domestic consensus in the United States on human rights. The lack of will on the part of the United States, or any other government, to fight abuses in countries that are currently or potentially important trading partners is seen in Asia as the total collapse of the administration's human rights policy. Whatever one thought of the MFN debate—and there were valid concerns about its substance and style—the way the United States justified its precipitate backdown dismayed Asian human rights activists from Sri Lanka to Japan and produced thinly disguised chortles of triumph from Asian governments. It is difficult to believe that any human rights–related economic threat by the United States against a country of East Asia would be taken seriously now because the will to enforce it is so obviously nonexistent.

Effective U.S. Human Rights Policy in East Asia

1. An effective U.S. policy on human rights should be rooted in the international system for protection of human rights and justified as much as possible in terms of international law rather than American values. This means that the United States must ratify the major international human rights treaties to which it is not yet party, such as the International Covenant on Economic, Social and Cultural Rights. It also means that human rights probably should be rhetorically delinked from democratization programs.

2. The United States should work with existing international human rights groups to develop multilateral coalitions that will have the United Nations' "thematic mechanisms" to visit, investigate, and make recommendations to governments that abuse human rights. These mechanisms include the Working Group on Arbitrary Detention; the Working Group on Enforced and Involuntary Disappearances; the Special Rapporteur on Torture and Other Forms of Cruel, Inhuman and Degrading Treatment; the Special Rapporteur on Summary

and Arbitrary Executions; and the Special Rapporteur on Religious Intolerance. Visits by the members of the Committee on Economic, Socia,l and Cultural Rights also should be encouraged. Multilateral pressure on countries with extensive political imprisonment to grant access to the International Committee of the Red Cross also would be useful. Japan would be more likely to join such efforts than to join in the imposition of economic sanctions. However, creating an effective coalition and keeping up the pressure following the U.N. visits—if indeed they take place—to implement the recommendations will still take time, resources, and political will.

3. An effective policy should include development efforts to promote the rule of law, as long as those efforts do not serve to enhance the legitimacy of abusive governments rather than to strengthen their legal system.

4. The United States should pay increasing attention to human rights and development issues, ensuring that political/civil and social/economic rights are treated as indivisible; that bilateral and multilateral aid, trade, and lending policies are consistent with human rights principles; and that groups that are particularly vulnerable to the negative impact of economic development, such as workers, be given high priority.

5. Multilateral efforts should not be seen as a substitute for bilateral measures, and the latter should include criticism of human rights abuses, both private and public. However much Asian governments may resent being publicly stigmatized, public criticism serves as both a form of pressure and a message of support to those who are working for human rights within a country. Appropriate criticism can take the form of anything from public statements at donor meetings to comments at regular State Department briefings, to avoidance of high-profile meetings with representatives of the country in question if the gravity of human rights abuses warrants.

6. The increasing economic importance of East Asia means that the administration should increasingly look to the private sector as a partner in supporting human rights initiatives. The U.S. government should lead, not follow, corporations in defining what those initiatives should be. Businesses need to have more exposure to the human rights, labor, and environmental NGOs working in the countries where they have commercial interests. Trade attachés at U.S. embassies in Asia should be as well versed in human rights issues as their colleagues who produce the State Department's annual report on human rights. They also should be prepared to introduce potential investors to appro-

priate NGOs for discussions on specific regional issues.

7. The administration needs to speak as much as possible with one voice. That does not mean reducing human rights concerns to the lowest common denominator among the State, Commerce, and Treasury departments and the Pentagon and National Security Council (NSC). As with every other foreign policy issue, the president should lead.

8. Economic sanctions, as provided for in U.S. law, should be the tool of last resort. If sanctions are threatened, they must be tied to specific, concrete objectives, and the threat must be credible. If sanctions are imposed, the administration should make clear to the target country precisely what it must do to get the sanctions lifted.

9. A human rights policy should not be tailored to considerations of what is acceptable to Asian governments, since any form of human rights criticism rarely is acceptable. Efficacy in securing human rights improvements is one test of a good policy but not the only one; in some situations abuses may be so grave that strong unilateral action is appropriate simply to send a message, even if the prospects for ending the abuses are slim.

10. A good policy should be sensitive to the concerns and priorities of human rights groups and activists within a country, to the extent that these can be assessed accurately.

The fact remains that international pressure on human rights is essential—as long as one is clear about ends and means. The aim of a human rights policy should be limited and specific: not to overthrow a government or change a political system but to stop—or at least reduce—violations of rights clearly stated in international agreements. A human rights policy that aims at long-term development and ignores ongoing abuses does not deserve the name.

Notes

1. The term "human rights," as is well understood by Asian governments but less so by American officials, is not a reference to some vague set of ethical standards or values but to a specific set of treaties, conventions, resolutions, and declarations of the United Nations, the most important of which is the Universal Declaration of Human Rights proclaimed in 1948. Countries do not sign the Universal Declaration; they agree to abide by its principles by virtue of their membership in the U.N. The other two documents making up the International Bill of Rights are full-fledged treaties, the International Covenant on Civil and Political Rights and the International Covenant on Economic, Social and Cultural Rights (ICESCR, which, incidentally, has not been ratified by the United States). Many East Asian governments are party to both: Japan, North Korea, South Korea, the Philippines, Vietnam,

and Cambodia. As North Korea's presence in the list indicates, ratifying the covenants is no guarantee of respect for their provisions, but it does indicate an acceptance of their legitimacy.

The broad rubric of civil and political rights is too often understood to mean only the right to elect one's representatives and participate in the political process freely, or the rights to freedom of expression, assembly, and association. It also however, includes the protection of physical integrity, such as the right not to be tortured or arbitrarily deprived of life; the right not to be arbitrarily detained; and the right to be protected against arbitrary interference with property.

Economic and social rights include the right to education, to a high standard of health, to work, to form trade unions, to enjoy an "adequate" standard of living, and to be free from hunger. Traditionally, they have been seen as more difficult to enforce than civil and political rights, in part because they seem tied to the question of resources, and in part because it is not always easy to pinpoint a perpetrator when they are violated. Human rights organizations, both in the West and in Asia, originally focused on political and civil rights, in part because violations and remedies were more obvious. If a prisoner is tortured, one can identify the individual or at least the agency responsible, and the remedy is clear—outlaw torture and punish the offenders; there is no obvious economic cost. If a country has a high illiteracy rate, it is not always so clear who is at fault, or whether a "violator" of the right to education can be determined. But proponents of more attention to economic and social rights argue that there are many instances where governments could use resources more effectively in order to guarantee the rights outlined in the ICESCR or where governments take away what people already have. In these cases, the violator is clear: when the government of Burma shut down all universities after 1988, it was a deliberate act violating the right to education that could have been easily reversed. Proponents also point out that while stopping some abuses of civil rights may be cost-free, there are clearly resource questions involved in setting up a good legal system. Increasingly, therefore, both Asian and Western human rights organizations see the two sets of rights as indivisible.

As economic and social rights also require positive action of governments, rather than noninterference, as in the case of most civil and political rights, they seemed at the time the ICESCR was passed by the General Assembly in 1977 to underscore the need for a strong centralized state and thus fit in well with the political agenda of many developing countries in the United Nations, as well as the socialist bloc. (For further reading on this issue, see Danilo Turk, "Final Report on the Realization of Economic, Social and Cultural Rights," UN Document E/CN.4/Sub.2/1992/16, July 3, 1992, pp. 3–9.)

2. In May 1994 President Clinton extended MFN to China unconditionally and renewed MFN again in 1995 and 1996. In 1995 congressional resolutions to overturn that decision never came to a vote. In 1996 a resolution to revoke MFN, fueled more by China's actions against Taiwan the previous March and by the right-to-life movement, was defeated overwhelmingly.

3. See, for example, "Statement by Foreign Minister Ali Alatas on Human Rights" at the 9th ASEAN-EC Ministerial Meeting in Luxembourg, May 30, 1991, in *News and Views INDONESIA* (July 15, 1991), p. 1; Speech by H. E. Liu Huaqiu, head of the Chinese Delegation at the World Conference on Human Rights, Vienna (June 15, 1993); Information Office of the State Council, "Human Rights in China," *Beijing Review* (Nov. 4–10, 1991); S. Wiryono, "Human Rights: Why the Confrontation?" *Nation* (Bangkok) (Apr. 1, 1993). In 1995 and 1996 the four countries that were most vocal about the concept had all but abandoned it in public speeches, but it was taken up with enthusiasm by representatives of Burma and Vietnam in various fora.

4. Information Office of the State Council, "Human Rights in China," *Beijing Review* (Nov. 4–10, 1991).

5. S. Wiryono, "Human Rights: Why the Confrontation?" *The Nation* (Bangkok) (Apr. 1, 1993).

6. Fareed Zakaria, "Culture Is Destiny: A Conversation with Lee Kuan Yew," *Foreign Affairs* (Mar./Apr. 1994), p. 111.

7. Bilahari Kausikan, "Asia's Different Standard," *Foreign Policy* (Fall 1993), p. 38.

8. John Bresnan, *Managing Indonesia* (New York: Columbia University Press, 1993), pp. 286–293.

9. In South Korea, abuses included the mysterious deaths of Professor Ch'oe Chong-kil and Chang Chun-ha in 1973, the torture of students and opposition assemblymen by the KCIA, and judicial executions in 1975 of alleged sympathizers of North Korea after military trials and the use of confessions extracted by torture. The number of political prisoners actually increased under Chun Doo-hwan, and included such well-known political figures as Kim Dae-jung. Torture was commonplace. In Indonesia, the first two decades of the New Order saw the incarceration of thousands of suspected Communists on the penal colony of Buru island, released only in 1979–80; the invasion of East Timor; the periodic suppression of student activists, leading members of the Jakarta intelligentsia, and suspected Muslim militants; and the 1983–85 "mysterious killings" in which an estimated 4,000 men were shot on the streets in a government-organized "anticrime" campaign.

10. "Why Voting Is Good for You," *Economist* (Aug. 27, 1994), p. 15.

11. Daniel Lerner, *The Passing of Traditional Society: Modernizing the Middle East* (Glencoe, IL: The Free Press, 1958), p. 12.

12. Bilahari Kausikan, "Asia's Different Standard," *Foreign Policy*, no. 92 (Fall 1993), p. 37.

13. Harold Crouch, "Democratic Prospects in Indonesia," *Asian Journal of Political Science* 1, no. 2 (Dec. 1993), p. 83.

14. Tony Saich, "The Search for Civil Society and Democracy in China," *Current History* (Sept. 1994), pp. 260–264.

15. Kishore Mahbubani, "Rights: The West Should Nag Less and Listen More,"

International Herald Tribune (Oct. 20, 1992).

16. See, for example, Neelan Tiruchelvam, "Development and the Protection of Human Rights," Paper presented at a conference organized by the Council of Europe, Strasbourg, France (Oct. 1992), pp. 3–4.

17. Mahbubani, "Rights." Aside from the fact that political realities, which Asian government so often deplore, would never have allowed those governments to be abandoned, the suggestion that the use of economic pressure amounts to the dismantling of governments is simply wrong.

18. The World Bank, *The East Asian Miracle: Economic Growth and Public Policy* (New York: Oxford University Press, 1993), p. 33.

19. Danilo Turk, "The Realization of Economic, Social and Cultural Rights," United Nations Document E/CN.4/Sub.2/1992/16, July 3, 1992, p. 25.

20. See Human Rights Watch/Asia and Human Rights in China, "Pressure Off, China Targets Activists," *Human Rights Watch Short Report* 6, no. 1 (1994).

21. Amar Bhattacharya and Mari Pangestu, "Indonesia: Development Transformation and Public Policy," *The Lessons of East Asia* (Washington, DC: World Bank, 1993), pp. 7–8.

22. The Indonesian government did set up a National Commission of Inquiry, the first time it had ever officially investigated a major incident of human rights abuse, but the commission did not do a thorough examination of deaths and disappearances. See Asia Watch, "Remembering History in East Timor" (Apr. 1993).

23. Human Rights Watch/Asia, *Limits of Openness: Human Rights in Indonesia and East Timor* (New York: Human Rights Watch, 1994), p. 93.

24. The first set of figures is from James W. Morley (ed.), *Driven by Growth* (Armonk, NY: M. E. Sharpe, 1993), p. 6, and the annual figures are in Richard D. Fisher, Jr., and John T. Dori, *U.S. and Asia Statistical Handbook*, (Washington, DC: The Heritage Foundation, 1994).

25. Won Soon Park, *The National Security Law*, (Los Angeles, CA: Korea NGOs Network for the UN World Conference on Human Rights, 1993), p. 121.

26. Tibet Information Network and Human Rights Watch, *Cutting Off the Serpent's Head: Tightening Control in Tibet, 1994–95"* (New York, NY: Human Rights Watch, 1996).

27. Steve Glain, "Kim Young Sam Presides Over Divisive Crackdown," *Asian Wall Street Journal Weekly* (Sept. 5, 1994), p. 1.

28. "Serious Violations of the Legal Rights and Interests of Workers by Some Foreign-Invested Enterprises," *Nineties* (Hong Kong) (Apr. 1994).

29. See, "China: New Arrests Linked to Worker Rights" *Human Rights Watch Newsletter* 6, no. 2 (Mar. 11, 1994).

30. In some cases, NGOs tend to be seen as the silver bullets for building civil society and contributing to democratization. But precisely because so much

Western funding was available for NGO work and because an explicit requirement for receiving funding was that the NGOs in question not be engaged in direct political work, some have suggested that the energies and talents of people who might have directly entered the political sphere have instead been channeled into nonpolitical community development, public interest, and human rights work—all immensely valuable but not particularly conducive to fostering a new generation of political leaders.

31. The World Bank, *The East Asian Miracle* (Oxford: Oxford University Press, 1993), p. 21.

32. The key elements of the "Asian concept" as formulated by Singapore, Indonesia, Malaysia, and China were economic development before political and civil rights; communal duties before individual freedoms; consensus rather than confrontation; and interpretation of international standards according to the culture, political system, and level of economic development of different countries.

33. "Jakarta Defends Timor Policy, Slams Activists," *Reuter* (July 27, 1994).

34. "Application of the ODA Principles," *Japan's ODA 1993* (Tokyo: Ministry of Foreign Affairs, 1994), p. 33.

35. Ibid.

36. Ibid., pp. 33–34.

37. "Malaysia PM Affirms Ban," *Guardian* (Manchester) (Mar. 17, 1994).

Chapter 7

American Stakes in Asian Problems

JAMES SHINN

Iow can the United States craft a coherent set of policies for the problems described in this book? In this chapter I assess the U.S. stake in the Asian transnational problems and evaluate the political feasibility of the policy recommendations proffered by the authors in this volume. All of the recommendations call for U.S. cooperation within a multilateral solution, so I then consider the stubborn institutional hurdles that stand in the way of multilateral solutions in Asia, and suggest a "recipe for success" in surmounting those barriers. I close by placing the transnational problems in broader perspective, within the context of overall U.S. foreign policy in Asia.

The Spillover to "Main Street"

America's stakes in the transnational problems are most direct in the three problems with the clearest "spillover transaction"—crime and drugs, illegal migrants, and refugees. These stakes are indirect in the case of pollution and infectious disease, and more attenuated with human rights and labor standards.

The numbers are eye-catching. For example, about 500,000 "hardcore" heroin addicts live in the United States. Two-thirds of their heroin supply is smuggled in from Southeast Asia. The social costs of the heroin plague are staggering, including not only law enforcement costs but health care costs as well; drug abuse cases clog the emergency rooms of every inner-city hospital. Between 50,000 to 100,000 illegal Asian migrants enter the United States every year. Half a million refugees from the Indochina wars have already settled in the United States, partly due to American guilt over its part in the Vietnam War. Both Asian legal and illegal migrants seek the United States as the ultimate sanctuary.

But drug addiction, crime, and illegal migration are domestic American problems with a long and ugly history. Asia is just one "supplier" of these ills. There are plenty of other sources for crime, drugs, and illegal migrants, in the event that Asian sources were cut off. For example, illegal Hispanic migrants outnumber Asian migrants by ten-to-one. Crack cocaine from South America has done more damage to the U.S. social fabric than heroin from Asia. Violence by the triads or yakuza in the United States pales (so far at least) by comparison with the turf wars between rival American drug dealers.

In contrast, the stakes for the United States in Asian environmental pollution and disease are less direct. These problems are hard to measure and even harder to predict. Nonetheless, environmental activists have colorfully publicized the threats posed to American public health by ozone depletion, to American food output by climate change, and even to American beachfront real estate by global warming. American foundations and think tanks have begun to elaborate a concept of "environmental security" in order to add some rigor to these more alarmist claims.

U.S. stakes in Asian public health problems are also indirect and, so far, are largely confined to speculation about a new virus, such as the Hong Kong "chicken flu," AIDs, or the Ebola virus, that may emerge from Asia's teeming urban slums to sweep across the Pacific.

What stakes does the United States have in Asian domestic labor and human rights abuses? When labor abuses are involved in export production, the link is reasonably clear. Activists can assert a moral responsibility of Americans not to buy items produced by child or prison laborers. But what if, as some Asian governments maintain, there is no physical transaction at all that link these problems with the United States?

Sidney Jones counters this claim with three arguments. Asian governments agreed to honor these basic rights when they ratified the U.N. Declaration of Human Rights in 1948. Asian governments are likely to treat foreigners the way they treat their own citizens, so the international community in general, and the United States in particular, has a stake in Asian human rights for the protection of their own citizens. Finally, human rights principles are the moral foundation of American foreign policy.

Loss of the Moral High Ground

But some Asian governments reject the notion that the United States or the international community has any "standing" under international law regarding how Asian governments deal with their own citizens in terms of basic human rights, labor rights, and particularly political rights. Some Asian spokesmen further suggest that the United States stands on no moral high ground when it comes to the transnational problems. They point a finger at the inability of the United States to solve its own domestic problems of drug addiction, crime, and illegal migrants. They contend that America's Vietnam War triggered the largest wave of refugees in Asia, that traveling Americans were the original vectors in the spread of the AIDS epidemic, and that the U.S. record of dealing with ethnic minorities is not without blemish. They are quick to remind environmental activists that the United States is the single largest producer of greenhouse gases. And they argue that a century ago, at comparable stages of development to the lower- income states of contemporary Asia, the United States was complicit in pillaging the natural environment of North America, shoving Native Americans off their land, and slaughtering whales throughout the Pacific.

Rules of Thumb

Although the scale and standing of U.S. stakes in Asia's transnational problems varies considerably, and in some cases is disputed by Asian governments, all the authors in this volume contend that the United States has a key role in crafting solutions. Their recommendations reveal some common "rules of thumb" for tackling the transnational problems.

1. *Governments must deal with both the supply and the demand side of these problems at the same time.* Washington must cooperate with Asian governments abroad to solve the transnational problems on a multilateral basis at the same time that it tackles these problems at home. For example, interdiction of Asian narcotics traffickers and snakeheads will not fix America's problems of narcotics addiction and illegal migrants. A multilateral regime to deal with the supply side of transnational problems in Asia will not work unless it is synchronized with domestic programs in the United States to suppress demand, such as eradicating drug addiction through treatment and public education, or cracking down on illegal migrants through labor documentation and site inspections.

2. *The transnational problems feed on one another and must be solved together.* Policies must be crafted in an intelligent, sequenced way so that successes in one problem area support progress in another. Solutions call for a root-and-branch approach. For example, criminals, illegal

migrants, and illicit drugs come together in one unsavory package: U.S. border controls are ineffective against well-financed and well-equipped snakeheads. By the same token, refugees and illegal migrants are the most frequent victims of labor abuses in the United States. And it is difficult to detect infectious disease transmission from Asia within a transpacific surge of illegal migrants.

3. *Free markets alone will not solve these problems. Solutions require more regulation and "good government."* But this bucks a trend toward deregulation in much of Asia and the United States. Free capital markets make drug smuggling and money laundering even easier, unless the U.S. Treasury Department imposes more regulations and paperwork and audits on money transfers. Free labor markets attract more illegal migrants, unless the Immigration and Naturalization Service (INS) does its job at the borders and the Labor Department cracks down on illegal sweatshops.

On a more positive note, the policy recommendations made in this volume are not prohibitively expensive. The institutions, personnel, and legal authorization to deal with the transnational problems are largely in place in the United States. What *is* required is some reallocation of effort, better coordination between agencies, and political willpower in Washington, D.C.

For example, in chapter 2 Stephen Flynn makes a strong case for redirecting drug interdiction funds to prevention and treatment. He argues that federal law enforcement should target the network of criminal enterprises themselves rather than try to nab drugs in transit. He suggests that these criminal enterprises are most vulnerable where they intersect with the regular business world, such as their extensive arrangements for money laundering. Unfortunately, federal efforts against Asian crime are balkanized among the Drug Enforcement Agency (DEA), the Federal Bureau of Investigation (FBI), the INS, the Coast Guard, and local police forces, with poor coordination in strategy and tactics. Flynn also points out how few Asian Americans work in any of these agencies, and he bemoans the paucity of American intelligence about Asian organized crime.

4. *Nongovernmental organizations (NGOs) play a crucial role in engaging the U.S. and Asian governments in the solution of a transnational problem.* NGOs can be collaborative or antagonistic with governments, and they can even work at cross-purposes—but they cannot be ignored from a policy standpoint. Reiterating a point made in chapter 1, not all NGOs are "good." Examples of "bad" NGOs are criminal gangs, egregious polluters, and labor abusers. In the new Asia, bad NGOs look increasingly corporate, with complex management structures, sophisticated finances, and cross-border strategic alliances. Fortunately, the problem-solving "good"

NGOs, such as religious institutions and citizen lobbies, are also getting more sophisticated and powerful. NGOs wield increasing influence within the U.S. policymaking process by defining the issues through the media, building consensus for solutions within Washington, and sometimes by stepping in themselves to help fix the problem directly.

For example, Human Rights Watch Asia keeps a close eye on political repression and is quick to call abuses to the attention of Congress and the Cable News Network. Likewise, organized religions are active, defending religious freedoms throughout Asia and aiding refugees, migrants, and the poor through their extensive networks in the region. Private philanthropic foundations have spearheaded institution-building programs to encourage the spread of the rule of law—a condition essential for both pollution clean up and to prevent human rights abuses. Private businesses have an enormous impact on labor standards in Asia when they enforce codes of conduct in their manufacturing operations or through their local contractors.

Each type of NGO has its own distinctive governance structure and institutional goals. Human Rights Watch Asia, the Sierra Club, the Roman Catholic Church, and the Nike Corporation rarely see eye to eye on all transnational problems. But NGOs are often skilled in setting aside their different agendas and making common cause in search for a solution to transnational problems in Asia.

NGOs can also be stubbornly independent-minded if the state is viewed as antagonistic to their objectives—whether the state is oppressing citizens in China, condoning labor abuses in Indonesia, abetting drug traffickers in Thailand, or riding roughshod over environmental concerns in Korea or Taiwan. NGOs can and will make their opposition known to the media, the world community, and sometimes on the streets. When they decide to make a stand on principles—whether on human rights or the rule of law—business firms are probably the most effective NGOs in getting the attention of Asian governments, especially by "voting with their feet" and transferring operations to less oppressive locales.

5. *The United States has limited leverage to solve these problems unilaterally.* Real solutions require cooperation with Asian allies and adversaries alike. Multilateral policies are awkward and time-consuming to craft, and are rarely appealing to national political leaders, but they are an essential tool in solving Asia's transnational problems.

All authors in this volume repeatedly invoke the mantra of multilateral solutions while recommending that the United States take a leadership role in constructing these multilateral solutions. None of them recommends that the United States should try to solve these problems on its own. The flow of migrants or drugs or pollutants is simply too dispersed, too complex, too quicksilver, to be stopped by the United States alone. All but one of the solutions proposed by our authors requires negotiation between governments to mount a coordinated response, based on a mutually acceptable give-and-take, rather than unilateral pressure.

The sole exception is labor standards and human rights. Sidney Jones does endorse unilateral pressure by the U.S. government on Asian governments. She applauds the use of trade sanctions to punish human rights violations by Asian states while admitting that such sanctions "should be the tool of last resort. If sanctions are threatened, they must be tied to specific, concrete objectives and the threat must be credible."

The same logic leads Jones to urge the United States to support a social clause in the World Trade Organization that requires minimum labor standards from all states as a way of condemning labor abuses; a multilateral agreement of this kind would be most effective in dealing with export-led Asian economies. She also notes the importance of the multilateral development banks (MDBs) to many Asian states—including China—and recommends that the United States should use its seat on MDB boards to tie lending decisions to human rights and labor rights standards.

Elizabeth Economy argues that the MDBs such as the World Bank have advanced the ecological cause in Asia by requiring environmental impact statements for big infrastructure projects (such as China's Three Gorges Dam) and by expanding the direct lending authority of the Global Environmental Facility. She would like to add environmental concerns to the Asia-Pacific Economic Cooperation (APEC) agenda, and believes that the U.S. government should encourage Japan's environmental leadership as part of the "common agenda" between Washington and Tokyo. Not surprisingly, Sadako Ogata and Johan Cels, given the former's role as leader of a powerful U.N. agency, see multilateral agencies as the best vehicle for solving the refugee problem. They carefully underline the importance of preventive diplomacy to head off future refugee problems and urge the United States to support a new paradigm for dealing with refugee problems, although they are wary of U.S. "compassion fatigue" towards refugee problems and appreciate Washington's disinclination to get involved in Asian "teacup" wars.

Flynn says the Asian drug problem must be tackled by a regional Asian multilateral organization and calls for an APEC organized crime task force as a first step. Crime has flourished in the gaps opened up by the freer flow of people, goods, and money throughout Asia, and can only be suppressed by legal measures that filter these flows. For example, he wants APEC to adopt measures in its investment code to fully disclose equity ownership, in order to flag criminal holdings in shippers and financial institutions that can be used for smuggling or money laundering. He recommends that APEC's proposed procedures for streamlining shipping manifests and customs clearance not become a carte blanche for drug smugglers. And Paul Smith believes that APEC attempts to standardize visa and immigration clearance procedures for "high-end" travelers, such as business travelers and tourists, may create procedures that can be later applied to regulate the flow of "low-end" migrant workers as well.

Political Reality Check

How workable are all of these recommendations? Are they mutually consistent? And are they politically feasible in the United States today?

Regarding the first rule of thumb for solving transnational problems—dealing with the supply and demand sides of the problems at the same time—Washington almost always deals with the Asian angle of a problem as an afterthought to a domestic, U.S.-centric solution. All the authors have stressed repeatedly that solutions to the transnational problems must be cooperative, not unilateral. Yet the U.S. Congress has little experience writing multilateral consultation into domestic legislation, particularly for hot-button social problems such as drug abuse and illegal immigration.

There is also a risk that the Asian "supply" of a transnational problem will be used as a scapegoat rather than as part of the solution. It is politically convenient to blame a country across the Pacific for U.S. problems rather than recognize illegal drugs and migrants as largely homegrown afflictions.

As for the second rule—the root-and-branch approach of dealing with interrelated aspects of transnational problems—any U.S. policy crafted to deal with these problems is likely to muddle through by trial and error, one problem at a time, more or less in isolation. History engenders little confidence that Washington can field a finely synchronized response to several transnational problems at the same time, such as a simultaneous "war" on illegal migrants, drugs, and the triads, despite the obvious benefits of doing so.

The third rule prescribes more "good government" regulation for dealing with these problems. On one hand, a prescription for more government—especially federal government—is out of step with the mood of the Republican majority in the U.S. Congress. On the other hand, solving domestic problems of drugs, crime, and illegal migrants is closely in step with the stated priorities of the Republican Party. Both skeptics of Washington and "America Firsters" would be delighted to see U.S. foreign policy in Asia support regulatory solutions to these nitty-gritty transnational problems, as opposed to Washington's traditional focus on military and economic concerns in the region.

Reshaping Washington's agencies' mandates to help tackle the Asian angle of domestic problems is time-consuming and tiresome. But if the two basic arguments of this volume are correct—that the transnational problems will rudely force themselves onto the foreign policy front burner, and the transnational problems will be increasingly perceived as integral to solving domestic U.S. social problems—then federal agencies may well embrace this new focus with the ardor born of bureaucratic self-preservation. For example, the Central Intelligence Agency may well discover a new mission in spying on triads and the yakuza if intelligence budgets shrink in the post–Cold War era.

NGOs are proliferating around every problem area, almost everywhere in Asia, so the outlook for the fourth rule of thumb is positive. Both Elizabeth Economy and Sidney Jones argue that environmental activists and human rights NGOs are increasingly vocal and are putting down deeper local roots in Asia. Less optimistically, it is difficult to judge if the "good" NGOs are growing faster than the "bad" NGOs, or to predict the outcome of the clash of wills between "bad" governments and "good" NGOs.

It is also hard to predict the outcome of the lobbying push-and-pull over these problems as Washington labors to craft a policy response, with a gaggle of single-issue interest groups and NGOs vying to prioritize their own cause. It is easy to recommend that the United States harness these NGOs to multilateral solutions for transnational problems, but the opposite effect appears to be taking place.

One result of this lobbying confusion is that the U.S. government often has squandered its limited political capital in Asia on the pursuit of multiple causes. Washington has imposed economic sanctions of one sort or another on almost every Asian state—friend and foe alike—for causes ranging from human rights to trade in endangered species. Officials of several different U.S. agencies have collided in Asian capitals, one official negotiating a trade agreement, one trying to extradite a drug smuggler, one criticizing the host government for labor abuses, and another official trying to promote U.S. exports of power generator equipment. This lack of coordination would be comical if it were not so counterproductive. Confusion over priorities has diluted the ability of the United States to solve any single transnational problem and has thoroughly confused Asian governments over U.S. priorities.

Yet the sensitivity of the U.S. government to aggressive lobbying is unlikely to change. Congress remains the quickest road for NGOs to pressure the president on transnational problems, but Congress shows no inclination to stop second-guessing the president on Asia foreign policy, and the Clinton administration has made limited progress in setting clear priorities in for Asia strategy.

The current political mood in Washington also bodes ill for the fifth rule of thumb, which places a priority on multilateral consultation and solutions. Multilateral institutions have few fans in Washington and little grass-roots support elsewhere in the United States. The United Nations is out of political favor, and it is difficult to work up much enthusiasm in Washington for either APEC or the Association of Southeast Asian Nations (ASEAN).

As for linking solutions to the transnational problems with the lending activities of the MDBs, free-market advocates in Washington are challenging the rationale for the MDBs in Asia. These banks are criticized for "wasting the taxpayers' money on a swollen bureaucracy and undercutting private markets." Indeed, the original mandate of the World Bank and the Asian Development Bank was to supply funds to less developed countries that could not borrow from private capital markets, as was frequently the case three decades ago. But today almost every Asian government can issue sovereign debt, and private direct investment has replaced bank lending as the biggest source of capital to Asian economies.

Finally, U.S. policymakers see APEC as some use in liberating Asian markets but have been disappointed by the backsliding from the liberalization commitments made in 1994 at the Bogor summit in Indonesia. Moreover, some Asian governments are stubbornly opposed to widening APEC's agenda to include topics other than trade. Human rights issues are a red flag to China; labor standards are a red flag to the ASEAN states.

Distaste and Sloth

Even if policymakers in Washington can summon the will to engage the United States in a solution to what is often perceived as an "Asian" problem, they still encounter the fact that it is remarkably difficult to craft a real multilateral solution to any of the transnational problems. The authors in this volume catalog a list of barriers, which can be distilled into two institutional roadblocks that I call "diplomatic distaste" and "multilateral sloth."

Foreign ministries dislike dealing with the transnational problems. These topics are viewed as pedestrian and rather gritty, in contrast to the "high politics" that generally engage diplomats. Diplomats are trained as generalists; few have the technical background necessary to deal knowledgeably with greenhouse gas emissions, infectious disease transmission, or narcotics smuggling. Moreover, lengthy experience with a single transnational policy problem can "type" an individual; few ambitious diplomats want to work on drug smuggling or illegal migrant problems for their entire career. Nor do diplomats enjoy dealing with NGOs, which they regard as unpredictable, unaccountable, and politically troublesome.

Those officials who do have the requisite technical background to deal with these problems usually are employed in government agencies that focus on domestic issues, such as law enforcement or labor ministries. But these agencies have limited international expertise and are reluctant to factor in the international equation when making policy.

The second institutional barrier is multilateral sloth. Multilateral mechanisms are slow moving and complex. Where established procedures exist, they move at a glacial pace; where procedures must be invented, they move only as far as the least common denominator.

Given this political backdrop and institutional barriers to a solution, can we predict which of Asia's transnational problems are most amenable to solutions and which will remain intractable? Based on the evidence presented in this volume, the closer the solution to a given transnational problem conforms to the following recipe, the better the odds of clearing both the political and institutional obstacles.

1. *The clearer and more physical the spillover transaction, the easier to craft a solution.* It is easy to prove that certain illicit narcotics were smuggled across borders; it is hard to prove the spillover transaction of labor standards. *The larger the scale of the spillover transaction to the underlying social problem, the better.* If a single microbe is responsible for a pan-Pacific epidemic, the easier it is to coordinate a solution. It is harder to make the case for pan-Pacific water pollution. *The more symmetrical the spillover, the better.* Few states gain from drug smuggling; some states do gain from illegal migration.

2. *The clearer the relationship between rising incomes and a transnational problem, the easier to craft a solution.* It helps if governments realize that time and higher incomes may not be on their side. It also helps if analysis can demonstrate how a particular transnational problem is a drag on econmic growth.

3. *The clearer the security threat that the problem poses to governments, the easier it is to craft a solution.* It is also helpful to delink the problems of labor standards and human rights from the broader problem of democratic political rights.

4. *The more value-neutral and technical the problem, the better.* States are much quicker to agree on transnational solutions with other states, governments with NGOs, and NGOs with other NGOs when ideology does not get in the way.

5. *The broader the "good" NGO community with a stake in a solution, the better.* It is helpful to have an NGO network in both the supply state and the demand state.

6. *If there is an international treaty or convention that provides a legal foundation for transnational cooperation, and a multilateral forum that can function with dispatch, the better the prognosis for a solution.* Whereas building a treaty or multilateral basis for cooperative solutions from scratch can take an eternity.

None of the transnational problems in this volume fits perfectly with this recipe, but as table 7.1 suggests, the Asian transnational problems most likely to be solved by multilateral cooperation are, in descending order: (1) drug trafficking; (2) infectious disease; (3) pollution; (4) illegal migration; (5) refugees; (6) population control; (7) labor abuse; and finally, (8) human rights abuses.

Based on the cases presented by our authors, the institutional barriers of diplomatic distaste and multilateral sloth can be minimized, if not eliminated, by two tactical prescriptions.

- Tackle the easier problems first and establish a track record of success— if only modest success—and a pattern of mutual gain between supply and demand states.

- Timing is key. It makes little sense to attempt a transnational solution until a domestic consensus has been reached on solving the wider social problem and until domestic politicians are ready to stand behind the solutions. Bureaucrats do not enjoy being out front.

No amount of tactical fiddling will solve these problems if the solutions are not consistent with the broader sweep of U.S. foreign policy— and U.S. policy objectives—in Asia, to which we now turn.

Strategic Vacuum

It is a bromide that U.S. foreign policy in Asia is "adrift" in the post–Cold War era, with many interests in the region but no overarching strategy to pursue them. The transnational problems make things worse by adding in more U.S. interests, yet providing no obvious grand strategy. In addition to this strategic vacuum, three longer-term patterns of U.S. engagement in Asia further cloud the prospect for solving the transnational problems.

- U.S. commercial stakes in Asia are less likely to be sacrificed to other objectives than during the Cold War. Commercial diplomacy is now "high politics" in Asia. The United States exported $200 billion to Asia in 1996, accounting for 3.5 percent of gross domestic product (GDP) and supporting 2.5 million domestic jobs. Washington will be less willing to use trade sanctions as a tool for solutions or support any policies in areas like crime or the environment that get in the way of making money.

- Although U.S. security interests in the region are in a period of transition, the prime mission of American military forces in Asia is still focused on Korea. Officers naturally resist diluting their war-fighting focus with "secondary" duties such as dealing with drug smuggling or organized crime, despite the profound connection between both of these problems and those of nuclear proliferation and terrorism.

- The United States is less inclined to exercise leadership in regime building and creating multilateral fora in Asia. There is a distinct lack of enthusiasm in Washington to expend limited political capital in the maintenance of "public goods" in Asia. U.S. officials are impatient with the slow pace and encumbrances of multilateral consultation. This increases the temptation for Washington to go it alone in dealing with political hot buttons such as narcotics smuggling, crime, and illegal migration, or for Washington to argue that Asian allies should provide the resources to solve these transnational problems while the United States provides a security umbrella for much of Asia. There is some logic for such a division of labor—until we come to the case of China.

China at the Center of Problems

U.S. foreign policy in Asia is increasingly preoccupied with the strategic puzzle of China's emergence as a great power. And China stands at the center of *all* of the transnational problems in Asia. For example, China itself produces little of the heroin that reaches the United States, but there is an epidemic of addiction in China's southern provinces, and Chinese triads account for the lion's share of drug smuggling within Asia and across the Pacific. China's megacities are a time bomb for infectious disease epidemics. China burns 1.2 billion tons of coal a year, has several of the most polluted cities on the planet, and will soon exceed the United States as a producer of greenhouse gases. The many illegal migrants who leave China each year are only a tiny fraction of China's estimated 100 million "floating" population of landless, jobless workers. And China plays a pivotal role in the debate over labor standards and human rights in Asia.

Not surprisingly, Beijing views the transnational problems as just one aspect of a more basic challenge to its ability to govern China. Indeed, many China watchers speculate whether the sheer scale of the problems of drugs, crime, pollution, public health, internal migration, and

Table 7.1: Transnational Problems Matrix

	Drugs	Infectious diseases	Pollution
Economic growth and rising incomes	Higher incomes spark more demand. Limited supply suppression.	Gains from sanitation and public health investment, and greater risk of "exotic" pandemics.	More pollution at "takeoff" stage of growth; less after $10K per capita GDP.
Pluralism and national security	Traffickers are a "clear and present danger," especially to weaker or failed states.	No direct connection; authoritarian states may be unwilling to admit scale of some pandemics, retarding treatment.	Some political friction.
Spillover scale and symmetry	Smuggling is important source of narcotics supply. No state gains from drugs: narrow elite may be enriched in short run, but in long run drugs highly corrosive.	Cross-border infection kicks off epidemics. All states have interest in solving these health threats.	Cross-border pollution far less than home grown pollutants. Higher income states can be motivated to pay lower-income states to pollute less.
Consensus, social values, and the media	Agreement on scale of problem, but deep disagreement on response. Interdiction is bigger news than treatment or prevention.	Value neutral. Wide agreement on need for prevention and treatment. Largely budgetary question. "Andromeda Strain" fears easiest to invoke.	Value neutral. Disagreement on economic tradeoffs. Only dramatic incidents make news.
NGO network	NGOs are overshadowed by traditional government organizations in both narcotics and public health problems, although specific "disease lobbies" have some clout.		Environmental NGOs proliferating, with links to lobbies in the West and Japan.
Legal foundation for multilateral cooperation	1971 U.N. Convention on Psychotropic Substances; UN Narcotics Control Board; UNNCB MOU with 6 Asian nations; ASEAN Ministry on Drugs (ASOD).	U.N. World Health Organization; Center for Disease Control (CDC).	Montreal Protocol; Rio Convention. Beijing Ministerial Declaration.

Illegal migration	Refugees	Labor abuses	Human rights problems
Income differentials cause migration. Long-term income growth can dampen supply.	Not a solution, except for economic refugees.	Slow improvement. Early growth brings some unique abuses.	No direct correlation. A middle class may eventually demand greater political rights.
Asian governments fear both illegal migrants and refugees as a bridgehead for possible subversion, espionage, terrorism, or even "slow motion invasion." West less interested in accepting refugees or intervening in "teacup wars."		Authoritarian states fear labor unions and human rights groups may lead to the "Polish disease" and topple their regimes. West less tolerant of internal repression by Asian "allies."	
Asia is largest source of illegal migrants worldwide. Chinese external migrants dwarfed by number of internal migrants. Poorer states depend on migrant remittances.	Refugees often a problem to host country, but may be welcome for economic reasons. Source countries cause problem but rarely accept responsibility.	Labor standards can spill over thorough international trade.	Authoritarian states deny any spillover from human rights issues.
Aware of problem but ambivalent about solution. *Golden Venture*-type disasters are good press.	Consensus rare on source of problem or solution. Refugee stories forgotten quickly.	No. Some Asian states claim this an economic, not political, problem.	No agreement except on most basic human rights. Media makes some dissidents famous, ignores others.
Social service NGOs and religious groups work with migrants and refugees, but there are few "policy" lobbies.		NGOs starting to publicize labor and human rights abuses to the world, invoking threat of consumer boycotts. Western unions and consumer groups pressing for higher standards and inspections. Unions banned in some Asian states.	Human rights NGOs are strong in West and Japan, and work with embryonic Asian human rights NGOs.
None. Some bilateral understandings.	U.N. 1951 Refugee Convention; 1967 Refugee Protocol—though many Asian countries have not signed.	U.N. ILO; some undertakings within WTO.	U.N. Charter and subsequent conventions; many signed but ignored in practice.

labor abuse eventually will overwhelm the Chinese government. All agree that these problems will absorb the energies of the Chinese state for decades. Solutions to these problems require *political* reform in China as well as continued *economic* reform. Without political reform, there is little hope of establishing a rule of law or rooting out corruption. Without law or effective regulation, there is no hope for solving pollution, illegal migration, labor abuse, or drug smuggling. Yet political reform is a dangerous road for an authoritarian regime to embark on.

In the event that the Beijing regime "muddles through" with only limited reform, then these problems may not topple the state, but they will sap its energies. A China besieged by transnational problems is an unlikely Asian hegemon in conventional security terms, but it is still a threat to the rest of Asia by virtue of "negative power projection" (such as the threat of swamping a neighboring state with millions of illegal migrants or refugees). China's neighbors are acutely aware of this threat, and they are deeply cautious about pressing for political change in China. On balance, they prefer a united, authoritarian China to a more pluralistic China that could degenerate into chaos.

All of China's neighbors, and the United States, agree that engagement with Beijing is more likely than confrontation to produce multilateral solutions to the transnational problems. Yet pressure on China to stop human rights abuses pulls the relationship toward confrontation, even as negotiations on problems such as the environment pull toward cooperation. The United States and China have an inherently difficult relationship, and the push-pull of the transnational problems do not make it any easier.

For example, the United States presses China to permit free emigration of political dissidents under the Jackson-Vanik amendment, while complaining about other illegal immigration from China. The United States presses China to reduce its fossil fuel pollution while blocking the export of nuclear generation equipment to China because of proliferation fears. Some Chinese interpret this inconsistency as evidence for underlying U.S. hostility to China; some Americans see these choices as forced upon Washington by a heavy-handed and corrupt regime in Beijing. The net result fuels the cycle of mutual suspicion and dims the prospects for transnational solutions.

Japan at the Center of Solutions

As central as China is to the transnational problems, Japan is central to regional solutions. For example, Japan generously supports regional public health efforts through multilateral health organizations such as the World Health Organization (WHO). Japan's environment is the cleanest in Asia, with good technology and effective regulation. The Japanese government has made environmentally sound development one of the pillars of its foreign aid programs, and Japan is far and away the largest aid donor in Asia.

Yet although Japan was a key actor in the Cambodian accords, which helped alleviate one of the most persistent refugee problems in Asia, it has remained largely closed to refugees itself, due to Japanese concerns about racial and cultural integration of refugees. Japanese government and businesses have developed a *modus vivendi* with yakuza criminal organizations that make a mockery of international law enforcement. And the Japanese government is extremely cautious about criticizing labor and human rights abuses in the region. As the largest aid donor and investor in Asia, Japan has great clout but is reluctant to "get out in front" on human rights issues. This official caution is sometimes attributed to a low-key diplomatic style, to long-term pragmatism, or to mere commercial opportunism. Whatever the reason, the net effect often leaves the U.S. government standing alone on questions of human rights, while U.S. businesses bear the brunt of Asian governments' displeasure at such criticisms.

Japan's policy toward the transnational problems in Asia reflects Tokyo's consistently long view about the evolution of the region. Japanese diplomats view quiet engagement and sustained economic development as the prerequisites to solving Asia's transnational problems, as the only practical way to modify the behavior of Asia's authoritarian states, ranging from the "soft authoritarian" states such as China, Vietnam, and Indonesia to—in the much longer run—Myanmar and even North Korea.

Engagement or Confrontation?

In the long run, resolving the transnational problems in Asia, even making limited progress toward solutions, will remove a major underlying irritant in relations with Asia's authoritarian states. Relations with China and Vietnam are already tense. Stirring issues of drugs and illegal migrants into this volatile mix can strain relations even more. But progress in dealing with these problems can build a record of successful collaboration and spawn interest groups on both sides with a stake in smoother relations.

For example, American and Chinese law enforcement agencies rarely see eye to eye on the ideological plane, but they have a vital common interest in suppressing the drug trade now coursing through China's southern provinces. Successful collaboration in nabbing drug smugglers will make it easier for these law enforcement agencies to collaborate on more delicate problems, such as extraditing triad kingpins or shutting down pirate compact disc (CD) factories. And it is hard for China to claim that international cooperation to suppress labor abuses is an "interference in domestic affairs" while simultaneously cooperating to suppress international drug trafficking.

A further benefit of engagement on the transnational problems is the useful "reality check" that it imposes on the West—particularly the United States—regarding the feasible speed of change in the authoritarian regimes in Asia. The authors in this volume make the case that transnational problems flourish in the event of a collapse of state authority; these problems breed in failed states. Cambodia and Burma are graphic examples, and North Korea may be the next. The nightmare scenario of a meltdown in China would result in a worsening of every one of the transnational problems discussed here.

Few experts contest the long-term desirability of increasing political pluralism in order to build a lasting peace in Asia. But close scrutiny of the transnational problems leads to the conclusion that a "soft landing" is preferable to a "hard landing," even for brutal or authoritarian regimes. The cost of a hard landing will be paid in the currency of rampant drug trafficking and crime, the spread of infectious disease, environmental devastation, miserable hordes of illegal migrants and refugees, abysmal working conditions in what employment remains, and human rights abuses of every kind.

But a strategy of accomodating an authoritarian regime, even in exchange for limited cooperation in suppressing a problem such as drug trafficking, may only prolong the scale of the other transnational problems, and delay the implementation of an effective multilateral solution. There are no easy choices, and few clear trade-offs. The traditional calculus of American security and economic strategy in Asia must now factor in the transnational problems as an urgent, complex policy objective in the region. These problems are no longer Fires Across the Water.

Index